Large-Group Treatment of Addictions[1]

by
Reg M. Reynolds, Ph.D., C.Psych. (Retired)
and Douglas A Quirk, M.A., C.Psych. (1931-1997)[2]

---

1 Most of the text in this manuscript was written by Douglas Quirk and edited/assembled by Reg Reynolds.
2 Formerly Chief Psychologist and Senior Psychologist at the Ontario Correctional Institute.

Copyright © 2023 by Reg M. Reynolds

Library of Congress Control Number:
      ISBN   eBook: 978-1-7776461-7-2
      Softcover: 9798395948465

I wish to express my appreciation to Joyce, the love of my life, who has put up with my obsessions for more than sixty years; and to the many volunteers whose tireless efforts supported so much of the research carried out by the Psychology Department at the Ontario Correctional Institute. (RR)

Table of Contents

PREFACE

This book presents a model to account for addictive behaviour in such a way that it can be modified using large-group treatment. It details (1) the development of a questionnaire to identify the motivations that drive addictions, (2) a detailed series of large-group treatment workshops for them, and (3) results that demonstrate their effectiveness. The text is taken primarily from two previous publications: *Large-Group Psychological Treatment Workshops* by Douglas Quirk and *Freedom from Addictions Second Edition* by Douglas Quirk and Reg Reynolds.

INTRODUCTION

Based on many years of clinical psychology practice, the authors formed the belief that:

(1) addiction results from the user's attempt to alleviate felt distress, and addictive behaviour mainly amounts to self-medication (Khantzian, 1974, 1999).
(2) a substance is only addictive if it relatively rapidly reduces an uncomfortable state and/or creates a desired or pleasant state. This is based on well known learning principles (see Skinner, 1953).
(3) a substance is only addictive for those people who experience and are uncomfortable with those specific habitual uncomfortable states that the substance alters. For example, people who are depressed do not get addicted to "downers" and people who are anxious do not get addicted to "uppers."
(4) the problems for which addicts seek chemical relief can more productively be addressed through psychological treatment,

and

(5) this can be most economically done through large-group psychological treatment. More than one hundred years of combined experience with various kinds of psychotherapies, which has led us to believe that many of the benefits of individual and small-group psychological treatment can also be obtained by the participants in large-group treatment workshops (supplemented where necessary by a relatively small amount of individual work) at a significantly lower cost.

LARGE-GROUP TREATMENT

In designing treatment workshops for maximum therapeutic benefit, we have made certain assumptions. First, it is assumed that it is necessary to build in evaluation at each stage of treatment program development and implementation, so that program delivery may be controlled by its results. Second, to ensure a powerful therapeutic effect, it is necessary that treatment be designed in such a way that it incorporates scientifically verified laws of learning and behaviour. Third, it is appropriate to include motivational elements as part of the treatment, rather than expect that only motivated clients will be referred. Fourth, treatment needs to be guided by the therapist (the expert) rather than by the client (where it becomes a case of the blind leading the blind). Fifth, it is necessary for the client both to be provided with information about the basic processes involved in his or her presenting problems and their treatment, and to be shown and sometimes guided through strategies for addressing and resolving them. And finally, it is desirable, if not always necessary, for clients to have an opportunity to practice using the information and strategies with which they are provided, to ensure that the treatment has really "taken," before turning the clients loose to function on their own.

In our experience, each of these treatment workshops usually takes about a day or two to complete, may be presented in either half-day or full-day sessions, and can be effective when delivered in groups as large as the space can accommodate. To date, they have been presented in full-day format (but allowing for coffee and lunch breaks), and there has been essentially no problem in maintaining attention and motivation of participants for that period of time. This has been accomplished partly by having two or more presenters who keep changing the pace of activities and level of excitement in their manner of presentation, and partly by the large-group format with its potential for contagious mutually-arousing interaction.

In the treatment workshops that we have offered, measures have been taken before and after each day-long workshop, so that the effect of each workshop could be evaluated, as well as any overall effect of the workshop series. In what follows, however, only the post-workshop scores are reported, for the sake of simplicity, since the scores shown are fully representative of pre- and post-workshop values, the pre- to post-workshop change scores, and subjective reports of improvements experienced by participants because of their workshop experiences.

Over the years that we have presented these workshops, (1) pre-post measures have shown that these treatment workshops produce measurable effects and (2) participants in these large group treatment programs have reported that they are able to use the instruction received and the skills that they have learned in day-to-day interactions. In addition, informal comparisons between the results of large-group treatment and the more intensive eight-to-ten-person group have been very favourable to the large-group approach. In those cases where the same measures have been employed, for example, the treatment workshops have generally produced better results.

Examples of the large-group workshop approach to treatment, are given in Appendix A. From the results of these examples, it can be seen that the large-group treatment workshop approach can be both efficient and effective.

LARGE-GROUP TREATMENT OF ADDICTIONS: THE ADDICURE STUDY

Many approaches have been proposed for addressing addictions, including individual and group psychotherapy and self-help groups such as Alcoholics Anonymous (AA) and Narcotics Anonymous (NA). Given the enormity of the problem, as witness the number of over-dose deaths each year, economies of treatment are incredibly important.

Typically, each approach to the treatment of addictions starts with an attempt to get to know the client/patient, most often through some sort of interview process. Psychologists, more than other professionals, are inclined to supplement that with psychological tests. Psychological tests vary in the extent to which they require interpretation, ranging from projective tests to straight self-report. It has been our experience that self-report questionnaires are usually sufficient for identifying the uncomfortable feeling states that motivate substance use/abuse and subsequent addictive behaviour. Since nothing that we judged suitable for identifying the motivations underlying addictions could be found, a questionnaire (ADDICAUSE) was developed (see Appendix B) to identify the psychological states that motivate addictive behaviours. It consists of 68 scales chosen to sample a wide variety of psychological states (see Appendix D).

For research purposes, the final pages of the ADDICAUSE questionnaire requests respondents to indicate all the following for each of 5 categories of foods, 3 categories of tobacco products, 10 categories of medications, 10 categories of alcoholic beverages, 13 categories of street drugs, and 3 categories of solvents:

<u>Y</u>: <u>Years of Use</u>: The respondent was asked to show the number of Years of Use of each substance.

9

U: <u>Strength of Use</u>: On an anchored scale from 0 to 7, for which each position was pre-defined for the respondent, he/she was asked to show the Strength of Use of each substance.

O: <u>Time Off</u>: The respondent was asked to show the number of months since he/she used each substance. (It quickly became clear that this score was meaningless within the context of its first application, a correctional treatment centre. The fact that the respondents were incarcerated at the time introduced an unmanageable element into responses in this category. For example, some of the respondents estimated time off from the last use of a particular substance while others gave the length of time they had been in prison.)

W: <u>Present Want</u>: On an anchored scale from 0 to 7, for which each position was pre-defined for the respondent, he/she was asked to show the strength of his/her present Want/Desire to use each substance. This score was intended to get at the addict who is deprived of access to his/her preferred addictive substance(s). (Once more, it soon became clear that this score was less than ideally useful for the incarcerate population on which it was first used. Many addicts, removed from access to their substances tend to experience a major decline in their addictive want which, unfortunately, may be reinstated as soon as access is again possible. In addition, many addicts are in denial and want to create a good impression by simply denying wanting substances, which also reduced the numbers of subjects acknowledging wants.)

Examination of the responses given to the ADDICAUSE questionnaire by thousands of *incarcerated* addicts identified a number of correlations between substance use/abuse and particular ADDICAUSE scales. Further statistical analysis led to the identification of nine factors or clusters of intercorrelated scales within the data. Examination of the scales in each of these clusters then led to the conceptual development of the targets for treatment.

For purposes of ease of differentiation among the several ADDICAUSE scales underlying each concept, those ADDICAUSE scales construed to be particularly relevant to each of nine concepts are presented in **bold** in the following table, and the ADDICAUSE scale(s) thought to be most representative are **<u>underlined</u>**.

#	General Concept	Treatment Name	Conceptual Contents and Related ADDICAUSE Scale Numbers
1	Failure	Creating SUCCESS	Failure/Punishment History/Expectation 03,**12**,13,20,**24,37,47,48**
2	Inflexibility	Creating FLEXIBILITY	Rigid/Inflexible Habits/ Adjustment 08.**12,36,37,47**
3	Excitement-Seeking	Creating EXCITEMENT	Apathy/Inhibition –> Stimulus-Hunger **12,20**,24,30,**37s**,40,**60n**
4	Gratification Need	Creating SATISFACTION	Immediate Satisfaction/ Relief Need 10,**12,13**,20,**24**,36,**37,40**, 44,**47**,48,53
5	Conflicted Values	Creating VALUES	Subcultural/Primitive/ Regressive Values **08**,12,**13,22,34**,36,**37**,40, 44,47,**48**
6	Guilt Intolerance	Creating INNOCENCE	Guilt-Proneness or Guilt Intolerance **02,08**,12,**30**,36,37,48,60
7	Distress	Creating HEALTH	Ill-Health/Stress/ Distress/Anxiety 03,08,**13**,34,37,**44,47**,53
8	Joylessness	Creating HAPPINESS	Depression/Joylessness/ Unfulfillment **02,03,08**,10,12,**13**,30,**36, 40**,44, 48,**53**

9	Weak Integratio	Creating INTEGRATION	A/Anti-Social Adjustment/Integration **02,03**,10,**12**,20,**22,<u>30</u>,34, **36**,40, **44**,48

For example, the first cluster listed above, which was given the label of Failure, was composed of the following ADDICAUSE scales, which are tentatively labelled in the table below according to the content of their items:

Scale Number	Scale Label
03	Reactive Depression
12	**Authority Rebellion**
13	Flat Depression
20	Hedonism
24	**Normal Resilience**
37	**Paroxysmality** (neurological)
47	**Physiological Anxiety**
<u>48</u>	**Punishment History and Expectation**

Although seeking to address as many addictive issues as possible, each treatment program was primarily designed to focus on a specific issue which could be represented as being related to a single ADDICAUSE scale (<u>underlined</u> in the above list of general concepts and their related ADDICAUSE scales). A brief description of the nine treatment programs is given below:

<u>Treatment 1</u> (Creating Success) was designed most specifically to affect ADDICAUSE Scale 4<u>8</u> (History of Punitive Reinforcements, i.e., failure expectations).

<u>Treatment 2</u> (Creating Flexibility) was designed most specifically to affect ADDICAUSE Scale 3<u>6</u> (Rigid Moralizations or fixed attitudes/beliefs).

<u>Treatment 3</u> (Creating Excitement) was designed most specifically to affect the 'S' aspect of ADDICAUSE Scale 3<u>7</u> (need pressure of 'grown up' ADDs/paroxysmals to pursue excitement) and the 'N' aspect of ADDICAUSE Scale 6<u>0</u> (the reinforcing effect of excitement achieved from use of exogenous events).

<u>Treatment 4</u> (Creating Satisfaction) was designed most specifically to affect ADDICAUSE Scale 4<u>7</u> (Physiological Anxiety, by turning the subject's attention to external sources of gratification thus to distract the person from preoccupation with internal distress). [3]

<u>Treatment 5</u> (Creating Values) was designed most specifically to affect ADDICAUSE Scale 2<u>2</u> (Subcultural Values, in order to foster the development of values which might support a pro-social adjustment and lifestyle).

<u>Treatment 6</u> (Creating Innocence) was designed most specifically to affect ADDICAUSE Scale 0<u>8</u> (Guilt Intolerance, or the poignant sense of guilt which the subject seeks to deny in defensive intolerance).

<u>Treatment 7</u> (Creating Health) was designed most specifically to affect ADDICAUSE Scale 4<u>4</u> (desire for Fast Lane Living, by altering the implicit motto: 'I will live fast, die young ...' with a focus of attention on health and its maintenance).

---

3 In retrospect, I wonder why we didn't include systematic relaxation, desensitization, and meditation as part of this treatment program., since they would target the physiological anxiety more directly. ☺

<u>Treatment 8</u> (Creating Happiness) was designed most specifically to affect ADDICAUSE Scale 4<u>0</u> (Pep Up Need, by countering the depressive undertones beneath this need with a continuous happy adjustment).

<u>Treatment 9</u> (Creating Integration) was designed most specifically to affect ADDICAUSE Scale 3<u>0</u> (Affect Denial). The generality of affect denial underlying several of the variables (including Guilt Intolerance, Rebelliousness in the face of Authority, Flat Depression, Hedonism, etc.) recommended this scale as the one most likely to represent the generality or inclusiveness of Treatment 9.

An expanded description of these nine treatment workshops is given in Appendix D, and a list of various components available for inclusion in treatment workshops is given in Appendix E.

RESULTS

Test Results

Statistical analysis of the relationship between attendance at the treatment workshops and the ADDICAUSE scores found that each of the treatments affected the participant's motivation for self-medicating as measured by the ADDICAUSE, and typically in the predicted direction. That is, each treatment lowered the kind of psychological motivation that it was predicted to lower, thereby reducing the participant's felt need to self-medicate for it. In this table, values of .05 or less (shown in Bold type) indicate a significant relationship between workshop attendance and the ADDICAUSE score. You might pay particular attention to the diagonal cells running from the upper left to the lower right, since these were the effects that were predicted. Main predictions are in <u>underlined</u> type, and significant relationships between treatment. In addition, however, significant outcomes are given in bold type whether or not they were predicted.

Effect of Treatment Workshops on the Sum of Response Values of All Twelve Items in Each Scale

ADDICAUSE Scale Name, and Scale Number Most Closely Associated with Workshop Listed	Tx #1	Tx #2	Tx #3	Tx #4	Tx #5	Tx #6	Tx #7	Tx #8	Tx #9
Punitive Rewards Hx, Scale 48 (Creating Success)	**.01**	.29	.38	.08	.09	.79	.46	.31	.97
Rigid Moralization, Scale 36 (Creating Flexibility)	.07	**.01**	.99	**.03**	.48	.39	.20	.07	**.00**
Paroxysmal Energy, Scale 37 (Creating Excitement)	.02	.06	**.02**	**.00**	**.02**	.32	.50	.35	.16
Physiologic Anxiety, Scale 47 (Creating Satisfaction)	.01	.10	.29	**.00**	.07	.53	.06	.26	.15
Subcultural Values, Scale 22 (Creating Values)	.40	.79	.70	.79	**.01**	.39	.16	.14	**.04**
Guilt Intolerance, Scale 08 (Creating Innocence)	.83	.49	.19	.17	.83	**.01**	.01	.01	**.003**
Fast Lane Living, Scale 44 (Creating Health)	.71	.73	.75	**.03**	.23	.50	**.02**	.10	.08
Pep Up Need, Scale 40 (Creating Happiness)	.40	.43	.15	.46	.30	.31	.26	**.04**	.01
Affect Denial, Scale 30 (Creating Integration)	.41	.16	.24	.29	.15	.80	.76	.42	**.01**

Two-tailed tests

These findings would seem to offer the clearest possible test confirming the construct validity of the ADDICAUSE questionnaire. That is, since the treatments were selected/designed based on the theory underlying the development of the test, the fact that the treatments did affect the test scores almost exactly as predicted should mean that the ADDICAUSE test, at the very least, represents its intended theory well.

The almost 'surgical precision' with which the treatments were successful in modifying the ADDICAUSE scales provides some additional information about the usefulness of the ADDICAUSE test. First, the fact that specific effects were achieved where intended (and mostly did not occur where they were not intended) strongly suggests that the ADDICAUSE scales are highly precise. Second, the fact that treatments, designed conceptually from the ADDICAUSE scales, modified the very ADDICAUSE scales at which they were targeted, strongly suggests that the content of the treatment workshops was well chosen for their intended motivational targets. Third, the fact that differential treatment was reliably achieved means not only that the ADDICAUSE scales are modifiable, but also that it is possible to target and modify a particular aspect of a person's presenting problem (which he/she wants to have modified) and at the same time not interfere with other aspects of the person (which he/she may not want to have modified).

In addition, like all demonstrations of effective 'directive' treatment, the present results again demonstrate that therapy need not be directed and instituted solely by the individual client. And finally, it seems clear that significant therapeutic effects can be achieved in interventions as brief as four or five hours in duration, and in groups as large as 55 participants. One importance of this observation is concerned with the need to find and use cost-effective procedures in an increasingly difficult economic climate for clients of treatment services.

Medium-term Post-Release Effects

Two years after all of the inmates involved in the ADDICURE study had been released from the sentences during which they were treated – what we would call medium term follow-up – justice system records were examined to see if the treatments had any lasting effect on subsequent criminal recidivism. In this medium-term-effects study, the following variables were examined:

<u>Recidivism</u>: Criminal recidivism subsequent to the sentence in which they were treated: 0 = None; 1 = Convicted recidivist.

<u>Counts</u>: Number of Counts of any subsequent offenses: 0 = None.

<u>Survival</u>: Number of months on the street from release to the point of criminal recidivism: 24 = Non-recidivist.

<u>Severity</u> of criminal recidivism: Aggregate sentence days (shown to be a good estimate of criminal seriousness (Quirk, Nutbrown and Reynolds, 1991) imposed for subsequent offenses: 0 = Non-recidivist. ***Severity scores were logarithmically transformed*** to deal with the problem of extreme seriousness scores obtained by some recidivists who perform very serious crimes, in contrast to the zero scores of non-recidivists.

<u>Kinds of Offenses</u>: Categories of subsequent offenses were recorded but were <u>not</u> used here because of the difficulty of processing that data.

Thus, the following table displays the results of the several treatments on four of these measures of subsequent criminal conduct. The results are not quite as clear as we might wish. However, Recidivism is significantly affected by all the treatments <u>except</u> the most general one (Treatment 9). As in previous tables, using F-Test probabilities for Medium-term (2-year) follow-up results on criminal recidivism, ***a value of .05 or less is indicative of a statistically significant effect of the treatment.***

TREATMENTS	RECIDIVISM	COUNTS		SEVERITY
Tx 1: SUCCESS	**.03**	.35	.92	.38
Tx 2: FLEXIBILITY	**.00**	.08	.27	**.04**
Tx 3: EXCITEMENT	**.03**	.28	.95	.31
Tx 4: SATISFACTION	**.02**	.53	.87	.17
Tx 5: VALUES	**.01**	**.05**	.28	.09
Tx 6: INNOCENCE	**.03**	.20	.55	.19
Tx 7: HEALTH	**.01**	.13	.39	.09
Tx 8: HAPPINESS	**.00**	.17	.26	**.02**
Tx 9: INTEGRATION	.42	.47	.55	.98

Two-tailed tests

Four of the nine treatments appear to have affected Offence Severity score to some degree, while the only workshop to have any effect on the number of offences (Counts) was Treatment 5, Values, and the only workshops to have any effect on the number of months on the street from release to the point of criminal recidivism (Survival) were Treatment 2 (Flexibility) and Treatment 8 (Happiness).

It should be noted, however, that *eight of the nine workshops resulted in less chance of these addicted inmates being reincarcerated within the two years post release*, and two of them resulted in any offences being of significantly less severity. This should be considered within following context:

(1) About 60% to 65% of the types of inmates treated at the O.C.I. tend to be convicted of further offenses within two years of their release if they serve their time at settings other than the O.C.I.

(2) About 45% of the types of inmates treated at the O.C.I. tend to be convicted of further offenses within two years of their release (Wolfus & Stasiak, 1991) if they serve their sentences at the O.C.I. and receive only the basic/regular treatment program there.

(3) Recidivism rates (percentages) found in the ADDICURE study for the control group (0 hours) and for experimental group members who attended 3 or more hours of treatment at varying numbers of the treatment workshops (1 or more, 2 or more, 3 or more, etc.) – see the following table – were as follows:

(a) Attendance at none (N=32) of the Addicure treatment workshops – the control group – results in a recidivism percentage, as indicated by the number of inmates reconvicted within the approximately two-year post release timeframe, of 38%, which is slightly less than the average of about 45% for the types of inmates treated at the O.C.I. as reported by Wolfus & Stasiak (1991).

(b) Attendance at one (N=86) or more (N=138) of the Addicure treatment workshops brings that recidivism percentage, as indicated by the number of inmates reconvicted within the approximately two-year post release timeframe, down to 30%.

(c) Attendance at two (N=7) or more (N=52) of the Addicure treatment workshops brings that recidivism percentage down to 23%.

(d) Attendance at three N=9) or more (N=45) of the Addicure treatment workshops brings that recidivism percentage down to 20%.

(e) Attendance at four (N=12) or more (N=36) of the Addicure treatment workshops brings that recidivism percentage down to 19%.

(f) Attendance at five (N=15) or more (N=24) of the Addicure treatment workshops brings that recidivism percentage down to

21%, and

(g) Attendance at six or more (N=9) of the Addicure treatment workshops brings that recidivism percentage down to 0%.

Numbers of subjects in each group (by number of Addicure workshops/ treatments received) and <u>Percentages</u> of Addicure Subjects convicted of further offenses, where Tx > 0 means 1 or more treatments; Tx > 1 means 2 or more treatments; etc.

Treatment "Amount"	Tx = 0	Tx > 0	Tx > 1	Tx > 2	Tx > 3	Tx > 4	Tx > 5
Number of Subjects	32	138	52	45	36	24	9
Recidivism Percentage	38	30	23	20	19	21	0

PREVENTION OF ADDICTIONS

If a brief treatment such as the above can influence addictive behaviours, can providing treatment for issues identified (e.g., by the ADDICAUSE questionnaire) before individuals become addicted be used to prevent the development of addictions? The truth is that we don't know. All we can do at this time is to use the light we do have to suggest how these questions might be answered in the future.

Many years ago, one of the authors was privileged to attend a meeting sponsored by the American Society for Humanistic Education. It brought together a large number of senior educators from all over the United States. Our task was to collate the opinions expressed concerning <u>the proper purposes and goals for education</u>. It was surprising to discover that standard content areas in academic education were virtually ignored by those attending. Indeed, upon inquiry, they had been expressly put aside as being of secondary importance. The goals that were conceived to be of primary importance were initiatives that would prepare the person for effective and adaptive social living and for participation in and contribution to the community, things like cooperativeness, assertiveness, self-confidence, courage, diplomacy, friendliness, positive attitudes, serenity, joyfulness, and the like – essentially the sorts of skills fostered in psychotherapy and in the programs discussed above.

It has been observed that, in contrast, standard academic education tends to concern itself primarily with developing verbal and numerical abilities, out of the more than 100 human abilities that might as easily have been selected, mainly because most jobs require some reading and mathematics. Quite apart from the purposes and the effects of educators choosing these two human abilities as predominant in education, the observation did remind us that it might it would be desirable to introduce into conventional education curricula those content areas concerned with precisely the same kinds of issues addressed in the treatment workshops discussed above.

Finally, the fact that failure is an important factor in the history of addiction (and, from another study, published as *A Simple and Effective Cure for Criminality,* a major factor in criminal behaviour as well), and since school is one of the most common contexts in which young people may experience failure, it is suggested that *ensuring* success in school – through better attention to those students who seem to be "falling through the cracks" – could go a long way towards preventing addiction.

APPENDIX A: EXAMPLES OF LARGE-GROUP TREATMENT WORKSHOPS

In general, the clientele to be served by the various workshop programs listed below will be relatively self- evident. For example, the Aggressiveness Program is designed to treat some kinds of aggressiveness, and only those clients who have problems with anger and its expression should be expected to get a lot of benefit from it. The Sexuality Program is intended for those individuals for whom sexuality is a problem; the Depression Program is intended for a subset of those individuals who are depressed; and so on. Some programs, such as the Stress Program and the Life-Enhancement Program, have wide applicability and may often be prescribed even when there is no apparent relevance to the presenting problem. It should be remembered, however, that this is not always the case, and an understanding of the participants' psychological needs is necessary for appropriate selection to programs. Trainers who undertake to use these program outlines must understand that it is their responsibility to assess all individuals who are referred to any of these programs to ensure, in consultation with the referral agent, that clients are provided with the most appropriate programs given their individual characteristics and needs.

AGGRESSIVENESS PROGRAM

The program for aggressiveness is designed to address all the major requirements for the management of most aggressiveness and its associated states. Components of the task are presented as separate, usually day-long, modules as described below. Experience to date suggests that treatment of this kind can be effective when delivered in groups as large as the space can accommodate.

1. <u>Orientation to Aggressiveness:</u>

The orientation to anger begins with a statement of purpose and an overview of what is to follow. The orientation continues with an explanation of the body's stress/emergency system, including the autonomic nervous system (ANS), the effects it has on the body's organs (especially cardiovascular, respiratory, muscular, sensory, alimentary, and endocrine systems), the nature of the ANS' activating sequences, the adrenal arousal-maintaining system, and the control of the immune system. The purpose of this part of the orientation is to provide the explanatory basis for the physiologic component of the anger and aggression management methods which follow.

To personalize the above information, participants are asked to complete and self-score questionnaires bearing upon the activators of anger in their own lives, and the strength of their anger response. The meanings of score ranges are discussed, permitting each participant to relate his personal experience to the various ANS functions. This allows some extension of the explanation about the physiological and psychological activating sequences/events affecting the ANS and anger arousal.

The second half of the orientation provides the first anger management interventions by offering strategy and practice in self-regulation of bodily functions. Self-regulation strategies are offered and demonstrated, with experiential training for (i) motor output pacing to provide time for self-regulation, (ii) re-labelling of the anger experience as being primarily ANS arousal, (iii) physical exercise as a means by which to use the energy produced by ANS arousal, (iv) respiratory self-regulation methods (the "calming" response), for quick stress relief and correcting cerebral oxygenation and (v) striate muscle relaxation for calming and to prepare for later systematic desensitization.

2. Relaxation/Calmness Training:

The second day-long module extends the striate muscle relaxation training to include experiential training in a wide variety of relaxation/calming methods. Participants practice (i) voluntary muscle relaxation, (ii) sub-hypnotic relaxation, (iii) autogenic training, (iv) self-programming relaxation, (v) yogic meditation, (vi) Zen meditation, (vii) mantra meditation, (vii) contemplative meditation, and (viii) seed thought meditation. The purpose of training participants in all these methods is to allow each to discover the method(s) which work best for him, so that he can use it/them along with the voluntary relaxation method employed in the later systematic desensitization to deepen his level of relaxation.

3. Resources Installation:

The third module involves experiential training of participants in the use of imagery as a therapeutic device. Participants are taught (i) to attend to internal imagery/representations of events in their lives, (ii) to enrich representational experience, (iii) to modify their representations of events to gain greater control over the meanings of events in their lives, (iv) to experience events in various ways which increase their sense of safety and ability to master events, and (v) to review and "install" those personal resources which might be used to alter personal internal representations. The purpose of this experiential training is to provide the participants with a sense of self-control and how to alter the effects of previous experiences.

4. Anger Circumstances Review:

With the above understandings and capabilities of calmness and self-regulation in place, the next module is concerned with the analysis of participants' past and possible future anger-arousing events. This is accomplished by (i) a general explanation of the range of types of activators to be considered, (ii) a series of self-scoring questionnaires which reflect personal status on various classes of anger-arousing stimuli, and which permit participants to personalize the preceding explanation, and (iii) an application of relapse prevention strategies to an examination of past and possible future anger situations. The purpose of this exercise is to help participants to discover the risk situations in which anger may occur, and to provide psychological inoculation against future potentially-anger-arousing situations.

5. Rational-Emotive Training:

With anger events/situations identified by participants, it is now meaningful to review those errors of thinking and cognitive coping strategies which contribute to participants' various anger situations or events. This module involves the use of self-scoring tests to identify some of each participant's errors of thinking, some instruction and small-group discussion to correct errors of thinking and to personalize cognitive strategies. Several cognitive strategies are considered, including (i) re-labelling of the situation and/or the subjective feelings, (ii) identification and modification of erroneous thinking as evidenced in self-talk, (iii) challenging of errors of thinking, (iv) reframing or the application of divergent thinking to a reconsideration of anger-arousing events, and (v) imagery restructuring and resources utilization to desensitize participants to their anger situations. The purpose of these procedures is to provide further cognitive anger inoculation.

6. Anger Responses Delay Training:

The next module extends the preceding one to include actions and social behaviours. In addition to the conventional methods for assertive responses training in social interactions to counter guilt and anxiety about aggressive responding and/or demanding under-assertiveness as anger derivatives, this module seeks to train participants experientially in the use of automatic delay of reactions in response to cues of anger. It extends the motor-output pacing method mentioned earlier to include small-group practice in the habits of automatic response delay. Its purpose is to extend coping and control strategies to the behavioural field and to social interactions.

7. Empathy Training:

The next module seeks to provide basic training in the skills of empathy. The nature of empathy and its role in achieving personal needs in the social context are described. Self-scoring tests of empathy are administered to allow the participants to personalize the discussion. Experiential exercises are conducted in effective listening skills, including (i) accurate empathy, (ii) respect, (iii) non-contingent positive regard, and (iv) extension of the three-part assertive statement to elicit empathic responses from others. The purpose of this module is to further extend coping and assertiveness skills to achieve improved outcomes in social contacts, and to develop feeling for others' needs.

8. Systematic Desensitization:

Systematic desensitization is usually part of any application of the Aggressiveness Program. The method follows Wolpe's procedure, employing the already-trained deep muscle relaxation, and coupling it repeatedly with a standard hierarchy of anger-arousing images selected based on anger tests administered to all participants as part of the anger circumstances review module. This procedure has been employed successfully with groups as large as 70 participants and presumably can be used with any size of group which the premises can accommodate.

Evaluation:

Short-term evaluation studies have been run with those modules of the Aggressiveness Program which were being offered at the time when the evaluative studies were being done. For this purpose, a self-rating monitoring method employing ratings analogous to Wolpe's Subjective Units of Disturbance (SUD's), but of several dimensions, was developed locally to measure change in a variety of subjective states. These scales were administered at the beginning and at the end of each day-long (approximately 4-hour) block of program time to varying numbers (due to availability) of participants in treatment workshops. Mean scores on the Anger and Self-Control sections of the self-rating questionnaire obtained following Orientation to Anger Management, Relaxation/ Calmness Training, Rational-Emotive Training, and a series of three Systematic Desensitization workshops are displayed in the Figure below. The following three components of this program could not easily be added to the table, but they are the second, fourth, and sixth parts of the program.: **Relax / Calmness, Systematic Desensitization.1, and Systematic Desensitization** 3.

Note: Lower scores indicate improvement

AGGRESSIVENESS TREATMENT PROGRAM

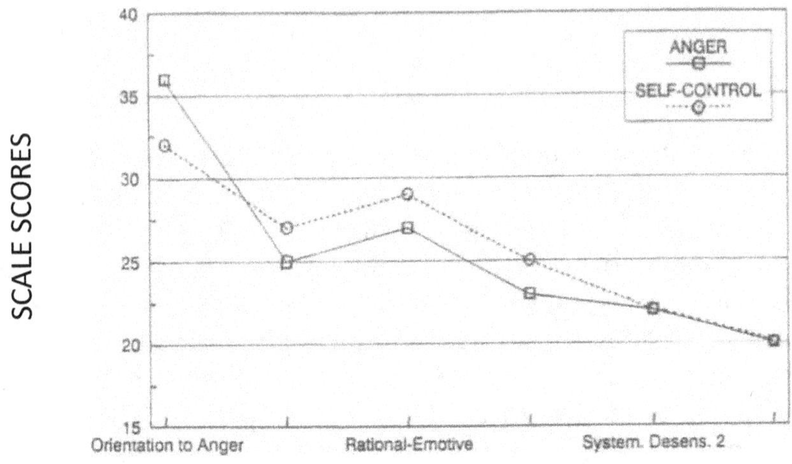

CONFLICT MANAGEMENT PROGRAM (generic)

The program for conflict management is designed to address all the major requirements for the management of most types of human conflict and their associated states. Components of the task are presented as separate modules described below. Experience to date suggests that treatment of this kind can be effective when delivered in groups as large as the space can accommodate.

1. Orientation to Conflict Management:

The orientation to conflict management begins with a statement of purpose and an overview of what is to follow. The orientation continues with an explanation of the main causes of human conflict, which, surprisingly to most participants, involves mainly the process of communication and the problems of language. This is followed by a further orientation to the nature of societal living and its advantages and responsibilities, and a review of the community's efforts at training people in socialization. The purpose of this orientation is to provide the explanatory basis for the management of conflict, as well as to break down some of the participants' pre-existing stereotypes by creating a degree of confusion in their minds.

To personalize the above information, participants are asked to provide conflict situations from their own experiences in social living. Each of these is analyzed in some detail for its informational contents and the communications involved. Alternative outcomes at each stage are elicited or provided to demonstrate the process by which conflict emerges and is maintained. This discussion tends to personalize both the issues at stake and the confusion experienced as former stereotypes are challenged.

The second half of the orientation examines the bifurcational and classificational nature of language, as a source of both stereotype and error, and its relevance to other societal systems. Demonstrations of the perceptual process, of information acquisition errors, of concept formation and of communication are made to illustrate the problems affecting language, information and communication, as a way of challenging the participants' notions about "reality" as it is presented to the senses. Some reassurance is provided to counter the disruptive effects of the confusion which is intentionally being created to disrupt existing stereotypes and old habits.

2. Assertive Training:

The second module addresses the concept of language as a set of communication skills. Experiential training is given in (i) in vivo assertion desensitization for a variety of conflictual and potentially conflictual interpersonal communication situations, (ii) self-talk and self-awareness procedures, (iii) restructuring of attributional errors, (iv) appropriate use of guilt and inhibition, and (v) the three-pan assertive statement The purpose of these exercises is to provide participants with improved tools for interpersonal communication, to develop a greater tolerance for assertiveness in self and others, to teach participants to more effectively employ the energies generated by the arousal associated with any approach to conflict, and to alleviate the development of conflict in daily communications with others.

3. Empathy Training:

The next module seeks to provide basic training in the skills of empathy. The nature of empathy and its role in achieving personal needs in the social context are described. Self-scoring tests of empathy are administered to allow the participants to personalize the discussion. Experiential exercises are conducted in effective listening skills, including (i) accurate empathy, (ii) respect, (iii) non-contingent positive regard, and (iv) extension of the three-part assertive statement to elicit empathic responses from others. The purpose of this module is to further extend coping and assertiveness skills to achieve improved outcomes in social contacts, and to develop feeling for others' needs.

4. Emotional Responsiveness Training:

Most people are unaware of the fact that conflict is almost never necessary in life. To the extent that the person feels and is focused on positive feelings and experiences, to that extent conflict does not need to occur. Consequently, the next module elaborates on the positive values referenced in the preceding module, using methods from assertive training to help participants to express and experience positive emotions and joyful experiences and to enjoy life more fully.

5. Life Values Review/Training:

A large amount of conflict arises in the context of competition. Competition usually involves Type "A" evaluative values and ignores the more socializing "Being" or "B" values. Accordingly, the next module asks participants to examine their values in detail, and challenges some of the pseudo-values which people have often construed as their basic values. The source of personal values in development are examined, and the discussion is personalized by reference to some self-scoring tests of personal values and of self-actualization needs. Participants are encouraged to examine their values and to decide upon the values that they might prefer to adopt among those which they can appreciate. Experiential exercises are introduced to help participants (i) to adjust their values and priorities to suit their own wishes, (ii) to use the values they have or wish to develop to remove the sources of their negative feelings and (iii) to reach toward greater joy in living.

Systematic Desensitization

Systematic desensitization is usually part of any application of the Conflict Management Program. The method follows Wolpe's procedure, employing trained deep muscle relaxation, and coupling it repeatedly with standard hierarchies of images related to anger, criticism, closeness, emotionality and friendliness, these arousal-images being selected on the basis of tests administered at the outset to all participants. The procedure has been employed successfully with groups as large as 70 participants and presumably can be used with any size of group which the premises can accommodate.

Evaluation:

Short-term evaluation studies have been run with those modules of the Conflict Management Program which were being offered at the time when the evaluative studies were being done. For this purpose, stress, anxiety and anger monitoring procedures have been administered at the beginning and at the end of each day-long (approximately 4-hour) block of program time to varying numbers (due to availability) of participants in treatment workshops.

The Willoughby Emotional Maturity Scale (WEMS), a 25-item scale of anxiety/neuroticism, has been used since the 1930's as a measure of change in psychotherapy. A self-rating monitoring method employing ratings analogous to Wolpe's Subjective Units of Disturbance (SUD), but of several dimensions was developed locally to measure change in ways supplementary to the WEMS. The mean scores on the WEMS and on the Anxiety and Anger sections of the locally developed self-rating questionnaire obtained following Orientation to Conflict Management, Assertive Training, Emotional Responsiveness Training and Life Values. **Assertive Training 1 and Emotional Responsiveness could not easily be added to the table but are the second and fourth components of this treatment workshop. Note that lower scores again indicate improvement.**

CONFLICT MANAGEMENT PROGRAM

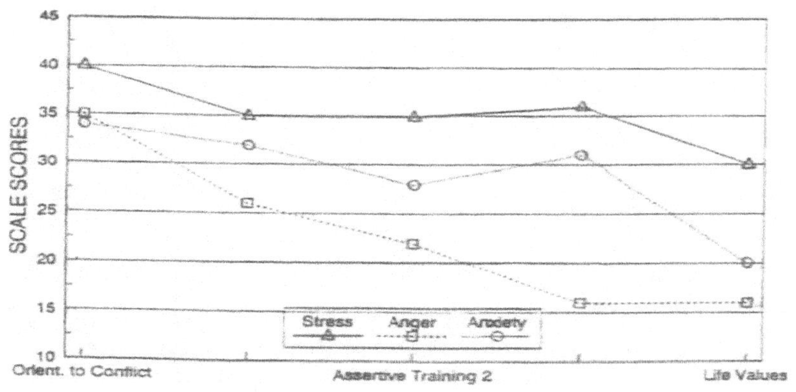

SEXUALITY PROGRAM, (generic)

The program for sexuality is designed to address all the major requirements for the treatment of most types of sexual problems. Components of the task depend, of course, upon the nature of the problem presented, but the core elements of the basic program are presented as separate modules described below. Experience to date suggests that treatment of this kind can be effective when delivered in groups as large as the space can accommodate.

1. Orientation to Sexuality:

The orientation to sexuality begins with a statement of purpose and an overview of what is to follow. It continues with an explanation of the main causes underlying sexual problems, the habits and thought patterns associated with each (including, as appropriate, the habits and thought patterns associated with deviant sexual behaviours, some of which are common to the various types of sexual offenses). This is followed by a further orientation to the nature of particular sexual problems or offenses relevant to the particular participants in the program. It is surprising how little basic knowledge is possessed by most people about the nature of sexuality and its anomalies, and the purpose of this orientation is to provide the explanatory basis for the program modules to follow.

To personalize the above information, participants are asked to complete and self-score some questionnaires bearing upon their views of sexuality and the sexual attitudes they hold. The meanings of score ranges are discussed, permitting each participant to relate his personal experience to the parameters of the general discussion. This allows some extension of the explanation about the various activating sequences/events affecting sexual motivations.

The second half of the orientation provides the first steps in management interventions by offering strategy and practice in self-regulation of thinking patterns. Self-regulation strategies are offered and demonstrated, with instruction/training for (i) various erotic arousal patterns, (ii) some of the other arousal sequences which affect sexuality, (iii) re-labelling of pseudo-erotic motivations for their real motivations, (iii) defining the components of these underlying motivations and tracking their sources, (iv) reframing source experiences to alleviate feelings of rejection, guilt, shame, anxiety, depression, etc., (v) reviewing the varieties of values which might be learned from past aversive sexual experience, and (vi) reviewing potential alternative habits of thought and action.

2. Human Sexuality Education:

The second module provides basic education about human sexuality. Both the biological and the psychosocial characteristics of both genders are reviewed in considerable detail along with the functions of both genders and means for self- and other-protection from conception and from disease. The phenomena discussed are presented in fairly graphic form, and the particular topics addressed in greater detail are chosen from participants responses to a checklist of topics which they wish to have covered. The dual purposes of this direct and informative approach to the topic of sexuality are to provide missing information and/or correct misinformation, and to decondition the private sensibilities of participants to overt conversation in this area in preparation for the remaining modules. In order to treat sexuality, it is necessary to remove some of the common taboos against straight and honest communication concerning sex.

3. Relationship Skills Training:

The third module moves beyond the basics of sexuality and directs attention to the contexts in which sexuality is normally experienced and which enrich the experiences of sex. The nature of human relationship, frequently never adequately experienced by those having sexual problems, is discussed in detail. The processes involved in each human relationship, whether sexual or not, are described, and some experiential training in these processes are offered. The means for adding enrichment to a relationship are presented, along with some preliminary discussion of social values and conventional mores. A brief course in empathy training is employed to provide both understanding and experience in the means by which individuals can obtain satisfaction for their social and other needs in the context of a relationship. Some indications of the relevance of this module and the next two modules are offered to participants.

4. Courting Skills Training:

The next module addresses the basic skills involved in courting. This module bridges relationships and the expression of sexuality. It provides information and some training in the cues used by both genders in the preliminaries of courting, and extensive information about the courting practices of various cultures with major focus on the North American scene. Sex roles and functions and the manner in which they change at various stages of development are discussed in detail. The enhancement of mutual sexual experience is emphasized throughout as that can be achieved through various courting activities, their maintenance and appropriate creative changes in them over time. Training is offered in the process of adapting oneself and one's personal characteristics to achieve greater acceptability to others, and to increase the joy of courting.

5. Emotional Responsiveness Training:

Perhaps the single most common feature of people who present with sexual difficulties is a general difficulty in experiencing, expressing, and enjoying their emotions. The final common module in the Sexuality Program is designed to alleviate this maladaptive inhibition of emotional responsiveness. Various methods from assertive training are employed to facilitate this task, along with several original models of emotional inhibition and defensiveness, and some methods for the delineation and achievement of personal development goals relating to the emotional life. The aim in this module is both personal experiential training and the enhancement and enrichment of the personal experience of emotions. All this is accomplished in a slow progression of steps, with full explanation at each stage. The effect tends to be to generate considerable excitement and a strong sense of the joy of emotions and the values they can support in daily living. The purpose of this exercise in this context is to help participants to set aside some of their unnecessary habitual controls which impair relationships, courting, and sexual gratification, and to pursue positive joy-giving experiences for themselves and their loved ones.

6. Additional:

Depending upon the nature of the presenting symptoms and circumstances, it may be necessary to implement any of several other treatment components for people with sexual difficulties, the reasons for which are exceedingly complex and impractical to detail here.

Evaluation:

Short-term evaluation studies have been run with some of the modules from the Sexuality Program. For this purpose, anxiety and anger monitoring procedures have been administered at the beginning and at the end of the Orientation to Sexuality, Human Sexuality Education, Courting Skills Training, and Emotional Responsiveness Training components of the Sexuality Program.

A self-rating monitoring method employing ratings analogous to Wolpe's Subjective Units of Disturbance (SUD), but of several dimensions, was developed locally to measure change in a variety of subjective states. These scales were administered at the end of each 4-hour block of program time to varying numbers (due to availability) of participants in treatment workshops. The mean scores on the Anxiety and Anger sections of the self-rating questionnaire obtained following Orientation to Sexuality, Human Sexuality Education, Courting Skills Training, and Emotional Responsiveness Training are displayed in the Figure below.

It is interesting to note that this program had more effect on Anxiety than on Anger – lower scores indicate improvement – possibly because many of the treatment subjects in this program were incarcerated because of problematic sexual behaviour rather than anger problems.

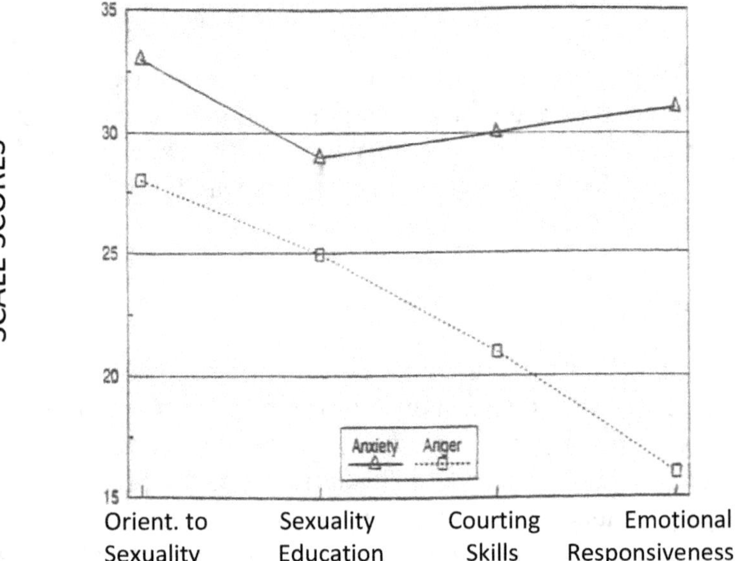

SCALE SCORES
35
30
25
20
15
Anxiety   Anger
Orient. to
Sexuality
Sexuality
Education
Courting
Skills
Emotional
Responsiveness

The program for stress management is designed to address all the major requirements for the management of stress and the effects of its associated states. Components of the task are presented as separate modules as described below. Experience to date suggests that treatment of this kind can be effective when delivered in groups as large as the space can accommodate.

1. Orientation to Stress:

The orientation to stress begins with a statement of purpose and an overview of what is to follow. The orientation continues with an explanation of the body's stress/emergency system, including the autonomic nervous system (ANS), the effects it has on the body's organs (especially cardiovascular, respiratory, muscular, sensory, alimentary, and endocrine systems), the nature of the ANS' activating sequences, the adrenal arousal-maintaining system, and the control of the immune system. The purpose of this part of the orientation is to provide the explanatory basis for the functional stress management methods which follow.

To personalize the above information, participants are asked to complete and self-score questionnaires bearing upon the activators of stress in their own lives, and the strength of their stress reactivity. The meanings of score ranges are discussed, permitting each participant to relate his personal experience to the various ANS functions. This allows some extension of the explanation about the physiological and psychological activating sequences/events affecting the ANS and stress arousal.

The second half of the orientation provides the first stress management interventions by offering strategy and practice in self-regulation of bodily functions. Self-regulation strategies are offered

41

and demonstrated, with experiential training for (i) motor output pacing for cardiovascular self-regulation, (ii) sleep self-regulation for periodic ANS regeneration, (iii) respiratory self-regulation methods for quick stress relief and correcting cerebral oxygenation (the "calming" response), and (iv) striate muscle relaxation for calming and to prepare for later systematic desensitization.

2. Relaxation/Calmness Training:

The second program module extends the striate muscle relaxation training to include experiential training in a wide variety of relaxation/calming methods. Participants practice (i) voluntary muscle relaxation, (ii) sub-hypnotic relaxation, (iii) autogenic training, (iv) self- programming relaxation, (v) yogic meditation, (vi) Zen meditation, (vii) mantra meditation, (vii) contemplative meditation, and (viii) seed thought meditation. The purpose of training participants in all these methods is to allow each to discover the methods which work best for him, so that he can use them along with the voluntary relaxation method employed in the later systematic desensitization to deepen his level of relaxation.

3. Resources Installation:

The third module involves experiential training of participants in the use of imagery as a therapeutic device. Participants are taught (i) to attend to internal imagery/representations of events in their lives, (ii) to enrich representational experience, (iii) to modify their representations of events to gain greater control over the meanings of events in their lives, (iv) to experience events in various ways which increase their sense of safety and ability to master events, and (v) to review and "install" those personal resources which might be used to alter personal internal representations. The purpose of this experiential training is to provide the participants with a sense of self-control and the means by which to alter the effects of previous experiences.

4. Stressor Events Review:

With the above understandings and capabilities of calmness and self-regulation in place, the next module is concerned with the analysis of participants' past and possible future stressor events. This is accomplished by (i) a general explanation of the range of types of stressors to be considered, (ii) a series of self-scoring questionnaires which reflect personal status on various classes of stressors, and which permit participants to personalize the preceding explanation, and (iii) an application of relapse prevention strategies to an examination of past and possible future stressors. The purpose of this exercise is to help participants to discover the risk situations in which stress may occur, as a form of psychological stress inoculation once the stress response is relieved.

5. Coping Strategies Training:

With stressor events/situations identified by participants, it is now meaningful to review those cognitive coping strategies which contribute to participants' various stressor situations or events. This module involves some instruction and some small-group discussion to correct errors of thinking and to personalize cognitive strategies. Several cognitive strategies are considered, including (i) re-labelling the situation and/or the subjective feelings, (ii) identification, challenging and modification of erroneous thinking as evidenced in self-talk, (iii) reframing or the application of divergent thinking to a reconsideration of stressor events, and (iv) imagery restructuring and resources utilization to desensitize the participants to their stressor situations. The purpose of these procedures is to provide further cognitive stress inoculation.

6. Assertive Training:

The next module extends the preceding one to include actions and social behaviours. In addition to the conventional methods for assertive responses training in social interactions to counter guilt and anxiety about aggressive responding and/or demanding under-assertiveness as stressor agents, this sub-program seeks to train participants experientially in the use of ANS stress-derived bodily energy both as a coping strategy and as an health-promoting anti-stress strategy (progressive in vivo desensitization). This module involves both instruction and small-group practice. Its purpose is to extend coping strategies to the behavioural field and to social interactions.

7. Stress Prevention Training:

The next module involves a direct use of relapse prevention strategies and materials both to create preparedness for future stressors, and to permit review of all the above means for managing stress; and it extends the above exercises by developing positive attitudes and feelings to replace negative ones. Procedures for resource accessing and future pacing, and additional cognitive strategies of an attitudinal and conceptual nature are introduced. The purpose of this exercise is review and consolidation, and some further future extension from the earlier sessions.

8. Systematic Desensitization:

Systematic desensitization is usually part of any application of the Stress Management program. The method follows Wolpe's procedure, employing the already-trained deep muscle relaxation, and coupling it repeatedly with a standard hierarchy of anxiety images selected based on anxiety tests administered to all participants as pan of the stressor events review sub-program. This procedure has been employed successfully with groups as large as 70 participants and presumably can be used with any size of group which the premises can accommodate.

Evaluation:

Short-term evaluation studies have been run with some of the modules from the Stress Program. For this purpose, stress and anxiety monitoring procedures have been administered at the beginning and at the end of the Orientation to Stress, Relaxation/Calmness Training, Assertive Training and Systematic Desensitization components of the Stress Program.

The Willoughby Emotional Maturity Scale (WEMS), a 25-item scale of anxiety/neuroticism, has been used since the 1930's as a measure of change in psychotherapy. A self-rating monitoring method employing ratings analogous to Wolpe's Subjective Units of Disturbance (SUD), but of several dimensions, was developed locally to measure change in ways supplementary to the WEMS. These scales were administered at end of each 4-hour block of sub-program time to varying numbers (due to availability) of participants in treatment workshops. The mean scores on the WEMS and on the Anxiety section of the self-rating questionnaire obtained following the workshops are displayed in the Figure below. Tables created in Word do not translate well for publishing in Kindle. In this table, the workshops in order are: Orientation to Conflict Management, Assertive Training 1, Assertive Training 2, Emotional Responsiveness Training, and Life Values Review/Training. And the vertical axis of the table refers to S scores.

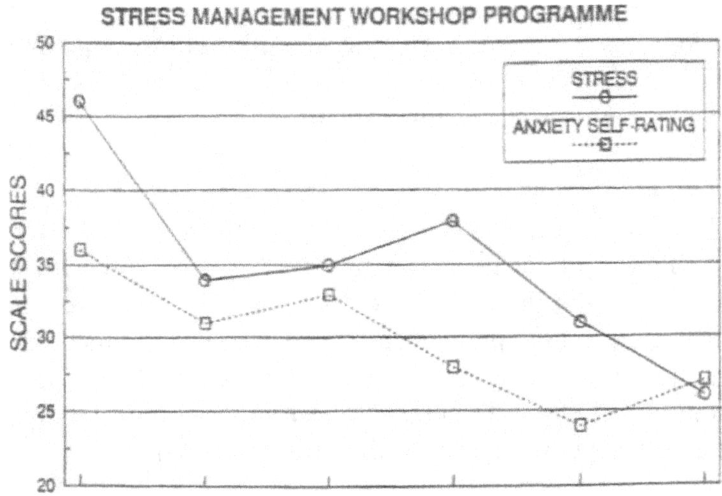

DISCUSSION

As clinical psychologists, we spent most of our careers helping individuals, and sometimes small groups, to solve their intra- and interpersonal problems and to lead more productive and personally satisfying lives. However, for many years, we have been intrigued by the idea of workshop-style (large-group) treatment programs, and we have come to believe that many of the benefits of individual and small-group psychological treatment can also be obtained by the participants in large-group treatment workshops, supplemented where necessary by a relatively small amount of individual work, at a significantly lower cost.

In designing these treatment workshops for maximum therapeutic benefit, we have made certain assumptions. First, it is assumed that it is necessary to build in evaluation at each stage of treatment program development and implementation, so that program delivery is controlled by its results. Second, it is appropriate to include motivational elements as part of the treatment, rather than expect that only motivated clients will be participating. Third, treatment needs to be guided by the therapist (the expert) rather than by the client (where it becomes a case of the blind leading the blind). Fourth, to ensure a powerful therapeutic effect, it is necessary that treatment be designed in such a way that it incorporates scientifically verified laws of learning and behaviour. Fifth, it is necessary for the client both to be provided with information about the basic processes involved in his or her presenting problems and their treatment, and to be shown strategies for addressing and resolving them. And finally, it is desirable, if not always necessary, for clients to have an opportunity to practice using the information and strategies with which they have been provided, so as to ensure that the treatment has really "taken," before turning the clients loose to function on their own.

In the treatment workshops that we have offered, measures have been taken before and after each day-long workshop, so that the effect of each workshop module could be evaluated, as well as any overall effect of the workshop series. In the pages that follow, only the post-workshop scores are reported, for the sake of simplicity. However, the scores shown are fully representative of pre- and post-workshop values, the pre- to post-workshop change scores, and subjective reports of improvements experienced by participants as a result of their workshop experiences.

Over the intervening years, (1) pre-post measures have shown that these treatment workshops produce measurable effects and (2) participants in these large group treatment programs have demonstrated that they are able to use the instruction received and the skills that they have learned in the treatment workshops in day-to-day interactions in their living-unit communities (cf *Freedom from Addictions* by Douglas Quirk and Reg Reynolds and *A Simple*

47

and Effective Cure for Criminality by Reg Reynolds and Douglas Quirk) In addition, informal comparisons between the results of large-group treatment and the more intensive eight-to-ten-person group have been very favourable to the large-group approach. In those cases where the same measures have been employed, for example, the treatment workshops have generally produced better results.

The present volume attempts to serve three functions. First, it provides for description and evaluation of four series of workshops offered at the Ontario Correctional Institute (where the authors were employed), each composed of several day-long modules – Anger Management (the Aggressiveness Program), Stress Management, Conflict Management, and Relationships and Human Sexuality (the Sexuality Program). Second, it outlines a variety of other workshops *which have been neither offered nor evaluated in precisely this format to date,* but which would be useful to the population in general. And finally, it shows how these workshops might be combined to address a variety of psychological problems encountered in everyday life..

In writing the descriptions of the various workshop programs, the authors have assumed that the purpose of each workshop will be relatively self-evident. For example, the Aggressiveness Program is designed to treat some kinds of aggressiveness, and only those clients who have problems with anger and its expression should be referred for it. The Sexuality Program is intended for those individuals for whom sexuality is a problem; the Depression Program is intended for a subset of those individuals who are depressed; and so on. Some programs, such as the Stress Program and the Life-Enhancement Program, have wide applicability and may often be prescribed even when there is no apparent relevance to the presenting problem.

In general, the clientele to be served by the various workshop programs will also be self- evident. However, this is not always the case, and an understanding of the participants' psychological needs is necessary for appropriate selection to programs. Trainers who undertake to use this program outline must understand that it is their responsibility to assess all individuals who are referred to any of these programs to ensure, in consultation with the referral agent, that clients are provided with the most appropriate programs given their individual characteristics and needs.

In our experience, the modules that comprise these treatment workshop programs usually take about a day or two to complete, may be presented in either half-day or full-day sessions, and can be effective when delivered in groups as large as the space can accommodate. To date, they have been presented in full-day format, and there has been essentially no problem in maintaining attention and motivation of participants for that period of time. This has been accomplished partly by having two or more presenters who keep changing the pace of activities and level of excitement in their manner of presentation, and partly by the large-group format with its potential for contagious mutually arousing interaction.

APPENDIX B: DEVELOPMENT OF THE ADDICAUSE QUESTIONNAIRE

Dimensional Concepts

With the help of colleagues, a wide variety of concepts which might conceivably be related to addiction and other sources of human suffering was assembled. Those which were chosen for as the basis for the short form of the <u>ADDICAUSE Questionnaire</u> displayed below.

Used Mainly as Verbs	Used Mainly as Nouns
Facilitate – Impede	Satisfied - Dissatisfied
Change - Persist	Facilitate - Impede
Fail - Succeed	Self - Other
Lose - Gain	Beauty – Ugliness
Approach - Avoid	Alone – Group
Sensitive - Insensitive	Bad – Good
Integrate - Disintegrate	Forwards-Backwards
Rigid - Change/Learn	Real – Unreal
Purpose - Random	Up – Down
Separate - Together	Isolated – Social
Sleep - Awaken	Pain – Pleasure
Power - Impotence	Active – Passive
Anxious - Depressed	Mind – Body
Tense - Relax	Error – Precise

A series of polar concepts was now available to serve as dimensions along which respondents might be able to express their participation in various types of motivations.

Numbers of Items Per Scale

The next question which needed to be addressed was the number of items to be written to provide scales to measure each variable. Psychometric lore suggested that the 'ideal' (maximizing predictive/outcome efficiency) number of correlated items in a scale would be 16, with a range of acceptability from 12 to 20. On the other hand, a great number of variables was to be scaled, which might suggest that minimizing the number of items per scale would be appropriate.

It was decided that each scale constructed would have cognitive and emotional elements and, due to our interest in Neuro-Linguistic Programming (NLP), visual, auditory, and kinaesthetic elements counter-balanced within its item composition, which might suggest that the number of items per scale would have to be a multiple of 6 and should favour larger numbers. Considering the uncertain value of the processing and sensory sub-scales, the anticipated length of the whole test recommended that 12 items be used in each scale, even if that would risk some imprecision in any sub-scales to be evaluated.

Means were explored to compensate for the risk to sub-scale reliabilities, given that sub-scales of only four items per scale each were being planned to measure the relative roles of visual, auditory and kinaesthetic factors in test respondents. In practice, it turned out that writing items to capture those visual, auditory and kinaesthetic factors added nothing particularly useful; however, neither did it appear to detract from the assessment process, so they were left as written.

Response Alternatives

The next question considered was the range of response alternatives to be made available to respondents. It was recognized that Likert-type scaling would have an advantage over binary (True/False) responding by extending the range of variability within each scale and sub-scale; and extending the response range might compensate for any impairment of reliability that might derive from the limited numbers of items in the sub-scales. Moreover, the polar nature of the concepts to be used recommended the idea of providing for distribution of responses along a scale. It was decided to employ Likert scaling for the response options offered.

But how many positions should the Likert response scales afford? The possibilities seemed restricted to 3, 5 or 7 positions as response options. On one hand, the larger the number of options, the wider and more discriminating should be the response distributions for each scale. On the other hand, many of the respondents to whom the test might be expected to be administered might well be incapable of highly refined discriminations within their experiences, so that a smaller number of options might be most appropriate. These two competing considerations suggested the selection of 5 response options: extremes, a middle, and somewhere in between. The response scale 0 to 4 was selected as the most likely to be an appropriate range for responding.

Item #	Verb	Object	Processing	Sense Modality	Response
1	X+	Y-	Cognitive	Visual	0 1 2 3 4
2	X+	Y-	Cognitive	Auditory	0 1 2 3 4
3	X+	Y-	Cognitive	Kinesthetic	0 1 2 3 4
4	X-	Y+	Cognitive	Visual	0 1 2 3 4
5	X-	Y+	Cognitive	Auditory	0 1 2 3 4
6	X-	Y+	Cognitive	Kinesthetic	0 1 2 3 4
7	X-	Y+	Affective	Visual	0 1 2 3 4
8	X-	Y+	Affective	Auditory	0 1 2 3 4
9	X-	Y+	Affective	Kinesthetic	0 1 2 3 4
10	X+	Y-	Affective	Visual	0 1 2 3 4
11	X+	Y-	Affective	Auditory	0 1 2 3 4
12	X+	Y-	Affective	Kinesthetic	0 1 2 3 4

<u>Item Construction</u>

A format or formula was constructed for each scale as follows.

Each of the 12 items for each scale or variable would start with the personal pronoun, continue with a verb based on one pole of each polar concept to be used for the scale, and conclude with an object based on the object to be used for that variable. The two poles of each dimension (represented by the '+' or '-' following the X or Y) would be counterbalanced in groups of three, but always tending in opposite directions with respect to each other to represent the probability that 'conflict' would be part of addiction-relevant variables.

The first six items of each scale would be expressed in 'cognitive' terms, while the last six would be expressed in 'affective' or emotional terms. In addition, visual, auditory, and kinaesthetic imagery would be woven into item contents in rotating order. Finally, the response options 0 to 4 would be used for every item.

For example, consider the items chosen for the second scale of the ADDICAUSE questionnaire, Group Enjoyment. The first six items of the second scale are cognitive (for example: "I *avoid* intimate groups when I can be in <u>large groups</u>" and "I *seek* the excitement and fun of <u>being with others</u>," while the final six items are affective: "I *keep from* feeling <u>isolated</u> as much as I can" and "I *enjoy seeing* friends and <u>going to parties</u>." Note that italics are added here (but not in the test itself) to emphasize the approach/avoidance dimension of this scale, and the underlining (also not in the test itself) is to highlight the object of the approach or avoidance. The other items in this scale follow a similar pattern but attempt to be phrased in auditory or kinaesthetic terms. For example, for the auditory sensory modality: "I *spend* as much time as I can <u>talking with others</u>" and "I *am most at ease* when I am <u>talking with friends</u>," and for the kinaesthetic sensory modality: "I *try to avoid* working at tasks I have to <u>do alone</u>" and "I *feel* least uptight when I am <u>doing social things</u>."

With this much constraint imposed on the writing of each item, it should not be surprising that the items almost 'wrote themselves.' Obviously, items written to a formula in this fashion would run the risk of being boring and repetitive. Some variation was afforded by using the two poles of each dimension, which were also employed in a counter-balanced fashion (see the + and − signs in the above table). In addition, for the sake of maintaining interest, an attempt was made to vary the apparent nature and content of each item slightly without putting aside the 'formula.'

Yet another constraint was imposed on the writing of items for the scales. The optimism or pessimism of the author of scales such as these could easily affect the nature of the scales written. Moreover, it seemed very likely that respondents would differ both in their own optimism or pessimism, and in the effect of each variable upon their addictive behaviours. To address these possible sources of respondent variability, two scales were constructed for most pairs of dimensional concepts. The items for the odd numbered of each pair of scales adopted a generally negative emotional tone, while the items for the even numbered of that pair of scales employed a generally positive emotional tone.

Where possible, no reference was made to uses of addictive substances, to minimize specific referencing to addictive contexts on the part of respondents while answering the questionnaire. That is, the attempt was made to obtain responses bearing on the general personality of the respondent regardless of whether he/she had used any substance or considered the issue in the question relevant to his/her addictive behaviour.

For research purposes, the final pages of the ADDICAUSE questionnaire requests respondents to indicate all the following for each of 5 categories of foods, 3 categories of tobacco products, 10 categories of medications, 10 categories of alcoholic beverages, 13 categories of street drugs, and 3 categories of solvents:

<u>Y</u>: <u>Years of Use</u>: The respondent was asked to show the number of Years of Use of each substance.

<u>U</u>: <u>Strength of Use</u>: On an anchored scale from 0 to 7, for which each position was pre-defined for the respondent, he/she was asked to show the Strength of Use of each substance.

<u>O</u>: <u>Time Off</u>: The respondent was asked to show the number of months since he/she used each substance. (It quickly became clear that this score was meaningless within the context of its first application, a correctional treatment centre. The fact that the respondents were incarcerated at the time introduced an unmanageable element into responses in this category. For example, some of the respondents estimated time off from the last use of a particular substance while others gave the length of time they had been in prison.)

<u>W</u>: <u>Present Want</u>: On an anchored scale from 0 to 7, for which each position was pre-defined for the respondent, he/she was asked to show the strength of his/her present Want/Desire to use each substance. This score was intended to get at the addict who is deprived of access to his/her preferred addictive substance(s). (Once more, it soon became clear that this score was less than ideally useful for the incarcerate population on which it was first used. Many addicts, removed from access to their substances tend to experience a major decline in their addictive want which, unfortunately, may be reinstated as soon as access is again possible. In addition, many addicts are in denial and want to create a good impression by simply denying wanting substances, which also reduced the numbers of subjects acknowledging wants.)

Also for research purposes, another three pages were included in the development stage of the ADDICAUSE questionnaire to collect additional information from the subjects in this treatment research study. The first of these pages asked the respondents to state their opinions about the 'causes' and the 'effects' of their uses of classes of substances. The 'cause' responses acquired were mostly rather vague (e.g., 'I wanted to try it'), or repetitive with respect to the 'effects' reported, or else were omitted. To obtain any information, the 'causes' and the 'effects' reported were combined as if, as they appeared to be, they were interchangeable. In order to make the resulting 'initial' cause scores generally comparable with the other scores, initial causes scores (Z scores)[4] were created by counting the number of times across substances that the respondent claimed a 'cause' or an 'effect' which could be classified and coded as related to the 68 ADDICAUSE scales. Thus, the initial cause (Z) score for each scale was the number of references to that scale among the respondent's claimed 'causes' and 'effects' of use of any of the listed classes of substances. This thinking resulted in three more scores for each of the 68 scales:

<u>S</u>: <u>Sum of Responses</u>: The circled numbers (response values) for all 12 items of each scale were <u>summed</u> together to form a total <u>S</u> score (Max=48).

<u>N</u>: <u>Number of Responses > 1</u>: The <u>number</u> of the twelve response values which reached 2 or more for each scale was <u>counted</u> to form a total <u>N</u> score (Max=12).

<u>Z</u>: <u>Number of Initial Causes</u>: The number of times the respondent claimed any given axis as a 'cause' or an 'effect' of his/her use of any of the five substance classes was <u>counted</u> to form a total <u>Z</u> score (Max=10).

These three pages were of limited utility and were dropped from the version of the ADDICAUSE questionnaire that is included in this manual.

---

4 Note that this is just a label for Number of Initial Causes,, not the statistic known as a Z score.

APPENDIX C: THE ADDICAUSE QUESTIONNAIRE

NAME: _________________________________

DATE:_________________ AGE:_____

Instructions: Some of the items in this questionnaire refer to the use of substances. If you have never used that kind of substance just circle 0 (i.e., "not at all"). Please answer every question. If you have trouble reading the words, please ask someone for help. Take as long as you need to do the questionnaire.

Please circle the number for each statement which most nearly applies to you *right now*. The numbers mean:

0 = "false," "no," "not me at all," "not now"
1 = "occasionally," "once in a while," "maybe sometimes"
2 = "about as often as not," "an average amount," "perhaps"
3 = "most often," "I guess so," "probably," "more than not"
4 = "true," "yes," "definitely," "sure do," "nearly always"

Scale 01:	
I avoid being noticed in social groups if I can	0 1 2 3 4
I avoid interacting with others if possible	0 1 2 3 4
I avoid social groups when I can	0 1 2 3 4
I try to spend as much time as I can by myself	0 1 2 3 4
I spend as much time as I can reading and thinking	0 1 2 3 4
I try to keep myself occupied by myself when I can	0 1 2 3 4
I am afraid to draw attention to myself in a group	0 1 2 3 4
I am uncomfortable having to interact with others	0 1 2 3 4
I am uptight or fearful in groups of people	0 1 2 3 4

I feel most comfortable being alone	0 1 2 3 4
I feel most at ease reading or thinking alone	0 1 2 3 4
I feel least uncomfortable working by myself	0 1 2 3 4
SocAnx[AvdSoc/ApprSelf]-(A)	
Scale 02:	
I avoid intimate groups when I can be in large ones	0 1 2 3 4
I avoid being alone as much as possible	0 1 2 3 4
I try to avoid working at tasks I have to do alone	0 1 2 3 4
I seek the excitement and fun of being with others	0 1 2 3 4
I spend as much time as I can talking with others	0 1 2 3 4
I feel most comfortable being part of a group	0 1 2 3 4
I keep from feeling isolated as much as I can	0 1 2 3 4
I am bored or irritable when I'm by myself	0 1 2 3 4
I feel a sense of emptiness when I'm alone	0 1 2 3 4
I enjoy seeing friends and going to parties	0 1 2 3 4
I am most at ease when I am talking with friends	0 1 2 3 4
I feel least uptight when I am doing social things	0 1 2 3 4
GrpEnj[Apprsoc/AvdSlf]+	
Scale 03:	
I give up when too many changes are happening	0 1 2 3 4
I tune out when too much is going on around me	0 1 2 3 4
I sometimes feel like there's a fist in my stomach	0 1 2 3 4
I try to cope when things look reasonably organized	0 1 2 3 4
I spend time with friends when I am fairly calm	0 1 2 3 4
I cling onto friends when my life runs smoothly	0 1 2 3 4
I feel down even when my world looks organized	0 1 2 3 4
I feel hurt by others even if they say they like me	0 1 2 3 4

I can't cope well even if things are going OK	0 1 2 3 4
I try to lift my spirits when I feel I can't cope	0 1 2 3 4
I seek help when I have too many problems to face	0 1 2 3 4
I try to find relief when I have too much stress	0 1 2 3 4
RctDepr[PasDisInt/ActInt]-(C)	
Scale 04:	
I am "cranked up" by changes I have to deal with	0 1 2 3 4
I want the volume up high when listening to music	0 1 2 3 4
I am most effective when under heavy pressure	0 1 2 3 4
I seek out high stress and risk-taking situations	0 1 2 3 4
I am drawn to active, noisy, exciting situations	0 1 2 3 4
I get into fast-moving, even if confusing, action	0 1 2 3 4
I have fun taking calculated risks	0 1 2 3 4
I enjoy "pulling a fast one" or "conning" somebody	0 1 2 3 4
I enjoy being in the "fast lane" in daily life	0 1 2 3 4
I enjoy watching many things going on at once	0 1 2 3 4
I like listening to more than one thing at a time	0 1 2 3 4
It's fun to have lots of things happening at once	0 1 2 3 4
StimHung[ActInt/PasDisint]+(I)	
Scale 05:	
It's hard work to improve the way I see things	0 1 2 3 4
I have to think hard to change the way I think	0 1 2 3 4
Changing myself to a purpose is a hard thing to do	0 1 2 3 4
I see no purpose to all the learning I have done	0 1 2 3 4
I think chance guided most of what I've learned	0 1 2 3 4
I can't make sense out of how we're expected to act	0 1 2 3 4

I see things the way I see them	0 1 2 3 4
I feel stuck in the way I think even if it hurts me	0 1 2 3 4
I've learned to act how I act	0 1 2 3 4
I see things the way they are	0 1 2 3 4
It's a dog-eat-dog world no matter what people say	0 1 2 3 4
I feel there's no way to change things anyway	0 1 2 3 4
RgdSlf[RgdPurp/LrnRand]-(cAd)	

Scale 06:	
I enjoy going along with the crowd I hang out with	0 1 2 3 4
I think the attitudes my group has are right	0 1 2 3 4
Friends are friends regardless of how anyone feels	0 1 2 3 4
I learn best from watching how others do things	0 1 2 3 4
I've learned to think the same way my friends do	0 1 2 3 4
I try to do things to fit in with my group	0 1 2 3 4
I enjoy seeing myself as acting like my group does	0 1 2 3 4
I think outsiders don't understand my group's ways	0 1 2 3 4
I need to feel I'm part of a group	0 1 2 3 4
I like to see things the way my friends do	0 1 2 3 4
I really enjoy the sense of sharing in my group	0 1 2 3 4
I like being influenced to do what my friends do	0 1 2 3 4
SocInfl[LrnSoc/RgdSlf]+(SRf)	
Scale 07:	
I see aggression as the worst thing people can do	0 1 2 3 4
I think people should try not to show their anger	0 1 2 3 4
I feel that angry feelings should be kept inside	0 1 2 3 4

I use up my anger by watching TV sports and movies	0 1 2 3 4
I often won't talk to people I'm irritated with	0 1 2 3 4
When I feel angry, I often won't do as I'm asked	0 1 2 3 4
A lot of human interaction is based on anger	0 1 2 3 4
It is natural to get angry about what others say	0 1 2 3 4
I feel angry at lots of things a lot of the time	0 1 2 3 4
I would do anything rather than express my anger	0 1 2 3 4
When I'm annoyed, it's hard for me to say so	0 1 2 3 4
I try to find ways to cool myself down when I'm angry	0 1 2 3 4
AggrInhb[AvdAct/ApprPas]-(T)	
Scale 08:	
My family disapproves of using alcohol or drugs	0 1 2 3 4
Most people disapprove of alcohol and drug use	0 1 2 3 4
I feel a bit guilty when using alcohol or drugs	0 1 2 3 4
I often see others as seeing what I do as shameful	0 1 2 3 4
People often want me to take the blame for things	0 1 2 3 4
I often feel guilty even when I've done no wrong	0 1 2 3 4
I feel there are far too many rules to follow	0 1 2 3 4
I hate having to do what others tell me to do	0 1 2 3 4
I feel that rules are just made to be broken	0 1 2 3 4
I often show I disapprove of others' disapproval	0 1 2 3 4
I often want to find ways to "stick it" to others	0 1 2 3 4
I enjoy being a rebel	0 1 2 3 4
GuiIntol[AvdPas/ApprAct:Gui]+(R)	
Scale 09:	
I find myself being alone most of the time	0 1 2 3 4

I do a lot of daydreaming about talking to friends	0 1 2 3 4
I need desperately to be with people	0 1 2 3 4
I do a lot of what I do just to be around others	0 1 2 3 4
I listen to the radio to feel I'm near other people	0 1 2 3 4
I go for walks to be involved in what others do	0 1 2 3 4
When I see other people together I feel an outsider	0 1 2 3 4
I hear others talking and I wish they'd talk to me	0 1 2 3 4
I feel empty inside unless I am with other people	0 1 2 3 4
I feel it is my way to be a loner	0 1 2 3 4
I think a lot to fill up the time when I'm alone	0 1 2 3 4
I feel lonely most of the time	0 1 2 3 4
Lonlin[PasSoc/ActAln]-(W)	
Scale 10:	
I get out with other people as much as I can	0 1 2 3 4
I spend as much time as I can talking with others	0 1 2 3 4
I feel the need to be close to other people	0 1 2 3 4
I picture myself participating in group activities	0 1 2 3 4
When alone, I think about what I can say to others	0 1 2 3 4
I let myself feel lonely to help me want company	0 1 2 3 4
When alone, I watch TV to see ways people relate	0 1 2 3 4
I think a lot about how to get along with others	0 1 2 3 4
I spend time alone to recharge for social contacts	0 1 2 3 4
I watch groups to see how others relate together	0 1 2 3 4
I listen to conversations to learn about people	0 1 2 3 4
I feel the need to be part of a group of friends	0 1 2 3 4
SocCntct[ActSoc/PasAln]+(SNd)	
Scale 11:	
It's better to "be in a fog" than to get to work	0 1 2 3 4

The demands of reality seem just too much for me	0 1 2 3 4
The pressure to do things just turns me off	0 1 2 3 4
It's a lot easier to daydream than to accomplish	0 1 2 3 4
I don't like being expected to be self-sufficient	0 1 2 3 4
I try to find ways to "get away from it all	0 1 2 3 4
I spend a lot of time daydreaming	0 1 2 3 4
I prefer to put off things I have to do	0 1 2 3 4
I find a lot of ways to "put in time	0 1 2 3 4
Tomorrow is a better day to do things than today is	0 1 2 3 4
I would like best not to have to do anything at all	0 1 2 3 4
I feel drowned in what others call "reality	0 1 2 3 4
RealDen[AvdReal/ApprUnr]-(U)	

Scale 12:	
It annoys me to have to deal with authorities	0 1 2 3 4
I hate being given orders by anyone	0 1 2 3 4
I think people older than me are mostly strange	0 1 2 3 4
I keep others from seeing when I am scared	0 1 2 3 4
I think of myself as something of a rebel	0 1 2 3 4
I put up a "tough" front for other people	0 1 2 3 4
In stores I always notice the surveillance devices	0 1 2 3 4
I feel angry at people who try to act too "good	0 1 2 3 4
I feel as though I've had a raw deal out of life	0 1 2 3 4
I hate rules and regulations	0 1 2 3 4
I feel I am criticized too much by others	0 1 2 3 4
I dislike having to pay sales tax on anything	0 1 2 3 4
AuthReb[AprUnr/AvdReal]+(II)	
Scale 13:	
Picturing the uncertain future just makes me	0 1 2 3 4

scared	
Even with planning you never know what will happen	0 1 2 3 4
If I'm sure of the future, I will be disappointed	0 1 2 3 4
When I picture my past, I become weak and depressed	0 1 2 3 4
I never amounted to much, so there's no hope I will	0 1 2 3 4
I feel my past left me empty and joyless	0 1 2 3 4
The future looks just as empty and flat as the past	0 1 2 3 4
I think life is good only in an imagined future	0 1 2 3 4
I feel afraid that life will continue as it was	0 1 2 3 4
Every picture of my past is upsetting or saddening	0 1 2 3 4
In the past I can only find rotten memories	0 1 2 3 4
My life feels like a joyless	0 1 2 3 4
FltDepr[ImpFrwd/PwrBck]-(L)	0 1 2 3 4
Scale 14:	
I can picture lots of resources I got from the past	0 1 2 3 4
I can remember many things which give me support	0 1 2 3 4
I can still feel many acts of caring from my past	0 1 2 3 4
I don't need to see now what the future holds	0 1 2 3 4
I can't stop all unhappy thoughts of the future	0 1 2 3 4
I know there will be lots of pains in the future	0 1 2 3 4
Not all the images from my past are pleasant	0 1 2 3 4
I likely remember as much hurt in my past as others	0 1 2 3 4
I can't help feeling sad about losses in my past	0 1 2 3 4
Picturing what I want will help me to achieve it	0 1 2 3 4
I can imagine lots of values and good in my	0 1 2 3 4

future	
The possibilities of the future make me feel good	0 1 2 3 4
VivSens[PwrFrwd/ImpBck]+	
Scale 15:	
I need to control the sharpness of my mental images	0 1 2 3 4
I want to empty my mind of its constant thoughts	0 1 2 3 4
I try to damp down the strength of my feelings	0 1 2 3 4
I see my body as being too uptight and too weak	0 1 2 3 4
I think my mind can't control my body's demands	0 1 2 3 4
I feel my emotions are often out of control	0 1 2 3 4
I need to see my life as more settled and slow	0 1 2 3 4
I want to be less bothered by my too sharp hearing	0 1 2 3 4
I feel emotions too strongly for me to bear	0 1 2 3 4
I need help to reduce the intensity of what I see	0 1 2 3 4
I need something to help me tune out my thoughts	0 1 2 3 4
I need some way to make my emotions affect me less	0 1 2 3 4
CntrlEfft[PwrMnd/ImpBdy]-(CNd)	
Scale 16:	
I see myself as being physically powerful	0 1 2 3 4
The way I speak exerts strong influence on others	0 1 2 3 4
My feelings are strong enough to win over others	0 1 2 3 4
I look for ways to make my vision of things cleared	0 1 2 3 4
I try to find ways to grasp life's meaning better	0 1 2 3 4
I want to increase the strength of my emotions	0 1 2 3 4

I have very powerful and forceful mental images	0 1 2 3 4
I impress others with the cleverness of my thoughts	0 1 2 3 4
I overwhelm others with the force of my emotions	0 1 2 3 4
I enjoy looking self-confident in whatever I do	0 1 2 3 4
I can control my body easily with my thoughts	0 1 2 3 4
My emotions are not strong enough to get in my way	0 1 2 3 4
SeEnhncCntrl[PwrMnd/ImpBdy]+(M)	

Scale 17:	
The grief I feel makes the future look empty	0 1 2 3 4
I feel helpless as I think about my losses	0 1 2 3 4
When I think about my losses I feel weak all over	0 1 2 3 4
I picture the happiness I had before my loss	0 1 2 3 4
I think of the fun I had in life before my grief	0 1 2 3 4
I wish I could get back the energy I used to have	0 1 2 3 4
As I picture my losses I only see empty space	0 1 2 3 4
As I think about the things I've lost I want to cry	0 1 2 3 4
I feel my losses are too heavy a burden to carry	0 1 2 3 4
The picture I have of myself is one of uselessness	0 1 2 3 4
I keep thinking about how things might have been	0 1 2 3 4
I feel a great weight of grief on me or inside me	0 1 2 3 4
Grief[PwrLss/ImpGn]-(Y)	
Scale 18:	
I think I look my best when drinking or doing drugs	0 1 2 3 4

I impress others when drinking or doing drugs	0 1 2 3 4
I am most self-confident when drinking/doing drugs	0 1 2 3 4
When drinking/doing drugs, I feel I am not a failure	0 1 2 3 4
I am accepted by others while drinking/doing drugs	0 1 2 3 4
I feel most sure of myself drinking or doing drugs	0 1 2 3 4
I really feel that I am better than other people	0 1 2 3 4
I feel I am very sensitive to others' motivations	0 1 2 3 4
I am sure others sense the power of my personality	0 1 2 3 4
I feel the need to be able to control other people	0 1 2 3 4
I feel the need to influence others' understanding	0 1 2 3 4
I feel the need to have power over others	0 1 2 3 4
SubsSeEnhnc[PwrGn/ImpLss]+(X)	
Scale 19:	
I try to avoid bright light or loud noise	0 1 2 3 4
I am super-sensitive to comments about my health	0 1 2 3 4
Pain and discomfort "get to me" too much	0 1 2 3 4
I almost always have pain somewhere in my body	0 1 2 3 4
I worry about injuring myself any more than I have	0 1 2 3 4
I am very careful not to strain my neck or back	0 1 2 3 4
I would like to forget life's pain and suffering	0 1 2 3 4
I worry about hurting or injuring myself	0 1 2 3 4
The world seems such a burden I often ignore pain	0 1 2 3 4
Life would look brighter without the pain I have	0 1 2 3 4

I'd be out with people more with less aches/pains	0 1 2 3 4
I'd enjoy being active without the burden of pain	0 1 2 3 4
PainSens[SensPn/InsnsPls]-(D)	
Scale 20:	
I see lots of fun situations to get involved in	0 1 2 3 4
I enjoy talking and laughing a lot with my friends	0 1 2 3 4
All sorts of things get me excited	0 1 2 3 4
I can get along OK in almost any situation/setting	0 1 2 3 4
I don't really care much what other people say	0 1 2 3 4
The minor injuries and pain I get don't trouble me	0 1 2 3 4
There are very few situations that bother me	0 1 2 3 4
Nobody succeeds in conning me or pushing me around	0 1 2 3 4
I can enjoy activities even when I've been injured	0 1 2 3 4
The main thing in life is to have a good time	0 1 2 3 4
I like conning or teasing those of the opposite sex	0 1 2 3 4
I'm always looking for exciting things to do	0 1 2 3 4
Hedon[SensPls/InsnsPn]+(JSHun}	
Scale 21:	
I seem to see the world better when I'm alone	0 1 2 3 4
I organize my thoughts best when nobody is around	0 1 2 3 4
I seem to feel most comfortable when I'm alone	0 1 2 3 4
When with others, I am distracted by their activity	0 1 2 3 4
I can't think clearly when others are talking	0 1 2 3 4

I don't like being part of most groups of people	0 1 2 3 4
It is easier not to be around where others are	0 1 2 3 4
I can't seem to find anything to say to others	0 1 2 3 4
Being with others feels like a burden to bear	0 1 2 3 4
I enjoy a sense of freedom when I'm alone	0 1 2 3 4
The conflict of life is not there when I'm alone	0 1 2 3 4
I feel I would like to be alone most of the time	0 1 2 3 4
SocWthdrw[BdSoc/GdAln]-(A)(O1)	

Scale 22:	
I like hanging around with the guys in a pub	0 1 2 3 4
Shooting-the-bull is a favourite pass-time of mine	0 1 2 3 4
I really like back-slapping un with the guys	0 1 2 3 4
Most people spend a lot of time drinking in pubs	0 1 2 3 4
I am proud of my use of alcohol and/or drugs	0 1 2 3 4
Most people use drugs and/or alcohol	0 1 2 3 4
I think what happens in life is a matter of luck	0 1 2 3 4
I think we need unions to protect workers	0 1 2 3 4
I'm an easy-going person, just out for a good time	0 1 2 3 4
It feels good to drink someone under the table	0 1 2 3 4
Telling jokes is the best kind of conversation	0 1 2 3 4
I am proud of the amount of booze I can drink	0 1 2 3 4
Subcult[GdSoc/BdAln]+(G)	
Scale 23:	
I dislike people who use their power over others	0 1 2 3 4
It's not fair to influence others to think your way	0 1 2 3 4
It's mean for people to force their will on others	0 1 2 3 4
I don't have the power to change anything much	0 1 2 3 4
I can't seem to change my thoughts or attitudes	0 1 2 3 4

I don't feel tough enough to handle strong feelings	0 1 2 3 4
I wish I could see how others get power over people	0 1 2 3 4
I hate others telling me how I should think	0 1 2 3 4
I don't like feeling always at the mercy of others	0 1 2 3 4
I usually feel others are pushing me around	0 1 2 3 4
I often think others influence me too much	0 1 2 3 4
I sometime feel as though I am always the follower	0 1 2 3 4
DpndInhib[PwrChg/ImpPrst]-(S+)	
Scale 24:	
I believe anybody can influence what happens	0 1 2 3 4
I think everybody's ideas contribute to any outcome	0 1 2 3 4
I feel heroes are ordinary people facing challenges	0 1 2 3 4
I view hanging on to a dream as one way to success	0 1 2 3 4
I think nothing lasts through time like an idea	0 1 2 3 4
I feel that sticking at a task is the way to win	0 1 2 3 4
I see lots in my life that I could usefully change	0 1 2 3 4
I can think of many ways to improve my joy in life	0 1 2 3 4
I am comfortable with my ability to change my life	0 1 2 3 4
I can live quite happily with things I can't change	0 1 2 3 4
I can make friends and enjoy them as well as anyone	0 1 2 3 4
I feel happy and content in spite of my limitations	0 1 2 3 4
NrmlRes[PwrChg/ImpPrst]+(ILoC)	

Scale 25:	
I watch people's actions to check on what they say	0 1 2 3 4
I often question the meaning behind what others say	0 1 2 3 4
I often wonder what others are doing behind my back	0 1 2 3 4
I'm amazed when people don't notice others tricks	0 1 2 3 4
I am surprised at how insensitive people often are	0 1 2 3 4
I am shocked how unaware people are of intentions	0 1 2 3 4
I can be less upset staying away from some people	0 1 2 3 4
I can sometimes forget others' meanness when alone	0 1 2 3 4
I often don't mind being away by myself	0 1 2 3 4
I fear I can see how people talk behind my back	0 1 2 3 4
I worry what others may say about me when I'm away	0 1 2 3 4
I get upset feeling some people's envy and anger	0 1 2 3 4
ParSens[SensSoc/InsnsAln]-(ch}	
Scale 26:	
I try to be with people who see things as they are	0 1 2 3 4
I try to keep those friends who talk reasonably	0 1 2 3 4
I relate to people who aren't always feeling hurt	0 1 2 3 4
I nearly always see things clearer when alone	0 1 2 3 4
I understand things best while thinking in private	0 1 2 3 4
I think it is best to work out hurt feelings alone	0 1 2 3 4
I like trying to see the world through others' eyes	0 1 2 3 4
I really enjoy hearing other people's insights	0 1 2 3 4

I enjoy feeling others' intensity in discussions	0 1 2 3 4
I like sitting alone and watching ordinary things	0 1 2 3 4
I enjoy solving puzzles and problems by myself	0 1 2 3 4
I like to just sit alone and feel nothing	0 1 2 3 4
RatnDef[SensSoc/InsnsAln]+(BC)	

Scale 27:	
I wish I didn't have to see every detail in a thing	0 1 2 3 4
I can't stop thinking until a thought is finished	0 1 2 3 4
I have to repeat some actions just so many times	0 1 2 3 4
I wonder if it could ever be OK to make a mistake	0 1 2 3 4
I think I'd like to say something less accurately	0 1 2 3 4
I guess some who make mistakes are doing their best	0 1 2 3 4
I analyse everything to be sure I see it correctly	0 1 2 3 4
I try hard to reason things out just right	0 1 2 3 4
I feel good whenever I do something accurately	0 1 2 3 4
I am annoyed when I see someone doing a job poorly	0 1 2 3 4
I am afraid of saying the wrong thing	0 1 2 3 4
I feel relieved when I avoid making an error	0 1 2 3 4
OppreInhb[PrcGd/ErrBd]- (BO-C)	
Scale 28:	
I like it when people analyse situations precisely	0 1 2 3 4
I approve of a person saying exactly what he means	0 1 2 3 4
I think well of myself when I do a task accurately	0 1 2 3 4
I try to see that things run well without mistakes	0 1 2 3 4
I like trying not to hurt other people's feelings	0 1 2 3 4

I approve of others' efforts to avoid making errors	0 1 2 3 4
I feel good when a mistake turns out not to be mine	0 1 2 3 4
I feel some people deserve to be criticized	0 1 2 3 4
I enjoy making mistakes when I learn from them	0 1 2 3 4
I am happy when people fail to see mean intentions	0 1 2 3 4
I am glad when people fail in trying to hurt others	0 1 2 3 4
I feel good when someone is too happy to feel hurt	0 1 2 3 4
Cmfrtlnhb[PrcGd/ErrBd]+(B+)(27)	
Scale 29:	
I worry I may blush in a group if I am noticed	0 1 2 3 4
I think I may lose my thought if talking in a group	0 1 2 3 4
I sense my hand is trembling noticeably in a group	0 1 2 3 4
I often imagine myself exposed in a group setting	0 1 2 3 4
I worry that other people know what I'm thinking	0 1 2 3 4
I feel others can read my feelings from my actions	0 1 2 3 4
I can see my body sag weakly when my mood is down	0 1 2 3 4
My voice sounds weak and whiny when I'm depressed	0 1 2 3 4
I feel unable to cope with things when I'm down	0 1 2 3 4
I get upsetting pictures in my mind of awful events	0 1 2 3 4
I think of scary situations at times	0 1 2 3 4

I sometimes fear I will lose control of myself	0 1 2 3 4
DistrbAff[AnxMnd/DprBdy]-(AC)	
Scale 30:	
I keep myself from being blue by being very active	0 1 2 3 4
I don't get down by telling myself I'm the greatest	0 1 2 3 4
I make myself feel high instead of being depressed	0 1 2 3 4
when I feel tired I make mental pictures of success	0 1 2 3 4
When I start worrying, I mask my thoughts with talk	0 1 2 3 4
When I feel scared, I energize myself with activity	0 1 2 3 4
I replace sad images with excited or happy ones	0 1 2 3 4
I control unhappy thoughts by actively making plans	0 1 2 3 4
I keep from feeling sad by distracting myself	0 1 2 3 4
When excited or uptight I just crank myself up more	0 1 2 3 4
When worried I try to solve complicated problems	0 1 2 3 4
When I feel scared I try to increase the sensations	0 1 2 3 4
AffDen[AvdBdy/ApprMnd]+(JCMa)(M)	
Scale 31:	
I see others as always putting themselves first	0 1 2 3 4
I don't appreciate other people's nasty remarks	0 1 2 3 4
I don't like the way people feel toward each other	0 1 2 3 4
If you spoil others they become very self-centred	0 1 2 3 4

I don't say nice things because others get too vain	0 1 2 3 4
I am disappointed when people laugh at others	0 1 2 3 4
I am disgusted when people show off or act vain	0 1 2 3 4
I get angry when someone criticizes me	0 1 2 3 4
I get annoyed when someone mimics someone else	0 1 2 3 4
I hate being made a fool of	0 1 2 3 4
I get angry when someone puts me down	0 1 2 3 4
I feel disgusted with some kinds of people	0 1 2 3 4
DwnOth[DsatsOth/SatsSlf]-(ch)(25)	

Scale 32:	
I find seeing my friends a rewarding experience	0 1 2 3 4
I get a lot of pleasure talking with friends	0 1 2 3 4
I feel fulfilled being close to the people I like	0 1 2 3 4
I find myself picking up the habits of my friends	0 1 2 3 4
I tend to talk and use the same ideas as my group	0 1 2 3 4
I seem to like doing the same things my group does	0 1 2 3 4
When my friends go somewhere, I usually go too	0 1 2 3 4
I have picked up a lot of the phrases my group uses	0 1 2 3 4
I have a lot of feelings for and about my friends	0 1 2 3 4
I get a lot of satisfaction from being in my group	0 1 2 3 4
I enjoy talking things over with my group	0 1 2 3 4
I like the feeling of closeness among my friends	0 1 2 3 4
GrpSats[SatsGrp/Hab]+(SRf)(0210)	
Scale 33:	
It's hard to get others to see things the right way	0 1 2 3 4
I think most people are pretty ignorant	0 1 2 3 4

It's frustrating to try to get others to act right	0 1 2 3 4
I wish others could be made to see things right	0 1 2 3 4
I try my best to help others understand my position	0 1 2 3 4
People must learn the way to act in each situation	0 1 2 3 4
Some jerks want to change how people see things	0 1 2 3 4
Some people are always trying to change the rules	0 1 2 3 4
I don't like people trying to change the way I am	0 1 2 3 4
It surprises me how right I am in how I see things	0 1 2 3 4
I am proud that my ideas are fixed and clear	0 1 2 3 4
I feel good that I act as I have always acted	0 1 2 3 4
Dgmat(GdPrst/BdChng]-(fCnstrcts)	
Scale 34:	
Other people all seem to see things the same way	0 1 2 3 4
You can tell how others will think about anything	0 1 2 3 4
Other people act like rubber stamps of each other	0 1 2 3 4
I prefer to see myself as "different" from others	0 1 2 3 4
My ideas are creative, different and original	0 1 2 3 4
I try to have unusual or different experiences	0 1 2 3 4
Most people lead dull colourless lives	0 1 2 3 4
Nothing ordinary is interesting enough	0 1 2 3 4
I feel sorry for "square" or "straight" people	0 1 2 3 4
I want to be seen by others as being different	0 1 2 3 4
My beliefs are different from most people's beliefs	0 1 2 3 4
I am different from the way others learned to be	0 1 2 3 4
DiffNd[BdPrst/GdChng]+(F)	

Scale 35:	
I dislike the way I present myself to others	0 1 2 3 4
I think I am mostly less a human than I should be	0 1 2 3 4
I lack self-confidence and I'm never sure of myself	0 1 2 3 4
I deserve some of the rotten things in my life	0 1 2 3 4
I am basically a socially-undesirable person	0 1 2 3 4
I expect to fail in most of the things I try to do	0 1 2 3 4
I think most other people dislike me and how I am	0 1 2 3 4
I am a failure in achieving society's standards	0 1 2 3 4
I am less worthwhile than most other people are	0 1 2 3 4
I have had bad luck in life and am mostly a nobody	0 1 2 3 4
I would like to get along much better with others	0 1 2 3 4
I would like to be a much nicer person than I am	0 1 2 3 4
SlfDeprc[BdSlf/GdOth]-(S)	
Scale 36:	
I see myself as a particularly good person	0 1 2 3 4
I only allow myself to think and say proper things	0 1 2 3 4
I am careful to behave myself always as I should	0 1 2 3 4
I don't like people who aren't clean and groomed	0 1 2 3 4
I disapprove of people using foul language	0 1 2 3 4
I think it's silly for people to make rude gestures	0 1 2 3 4
Some people don't know how to sit or walk properly	0 1 2 3 4
I wish people would try to speak better English	0 1 2 3 4
People should do as they want others to do for them	0 1 2 3 4
I feel that I follow the straight and narrow path	0 1 2 3 4

I understand and obey the spiritual and legal laws	0 1 2 3 4
I feel that those who find fault with me are wrong	0 1 2 3 4
RgdMrlsm[GdSlf/BdOth]+(ConvPhVi)	

Scale 37:	
There is one kind of alcohol that changes how I act	0 1 2 3 4
I sometimes get drunk on just a couple of drinks	0 1 2 3 4
I sometimes go into "blind rages"	0 1 2 3 4
Learning to read was harder for me than other kids	0 1 2 3 4
Doing arithmetic was harder for me than other kids	0 1 2 3 4
Sometimes I do things I would never intend to do	0 1 2 3 4
I sometimes suddenly get depressed for no reason	0 1 2 3 4
I sometimes "lose control" when I'm drinking	0 1 2 3 4
I tend to be a binge drinker	0 1 2 3 4
At times I get an odd feeling - a breeze or smell	0 1 2 3 4
I sometimes think there must be a devil in me	0 1 2 3 4
I was told I was very "hyperactive" as a child	0 1 2 3 4
Paroxys[ImpFclt/PwrImpd]-(N)	
Scale 38:	0 1 2 3 4
I hate losing my freedom almost most of all	0 1 2 3 4
I feel too restricted by rules and authorities	0 1 2 3 4
Above all, I just want to be free to be myself	0 1 2 3 4
I feel I must always be able to see outside	0 1 2 3 4
It's hard for me to stop attending to my thoughts	0 1 2 3 4

I like to break rules just for the fun of it	0 1 2 3 4
I dislike riding in elevators, subways or planes	0 1 2 3 4
Others' criticism feels like it restricts/stops me	0 1 2 3 4
I feel very uncomfortable in a confined space	0 1 2 3 4
I'd freak out if trapped under a collapsed building	0 1 2 3 4
I get very upset if someone disagrees with me	0 1 2 3 4
I often feel that other people control what I do	0 1 2 3 4
RegIntol[ImpImpd/PwrFc1t]+(K:Cls)	
Scale 39:	
I would like to be by myself away from people	0 1 2 3 4
I would like to have a good long time just to sleep	0 1 2 3 4
I have to make heroic efforts just to survive	0 1 2 3 4
I need some things so badly I almost can't stand it	0 1 2 3 4
Just too much is expected of me by others	0 1 2 3 4
I feel cramps and inner aches much too strongly	0 1 2 3 4
Things are just too upsetting for me to handle	0 1 2 3 4
I feel that I have to work much too hard	0 1 2 3 4
Pain and discomfort get to me too much	0 1 2 3 4
Mostly I feel just plain weak and tired	0 1 2 3 4
I feel sickly and unable to get myself going	0 1 2 3 4
I am tired out and exhausted most of the time	0 1 2 3 4
EffStr[PwrImpd/ImpFclt]-(ECQ)(66)	
Scale 40:	
I look for ways to use ideas that excite me	0 1 2 3 4
I enjoy thinking lots about things that interest me	0 1 2 3 4
I get excited when a task I'm doing interests me	0 1 2 3 4
I don't let myself see difficulties in my way	0 1 2 3 4
I stop thoughts that might make me want to give	0 1 2 3 4

up	
I won't let myself get hopeless/down about anything	0 1 2 3 4
I look for and solve barriers that are in my way	0 1 2 3 4
I consider what others say to adjust my actions	0 1 2 3 4
I may let myself feel down to enjoy cranking back up	0 1 2 3 4
I may ignore something just to keep myself on edge	0 1 2 3 4
I stop thinking about a thing to add to anticipation	0 1 2 3 4
At times I hold back excitement so it gets stronger	0 1 2 3 4
PepNd[PwrFclt/ImpInfclt]+(JC)	
Scale 41:	
Once I see a thing one way I can't see it another	0 1 2 3 4
It is hard to change my ideas once they are fixed	0 1 2 3 4
If people hurt me I forget any good they did before	0 1 2 3 4
It's hard to teach this "old dog" new tricks	0 1 2 3 4
I've learned to be careful from lots of hard knocks	0 1 2 3 4
I've been "burned" often enough not to trust others	0 1 2 3 4
For me to warm up, I need to be shown others care	0 1 2 3 4
I need a lot of evidence to believe what others say	0 1 2 3 4
I believe you're either for me or against me	0 1 2 3 4
Don't teach me how to do a task. I learn for myself	0 1 2 3 4
Once I have my mind made up, don't try to change it	0 1 2 3 4

People should leave me alone to do things my way	0 1 2 3 4
RgdHab[HbtPrst/LrnChng]-(chchr)	

Scale 42:	
I am ready to try anything that may be fun	0 1 2 3 4
I like learning all I can about how others think	0 1 2 3 4
I want to have every experience possible in my life	0 1 2 3 4
Others seem to want to restrict themselves narrowly	0 1 2 3 4
I know the way I think is the best way for me	0 1 2 3 4
I believe I will always feel much as I do now	0 1 2 3 4
I want my point of view to keep on growing always	0 1 2 3 4
I keep hearing about new ways to gain enjoyment	0 1 2 3 4
I attend to how I feel so I can keep myself happy	0 1 2 3 4
I make sure others see me as cheerful and lively	0 1 2 3 4
My conversation is always easy-going and positive	0 1 2 3 4
I won't allow myself to feel down and blue ever	0 1 2 3 4
EasGoEnj[LrnChng/Rgdprs]+(MaSHu)	

Scale 43:	
I avoid active exercise whenever possible	0 1 2 3 4
I stay underweight even though I eat too much	0 1 2 3 4
I tend mostly to breathe in my chest (not diaphragm)	0 1 2 3 4
My muscles don't seem as strong as they should be	0 1 2 3 4
I am definitely much over-weight or under-	0 1 2 3 4

weight	
Everything I eat seems to go to fat	0 1 2 3 4
I drink a lot of fluids all the time	0 1 2 3 4
I tend to eat until I'm stuffed	0 1 2 3 4
I average more than two bowel movements a day	0 1 2 3 4
I am tired out unless I eat a lot	0 1 2 3 4
I am constantly restless, on edge and active	0 1 2 3 4
I need to eat the whole time just to keep going	0 1 2 3 4
MetabDis[AvdPwr/ApprImp]-(P)	
Scale 44:	
I intend to live in "the fast lane"	0 1 2 3 4
I enjoy keeping lots of projects going at once	0 1 2 3 4
I keep myself cranked up and high as I can	0 1 2 3 4
I dislike seeing life going along slowly	0 1 2 3 4
I hate it when people can't be quick and decisive	0 1 2 3 4
I won't be slowed down by anyone if I can help it	0 1 2 3 4
People are mostly just sheep who will buy anything	0 1 2 3 4
I'll keep conning others as long as they let me	0 1 2 3 4
I won't slow down and let someone get ahead of me	0 1 2 3 4
I'll live fast, die young and be a handsome corpse	0 1 2 3 4
I don't mind if my life is short if it's exciting	0 1 2 3 4
I want power and the feeling power gives me	0 1 2 3 4
FstLnLv[ApprPwr/AvdImp]+(J)	
Scale 45:	
I use two or more spoonfuls of sugar in my coffee	0 1 2 3 4
I have more than 5 colas or 5 cups of coffee a day	0 1 2 3 4

Normally, I nearly always go without breakfast	0 1 2 3 4
I feel "on edge" mid-mornings and mid-afternoons	0 1 2 3 4
I feel excited or restless after coffee or snacks	0 1 2 3 4
I tend to eat candies or chocolate to get me going	0 1 2 3 4
An alcoholic beverage or fruit drink will pep me up	0 1 2 3 4
I usually wake up in the morning drained and weak	0 1 2 3 4
I'm often just too tired to be able to work hard	0 1 2 3 4
I tend to feel down and weak before meals	0 1 2 3 4
I often feel a knawing pain in my gut before meals	0 1 2 3 4
I'm mostly pretty tired and "wiped out"	0 1 2 3 4
Hypoglyc[InsBdy/SensMnd]-(O)	
Scale 46:	
I probably put more strain on my body than I should	0 1 2 3 4
I guess my life style demands a lot of my body	0 1 2 3 4
My body seems to tolerate a lot before it wipes out	0 1 2 3 4
I can visualize things very well in my imagination	0 1 2 3 4
I think my mind is particularly sensitive to ideas	0 1 2 3 4
My feelings are very sensitive and react strongly	0 1 2 3 4
I often forget about looking after my health	0 1 2 3 4
I do quite a few things I know are not good for me	0 1 2 3 4
I guess the things I do put a lot of strain on me	0 1 2 3 4
I'm likely to get sick in the spring and fall	0 1 2 3 4
I seem often to get sick when I'm on vacation	0 1 2 3 4
I have rashes, colds, allergies or bronchitis a lot	0 1 2 3 4

AllrgStr[SnsBdy/InsnsMnd]+(Q)	

Scale 47:	
I'm not sure I could deal well with an emergency	0 1 2 3 4
I lie awake at night worrying	0 1 2 3 4
Getting things done often uses up lots of my energy	0 1 2 3 4
I tend to lose interest in things quite quickly	0 1 2 3 4
I worry about making an embarrassing social mistake	0 1 2 3 4
I often wake up with a jolt or a big twitch	0 1 2 3 4
I can get badly shaken up by troubles I meet	0 1 2 3 4
I can't remain calm if others don't like me	0 1 2 3 4
I can't calm down easily if something upsets me	0 1 2 3 4
I am often restless, twitchy or uncomfortable	0 1 2 3 4
I often feel jealous or possessive of those I like	0 1 2 3 4
I tend to tremble or sweat in certain situations	0 1 2 3 4
PhysAnx[PwrBdy/ImpMnd]-(CQ)	
Scale 48:	
I have received a lot of punishment in my life	0 1 2 3 4
I believe that most people I know don't like me	0 1 2 3 4
I seem to get in situations where I get in trouble	0 1 2 3 4
I believe that life is pretty punishing	0 1 2 3 4
Criticism is the main kind of attention others give	0 1 2 3 4
I just expect to have a hangover after drinking	0 1 2 3 4
A gift makes me wonder what the giver wants back	0 1 2 3 4
I guess I learn best if my mistakes are pointed out	0 1 2 3 4
I often try to find ways to "raise a little hell	0 1 2 3 4

Parents who shout at kids are giving them attention	0 1 2 3 4
I wonder if punishment is one sign of parents' love	0 1 2 3 4
When someone finishes giving me hell, I feel better	0 1 2 3 4
PunRf[BadLrn/GdRgd]+(I)	
Scale 49:	
I always find faults even in very beautiful scenes	0 1 2 3 4
I never seem to hear music which is perfect enough	0 1 2 3 4
I know that strong feelings will lead to pain	0 1 2 3 4
I find ways to ignore ugliness and confusion	0 1 2 3 4
I don't pay attention to ugliness and chaos in life	0 1 2 3 4
I control unpleasant feelings so I don't get upset	0 1 2 3 4
I feel there is too much that is ugly in life	0 1 2 3 4
I feel the conflict and demands of others too much	0 1 2 3 4
I am too sensitive to pain and unpleasant feelings	0 1 2 3 4
I don't allow myself to get excited by beauty	0 1 2 3 4
I hold back from getting involved in nice music	0 1 2 3 4
I keep myself from feeling pain or sorrow too much	0 1 2 3 4
AffAvdnc[SnsUgl/InsnsBty]-(BL)	
Scale 50:	
I must be conscious of the world's ugliness too	0 1 2 3 4
I listen to all music including the awful stuff	0 1 2 3 4
I let myself feel pain so I can enjoy pleasure more	0 1 2 3 4
I suppose I miss much of the beauty of life	0 1 2 3 4
I prefer listening to noisy and not beautiful	0 1 2 3 4

music	
I don't seem to have many nice pleasant feelings	0 1 2 3 4
I feel the beauty of nature too strongly	0 1 2 3 4
I get too involved in listening to classical music	0 1 2 3 4
I feel used by others because I care too much	0 1 2 3 4
I don't care if things look ugly or deformed	0 1 2 3 4
I'm not bothered by hearing harsh or too loud talk	0 1 2 3 4
I try to prevent unpleasant and disgusted feelings	0 1 2 3 4
CntrlSns[SnsBty/InsnsUgl]+(BL)	
Scale 51:	
I get really upset when things go wrong	0 1 2 3 4
I can feel guilt or remorse over just little things	0 1 2 3 4
I get very upset if I can't do something just right	0 1 2 3 4
If people are hostile to me I quickly forgive them	0 1 2 3 4
People say I am a bit too defensive	0 1 2 3 4
I don't dare tell people what I really feel	0 1 2 3 4
I often feel worthless when I'm around other people	0 1 2 3 4
Personal criticism upsets me greatly	0 1 2 3 4
I feel I need my friends more than they need me	0 1 2 3 4
I feel I often look like I'd done something wrong	0 1 2 3 4
If something is expected of me I feel I must do it	0 1 2 3 4
I often feel as though I had done something wrong	0 1 2 3 4
GuiPrn[PasPwr/ActImp]-(R)	

Scale 52:	
I will come on strong to anybody who challenges me	0 1 2 3 4
I am always ready to react to any insult I receive	0 1 2 3 4

I'm on quite a "short fuse," so don't come on to me	0 1 2 3 4
I may keep from letting go for a while if I have to	0 1 2 3 4
I do try to talk some annoyances out first	0 1 2 3 4
I can stay cool for a while, but it's pretty hard	0 1 2 3 4
I can see that it is sometimes best to be friendly	0 1 2 3 4
At first I may give someone time to get it right	0 1 2 3 4
Sometimes I hold back my anger for a while	0 1 2 3 4
I can't help it if people do things to make me mad	0 1 2 3 4
I get angry easily at the things people say	0 1 2 3 4
Although I may not act it out, I often feel angry	0 1 2 3 4
AngHst[PwrAct/ImpPas]+(AgT)	
Scale 53:	
My body keeps being weak and without any energy	0 1 2 3 4
I think that one of these days I'll wake up healthy	0 1 2 3 4
I seem to be waiting a long time to feel better	0 1 2 3 4
My mind is constantly occupied with my being sick	0 1 2 3 4
I keep wondering "Why me?" when others are healthy	0 1 2 3 4
I seem totally obsessed with my upset feelings	0 1 2 3 4
Each day, all I see is a bleak and empty day ahead	0 1 2 3 4
Every thought leads me back to my unhappy state	0 1 2 3 4
I keep "taking my emotional pulse" to see how I am	0 1 2 3 4
Whatever I do, I have too little energy to do it	0 1 2 3 4
I do what my doctors tell me, but it doesn't help	0 1 2 3 4

No matter what I try, I just can't get going	0 1 2 3 4
SomDepr[PasBdy/ActMnd]-(QC)	
Scale 54:	
I have tried many things to be attractive to others	0 1 2 3 4
I tell myself I must find ways to shape up my body	0 1 2 3 4
I go out with friends a lot to feel people care	0 1 2 3 4
No matter how I look at it, I can't find solutions	0 1 2 3 4
Everything I find to do turns out to be impossible	0 1 2 3 4
I feel I need someone else to tell me what to do	0 1 2 3 4
I see that others' needs are met, but mine aren't	0 1 2 3 4
I ask for others' advice, but it doesn't help	0 1 2 3 4
I feel resentful that others get what they want	0 1 2 3 4
It's just too hard to diet or exercise to firm up	0 1 2 3 4
I think others should help me more than they do	0 1 2 3 4
I feel I can't improve things without lots of push	0 1 2 3 4
HungHrt[ActMnd/PasBdy]+(Dpnd)	
Scale 55:	
I used to feel attractive to others, but not now	0 1 2 3 4
My ideas are not creative or interesting enough now	0 1 2 3 4
Most things I do seem to fall short of acceptance	0 1 2 3 4
Most people find ways to be attractive to others	0 1 2 3 4
Others always have interesting things to talk about	0 1 2 3 4
Others seem to feel good about themselves	0 1 2 3 4
Whatever I do to please others, it's never enough	0 1 2 3 4
I don't seem able to make interesting conversation	0 1 2 3 4
I can't seem to express my feelings well enough	0 1 2 3 4
I seem often to lose those I feel close to	0 1 2 3 4

I can't convince others to stay in close contact	0 1 2 3 4
People won't try to hang on to good relationships	0 1 2 3 4
ImpSeEst[Lss0th/GnSlf]-(chL)	
Scale 56:	
I like people being near by even if I don't see them	0 1 2 3 4
Most of my friends seem to find fault with everyone	0 1 2 3 4
Most of my friends control their feelings well	0 1 2 3 4
My friends all like to be the centre of attention	0 1 2 3 4
It's hard to get a word in edgeways with my friends	0 1 2 3 4
My friends are nice people but they are hard to like	0 1 2 3 4
My friends notice me, but mostly when I'm not there	0 1 2 3 4
When I'm not present my group likely talks about me	0 1 2 3 4
I feel my friends miss me when we're not together	0 1 2 3 4
I miss my friends when we are away from each other	0 1 2 3 4
Recalling others' criticism is company when alone	0 1 2 3 4
I miss my friends even though they often let me down	0 1 2 3 4
MskdDsappt[Lss0th/GnSlf]+(chB)	

Scale 57:	
Others seem not to want my company	0 1 2 3 4
Other people don't seem to want to talk to me	0 1 2 3 4

I feel that other people just don't like me	0 1 2 3 4
I think it is my fate to be alone mostly	0 1 2 3 4
I spend a lot of time in my own head, thinking	0 1 2 3 4
I feel that others want to avoid being with me	0 1 2 3 4
I'm not sure I enjoy other people's company much	0 1 2 3 4
I feel most comfortable alone with my thoughts	0 1 2 3 4
I think I don't like other people very much	0 1 2 3 4
I notice when others are together they cut me out	0 1 2 3 4
I'm usually excluded from others' conversations	0 1 2 3 4
I feel most rejected by those I most care for	0 1 2 3 4
Rejectn(SepOth/TogSlf]-	
Scale 58:	
I want to spend time together with other people	0 1 2 3 4
I want to feel I can communicate with others	0 1 2 3 4
I try to be with people who are on my wave length	0 1 2 3 4
I avoid people who see things differently from me	0 1 2 3 4
I don't need people who think in strange ways	0 1 2 3 4
I avoid those who don't feel about things as I do	0 1 2 3 4
I visualize how to share my ideas with my friends	0 1 2 3 4
I think things out alone and then tell my friends	0 1 2 3 4
Even when alone I still feel I'm with my friends	0 1 2 3 4
My group has a bond of understanding when apart	0 1 2 3 4
What I need most is to communicate with others	0 1 2 3 4
I feel empty when I have nobody to talk with	0 1 2 3 4
CommNd[TogOth/SepSlf]+	
Scale 59:	

I must have some way to calm my nervous tension	0 1 2 3 4
I can't take my uptight worrying about the future	0 1 2 3 4
I'd do anything to settle down my nervousness	0 1 2 3 4
I'd be happy if I could get rid of my uptightness	0 1 2 3 4
I can talk comfortably when I stop worrying	0 1 2 3 4
I enjoy everything when I can relax my nerves	0 1 2 3 4
I feel good when I can stop things bothering me	0 1 2 3 4
I can think clearly when I finally stop worrying	0 1 2 3 4
I am confident when I can calm my nerves down	0 1 2 3 4
I like bow I see things when I get settled down	0 1 2 3 4
I enjoy calming down and talking more slowly	0 1 2 3 4
I feel good when I'm calm and less hyper or up	0 1 2 3 4
CalmNerve[AvdPn/ApprPls]-(Q)	
Scale 60:	
I look for ways to keep cranked up and going	0 1 2 3 4
I think I need the buzz I get from some things	0 1 2 3 4
Nothing can replace the high some things give me	0 1 2 3 4
I don't like feeling down and like an "under dog	0 1 2 3 4
I don't like to feel my thoughts running slowly	0 1 2 3 4
I must avoid feeling old and slowed down	0 1 2 3 4
I like the lift I get from some substances	0 1 2 3 4
I like to feel my thoughts are sharp and right on	0 1 2 3 4
I enjoy getting myself active and excited	0 1 2 3 4
I can't take it when everything is slow and boring	0 1 2 3 4
Whatever the cost, I need to feel bright and alive	0 1 2 3 4
I won't stand feeling down, useless or a nothing	0 1 2 3 4
SubsUp[AprUp/AvdDwn]+(L-)	
Scale 61:	
I cannot let myself see myself as a failure	0 1 2 3 4

I want to put any failures out of my mind	0 1 2 3 4
I will not let myself feel like a failure	0 1 2 3 4
I can see myself as a success with a little help	0 1 2 3 4
I think of successes best when I forget the past	0 1 2 3 4
When I feel confident, I feel like a real success	0 1 2 3 4
I want to see myself as not failing at anything	0 1 2 3 4
It feels good to be able to forget some failures	0 1 2 3 4
I can't feel that I might fail in a relationship	0 1 2 3 4
Some things help me see myself as a great success	0 1 2 3 4
I want ways to help me feel specially successful	0 1 2 3 4
I need to feel that I am totally successful	0 1 2 3 4
FrgtFail[LssFai/GnSuc]-(SubNd)	

Scale 62:	
I always seek new and different experiences	0 1 2 3 4
I think of ways to think of things differently	0 1 2 3 4
I try to do things to change the ways I feel	0 1 2 3 4
I look for ways to escape the same old routines	0 1 2 3 4
I'm sick of the same old familiar lines and talk	0 1 2 3 4
I try to avoid others' "stuck in the mud" ways	0 1 2 3 4
I want to see and experience success in my life	0 1 2 3 4
I want to talk smoothly with the other sex	0 1 2 3 4
I want to succeed and have more fun in sex	0 1 2 3 4
I must avoid not being sexually attractive	0 1 2 3 4
I must avoid turning others off by how I relate	0 1 2 3 4
I must not fail in enjoying sexual experiences	0 1 2 3 4
DiffExp[GnSucChg/LssFaiPrs]+(F)	
Scale 63:	
I could easily be depressed and bored if I tried	0 1 2 3 4
I could think unpleasant thoughts if I let myself	0 1 2 3 4

I could feel disgusted and down if I let go	0 1 2 3 4
I would sit and do nothing if I didn't fight it	0 1 2 3 4
My mind would go blank if I let it	0 1 2 3 4
I would feel totally bored if I didn't prevent it	0 1 2 3 4
I keep myself up and active as much as I can	0 1 2 3 4
I challenge myself to talk in a lively and up way	0 1 2 3 4
I keep my feelings cranked up as much as I can	0 1 2 3 4
I try to avoid slipping back into giving up	0 1 2 3 4
I keep thinking of ways to churn up excitement	0 1 2 3 4
I avoid letting myself feel depressed or bored	0 1 2 3 4
AvdDepr[AvdPas/AppAct]-(LMa) (Na)	
Scale 64	
I always want to look as confident as possible	0 1 2 3 4
I enjoy being very assertive in what I say	0 1 2 3 4
I like to take risks that make me feel daring	0 1 2 3 4
I avoid letting anyone see me as less than competent	0 1 2 3 4
I don't want to come on in a weak way to anyone	0 1 2 3 4
I don't want anyone to think that I am scared	0 1 2 3 4
I like to build myself up to be super-confident	0 1 2 3 4
I like to come on strongly and aggressively	0 1 2 3 4
I like to take any risk to feel extra daring	0 1 2 3 4
I want to be seen by others as strong and great	0 1 2 3 4
I want to speak with the voice of authority	0 1 2 3 4
I want to feel up and on top of the world	0 1 2 3 4
AssrtConf[AprAct/AvdPas]+(MX)	
Scale 65:	
Others are apt to come on to attractive people	0 1 2 3 4
It's hard to say no to someone who is special	0 1 2 3 4
People with power may take advantage of others	0 1 2 3 4
I can't help my appearance with my skin	0 1 2 3 4

blemishes	
It's odd they don't make clothes I like to fit me	0 1 2 3 4
But for my weight, I might be quite attractive	0 1 2 3 4
I don't get too much attention not looking my best	0 1 2 3 4
Not being at my best saves me a lot of hassles	0 1 2 3 4
I don't mind the things that spoil my appearance	0 1 2 3 4
I'd rather not have that "come on" look	0 1 2 3 4
I prefer it when people don't notice me	0 1 2 3 4
I feel safer not being too attractive/interesting	0 1 2 3 4
AvdAttr[AvdBty/AppUgl]-(iVAnorx)	
Scale 66:	
I find it hard to get to sleep or stay asleep	0 1 2 3 4
I can't turn my mind off so I can get to sleep	0 1 2 3 4
It's hard to find a comfortable sleeping position	0 1 2 3 4
When lying in bed I often picture things to do	0 1 2 3 4
My mind keeps going over past events and plans	0 1 2 3 4
In bed, my body is restless - not ready for sleep	0 1 2 3 4
I may have vivid dreams when I go to bed at night	0 1 2 3 4
I worry that I may not wake up if I go to sleep	0 1 2 3 4
I'm almost afraid to go to sleep at night	0 1 2 3 4
I prefer to have a night-light on when I'm in bed	0 1 2 3 4
In bed, I worry I won't be able to fall asleep	0 1 2 3 4
I'm often awakened by a jolt when falling asleep	0 1 2 3 4
SlpImp[ImpSlp/FacAwk]-(Slp)	
Scale 67:	
I try to have many places where I can relax	0 1 2 3 4
I like to get away from noise often to calm down	0 1 2 3 4
I try to find peaceful times when I can relax	0 1 2 3 4
I can unwind and relax myself in several settings	0 1 2 3 4

I have many ways to talk myself down when uptight	0 1 2 3 4
I try to calm down when I am tense or "hyper	0 1 2 3 4
I like to see my body's tension being relieved	0 1 2 3 4
I enjoy telling myself to calm down when I'm tense	0 1 2 3 4
I enjoy the feeling of calming tension in my body	0 1 2 3 4
I like to see myself as comfortable and calm	0 1 2 3 4
I like to talk calmly and comfortably to others	0 1 2 3 4
I feel good when I'm all relaxed and comfortable	0 1 2 3 4
ClmRelNd[FacClm/ImpTns]+(Rel)	
Scale 68:	
I seek other's help to change how I see life	0 1 2 3 4
I ask others to help me change my thinking	0 1 2 3 4
I go where others know how to enjoy life more	0 1 2 3 4
I can't see things differently by myself	0 1 2 3 4
I ask others to tell me how to enjoy life better	0 1 2 3 4
I depend on others to help me feel good	0 1 2 3 4
I can't find exciting experiences on my own	0 1 2 3 4
I need to be told how to make my life tolerable	0 1 2 3 4
I need others to find ways to make my life good	0 1 2 3 4
Others show me exciting ways to colour up life	0 1 2 3 4
Others help me find enjoyable ways to have fun	0 1 2 3 4
I learn from others how to make life feel great	0 1 2 3 4

SubsDep[PasSlf/ActOth]-(Sub)

C:_____ E:_____ V:_____ A:_____ K:_____ S:_____ N:_____ Z:_____

<u>Instructions</u>:   For each kind of potentially addictive substance, please thoughtfully write down what you think were the CAUSES

and the EFFECTS of using each of the substances listed. "Causes" are WHY you started its use, and "effects" are HOW you felt after use.

1. **Foods** (e.g., coffee, cola, chocolate, sweets, salty things):

CAUSES:____

EFFECTS:____

____

2. **Tobacco** (e.g., cigarettes, cigars, pipe, chewing tobacco):

CAUSES:____

____

EFFECTS:____

____

3. **Medications**: (e.g., tranquillizers, anti-depressants, pain meds):

CAUSES:{ }Prescribed,
  or: (specify) ____

EFFECTS:____

____

4. **Alcohol** (e.g., beer, wine, hard liquor, others):

CAUSES:____

EFFECTS:____

____

5. **Street Drugs** (e.g., pot, hash, LSD, cocaine, heroin, mushrooms):

CAUSES:____

____

EFFECTS:____

____

VERY IMPORTANT Instructions: PLEASE read this page carefully and understand HOW to do the ratings requested BEFORE you go on to the last page to complete the ratings. The ratings you make need to communicate information to us, and so it is necessary that some standards be used in how people respond to the next page.

For **ANY** and **EVERY** kind of potentially addictive FOOD, MEDICATION, TOBACCO, ALCOHOL, SOLVENT, STREET DRUG or other substance you have ever used, please mark (a) the NAME of the substance if it not listed, (b) the LENGTH OF TIME YOU USED IT (in YEARS or MONTHS and circle years or months), (c) HOW STRONG YOUR USE WAS (using the rating method shown below), (d) if you stopped, HOW LONG AGO YOU STOPPED USING it, and (e) HOW STRONGLY YOU WOULD **NOW** LIKE TO USE it while you are here (using the same rating method shown below). Just check the N/A box if you <u>NEVER</u> used the named substance.

<u>PLEASE</u> read the instructions for the rating method which follow.

<u>RATINGS</u>: <u>HOW TO ESTIMATE "STRENGTH OF USE" <u>and</u> <u>PRESENT WANT"</u>:

<u>Step <u>A</u></u>: First, we have to define <u>**ONE USE**</u> (whether actually used in the past, or wanting use now): <u>**ONE USE**</u> is <u>defined</u> as **every time** you use a substance (1 to 3 of anything in a row or on one occasion) is <u>"**ONE USE**"</u>. [<u>Examples</u> of <u>**ONE USE**</u> might include: one to three glasses of wine with a meal, <u>or</u> one to three cigarettes in a row, <u>or</u> one hit of a drug, <u>or</u> one to three pills popped at a time, <u>or</u> one to three shots of hard liquor in a row, <u>or</u> one or two beers, <u>or</u> one can/bottle of cola, <u>or</u> one to two cups of coffee at a time, <u>or</u> one fill of a pipe, <u>or</u> one session of gas or glue sniffing]

<u>Step <u>B</u></u>: Now, <u>using the above definition of "ONE USE"</u>, please rate your <u>**STRENGTH**</u> of <u>**either**</u> past <u>**USE**</u> <u>**or**</u> present <u>**WANT**</u> for <u>each</u> type of substance, estimated from the following table:-
0 = None or No Use or Want = <u>Up to **less than 1 use** per month</u>.
1 = Slight Use or Want = <u>from **1** to **less than 2 uses** per month</u>.
2 = Some Use/Want = **2 uses** a month to **less than 1 use** a day.
3 = Considerable Use/Want = **1 use** to **less than 5 uses** a day.
4 = **B** = Binging = <u>any</u> <u>**"binge" use**</u>.
5 = Heavy Use/Want = **5 uses** to **less than 10 uses** a day.
6 = Very Heavy Use/Want = **10 uses** to **less than 15 uses** a day.
7 = Extreme Use/Want = <u>anything **above 15 uses** per day</u>.

PLEASE USE THE ABOVE RATING METHOD TO COMPLETE THE NEXT PAGES

SUBSTANCES: Kind of Chemical	Used	Not Used	How long used (indicate whether Years or Months)	Use Rating Above for How Strong / Heavy	Months Off, i.e., months since used	Use Rating Above for How Strong Want NOW
FOODS	[ ]	N/A	(Never used except in moderation)			
OverEating	[ ]	N/A	____ Years / Mths	0 1 2 3 4 5 6 7	____ Mths	0 1 2 3 4 5 6 7
Coffee	[ ]	N/A	____ Years / Mths	0 1 2 3 4 5 6 7	____ Mths	0 1 2 3 4 5 6 7
Cola	[ ]	N/A	____ Years / Mths	0 1 2 3 4 5 6 7	____ Mths	0 1 2 3 4 5 6 7
Chocolate	[ ]	N/A	____ Years / Mths	0 1 2 3 4 5 6 7	____ Mths	0 1 2 3 4 5 6 7
Chips/Nuts	[ ]	N/A	____ Years / Mths	0 1 2 3 4 5 6 7	____ Mths	0 1 2 3 4 5 6 7
TOBACCO	[ ]	N/A	____ Years / Mths	0 1 2 3 4 5 6 7	____ Mths	0 1 2 3 4 5 6 7
Cigarettes	[ ]	N/A	____ Years / Mths	0 1 2 3 4 5 6 7	____ Mths	0 1 2 3 4 5 6 7
Pipe/Cigar	[ ]	N/A	____ Years / Mths	0 1 2 3 4 5 6 7	____ Mths	0 1 2 3 4 5 6 7
Chewing Tobacco	[ ]	N/A	____ Years / Mths	0 1 2 3 4 5 6 7	____ Mths	0 1 2 3 4 5 6 7
MEDICATION	[ ]	N/A	____ Years / Mths	0 1 2 3 4 5 6 7	Mths	0 1 2 3 4 5 6 7
Valium	[ ]	N/A	____ Years /	0 1 2 3 4 5	____ Mths	0 1 2 3 4 5

			Mths	6 7		6 7
Tranquilizers	[ ]	N/A	______ Years / Mths	0 1 2 3 4 5 6 7	______ Mths	0 1 2 3 4 5 6 7
Narcotic	[ ]	N/A	______ Years / Mths	0 1 2 3 4 5 6 7	______ Mths	0 1 2 3 4 5 6 7
Barbiturate	[ ]	N/A	______ Years / Mths	0 1 2 3 4 5 6 7	______ Mths	0 1 2 3 4 5 6 7
Downers	[ ]	N/A	______ Years / Mths	0 1 2 3 4 5 6 7	______ Mths	0 1 2 3 4 5 6 7
Uppers	[ ]	N/A	______ Years / Mths	0 1 2 3 4 5 6 7	______ Mths	0 1 2 3 4 5 6 7
Ritalin	[ ]	N/A	______ Years / Mths	0 1 2 3 4 5 6 7	______ Mths	0 1 2 3 4 5 6 7
Pain Meds	[ ]	N/A	______ Years / Mths	0 1 2 3 4 5 6 7	______ Mths	0 1 2 3 4 5 6 7
Seltzers	[ ]	N/A	______ Years / Mths	0 1 2 3 4 5 6 7	______ Mths	0 1 2 3 4 5 6 7
Antibiotics	[ ]	N/A	______ Years / Mths	0 1 2 3 4 5 6 7	______ Mths	0 1 2 3 4 5 6 7
ALCOHOL	[ ]	N/A	______ Years / Mths	0 1 2 3 4 5 6 7	______ Mths	0 1 2 3 4 5 6 7
Beer/Ale	[ ]	N/A	______ Years / Mths	0 1 2 3 4 5 6 7	______ Mths	0 1 2 3 4 5 6 7
Rum	[ ]	N/A	______ Years / Mths	0 1 2 3 4 5 6 7	______ Mths	0 1 2 3 4 5 6 7
Rye	[ ]	N/A	______ Years / Mths	0 1 2 3 4 5 6 7	______ Mths	0 1 2 3 4 5 6 7
Gin/Vodka	[ ]	N/A	______	0 1 2	______	0 1 2

			Years / Mths	3 4 5 6 7	Mths	3 4 5 6 7
Scotch	[ ]	N/A	______ Years / Mths	0 1 2 3 4 5 6 7	______ Mths	0 1 2 3 4 5 6 7
Home Brew	[ ]	N/A	______ Years / Mths	0 1 2 3 4 5 6 7	______ Mths	0 1 2 3 4 5 6 7
Brandy	[ ]	N/A	______ Years / Mths	0 1 2 3 4 5 6 7	______ Mths	0 1 2 3 4 5 6 7
Wine	[ ]	N/A	______ Years / Mths	0 1 2 3 4 5 6 7	______ Mths	0 1 2 3 4 5 6 7
Solvents	[ ]	N/A	______ Years / Mths	0 1 2 3 4 5 6 7	______ Mths	0 1 2 3 4 5 6 7
Other	[ ]	N/A	______ Years / Mths	0 1 2 3 4 5 6 7	______ Mths	0 1 2 3 4 5 6 7
DRUGS	[ ]	N/A	______ Years / Mths	0 1 2 3 4 5 6 7	______ Mths	0 1 2 3 4 5 6 7
Marijuana	[ ]	N/A	______ Years / Mths	0 1 2 3 4 5 6 7	______ Mths	0 1 2 3 4 5 6 7
Hashish	[ ]	N/A	______ Years / Mths	0 1 2 3 4 5 6 7	______ Mths	0 1 2 3 4 5 6 7
Opium	[ ]	N/A	______ Years / Mths	0 1 2 3 4 5 6 7	______ Mths	0 1 2 3 4 5 6 7
Mushrooms	[ ]	N/A	______ Years / Mths	0 1 2 3 4 5 6 7	______ Mths	0 1 2 3 4 5 6 7
Peyote	[ ]	N/A	______ Years / Mths	0 1 2 3 4 5 6 7	Mths	0 1 2 3 4 5 6 7
PCP	[ ]	N/A	______ Years /	0 1 2 3 4 5	Mths	0 1 2 3 4 5

				Mths	6 7		6 7
Heroin	[ ]	N/A	____ Years / Mths		0 1 2 3 4 5 6 7	____ Mths	0 1 2 3 4 5 6 7
Morphine	[ ]	N/A	____ Years / Mths		0 1 2 3 4 5 6 7	____ Mths	0 1 2 3 4 5 6 7
LSD	[ ]	N/A	____ Years / Mths		0 1 2 3 4 5 6 7	____ Mths	0 1 2 3 4 5 6 7
Speed	[ ]	N/A	____ Years / Mths		0 1 2 3 4 5 6 7	____ Mths	0 1 2 3 4 5 6 7
Cocaine	[ ]	N/A	____ Years / Mths		0 1 2 3 4 5 6 7	____ Mths	0 1 2 3 4 5 6 7
Crack	[ ]	N/A	____ Years / Mths		0 1 2 3 4 5 6 7	____ Mths	0 1 2 3 4 5 6 7
Other	[ ]	N/A	____ Years / Mths		0 1 2 3 4 5 6 7	____ Mths	0 1 2 3 4 5 6 7
SOLVENTS	[ ]	N/A	____ Years / Mths		0 1 2 3 4 5 6 7	____ Mths	0 1 2 3 4 5 6 7
Gasoline	[ ]	N/A	____ Years / Mths		0 1 2 3 4 5 6 7	____ Mths	0 1 2 3 4 5 6 7
Glue	[ ]	N/A	____ Years / Mths		0 1 2 3 4 5 6 7	____ Mths	0 1 2 3 4 5 6 7
Other	[ ]	N/A	____ Years / Mths		0 1 2 3 4 5 6 7	____ Mths	0 1 2 3 4 5 6 7

103

APPENDIX D: EXPANDED DESCRIPTION OF THE NINE LARGE-GROUP TREATEMENT WORKSHOPS FOR THE TREATMENT OF ADDICTIONS

These descriptions are offered here as an example of what might be included in workshops designed for any other group of addicts in need to treatment. However, remember that these particular treatment workshops may or may not meet the needs of other addicts, and the treatments provided to any particular subject or group of subjects should always be based on the motivations identified in their responses to the ADDICAUSE questionnaire.

Treatment 1: Creating SUCCESS

The <u>main target</u> of this treatment program is the sense of <u>failure</u> experienced by many addicts both throughout their histories (as seen in their proneness to report and expect punishment and failure) and in their unsuccessful attempts to stop their addictive behaviours. Failure is a punishing experience for them, and they often seek to forget it. These parameters define the strategy.

It is difficult to set out to reduce the sense of failure as it is often denied; and focusing on it seems mainly to impair involvement or participation. To seek to enhance their unrealistic view of their success and importance, however, is inappropriate too. It affords more practice in avoiding reality. The solution seemed to be to help participants to succeed in various ways.

Block 1: Orientation:

We always start with house-keeping considerations about the day's schedule and components. Then we proceed to the orientation. Estimate the percentage of the time you were a failure in things you have done in your life. Guess at the percentage. (Responses typically vary from 20% to 95%). Actually, the percentage for all of us is a flat 0%.

Failure is not a characteristic of how humans do things. It is an idea derived from others' judgements, and the notion that you failed comes from accepting another's judgement. Doing one thing successfully, fails to do another. Others might have thought you ought to be or were doing something different from what you were actually trying to do – that is, to do something they thought you were, but you were not trying to do. But, simply and flatly, they were wrong.

Judgements of what you ought to have been trying to do are based on values, or what seems important to you or to the other person. You will always have been trying to do what <u>you</u> thought it was important to do, or what <u>you</u> valued.

You may not know that you know, but you do know what you want to do. And you learn very well to do the things you want to do. Humans are enormously competent learning machines. Sometimes we may end up doing something less well than we might have wished or liked. This may be because weak attention/concentration may get in the way or because we haven't practised it enough or haven't figured out the best strategy for doing it. But it is most likely to be that, <u>after the fact</u>, you see ways of doing it differently or of 'succeeding' in a different (by then viewed as a better) way.

Your imagined or affirmed failures of the past occurred either (a) because you were trying to do something different from what someone else thought you should have been trying to do, or (b) because, viewed from after-the-fact, you picked a poor strategy for what you wanted to do, perhaps because you were already older by the time you judged yourself, or (c) because you hadn't yet learned how to do what you wanted to do as well as you, later, thought you should have. Does that mean there's anything wrong with you, or that you were a bad or incompetent person? It does not. In fact, the only people who make no mistakes are those who don't do anything. Feedback from efforts is not failure; it is part of successful learning. It may mean that you need (a) to learn how to share or communicate with yourself or others what you are trying to do at any given time, (b) to get some (treatment) help in finding new or different strategies by which to do things, or (c) to do some more learning about how to do something.

(a) If you want to learn how to communicate about your intentions better, you might take a values training program or an assertive training program. (b) You are currently involved actively in learning new strategies in your various treatment programs. (c) Right now, let's think about how learning is done.

The "learning circle" [draw 'O' with arrows and stages: –> Knowledge/Skill –> Interest/Motivation –> Effort –> Learning –>]. The point of entry is <u>effort</u> to learn. But if you think of yourself as a failure, or if you think you can't learn, or if you think that effort expenditure seems like too much work, how can you arouse the effort to learn? So much depends on our attitudes.

Life is activity. If you are inactive, you will feel more or less dead. Waiting for things to happen is an approach left over from childhood. If you want anything in life, it is up to you to do something about it. As adults, nobody gives us anything. We are responsible to ourselves to get anything we want. The most important thing in life is simply 'doing' or activity. Of course, the strategies we use and how we do things are also important. Today's purpose is to find strategies to succeed.

<u>Block 2</u>: <u>Tools</u>:

Here are some simple tools for learning that you could use on your own to help in recognizing your immense successes.

First, your own <u>attitudes or expectations</u> will decide how quickly and easily you learn. [Flash cards with different numbers of random dots on each]. Quickly now, how many dots on this card? [Response given] Right! How many on this card? [Response] Right! (etc.). That was easy, wasn't it? Just like learning. [Slack's Estimate the Number of Dots task]. You need to believe in yourself, to know how really good you are, and to trust in the wonderful programming and capacity of your marvellous brain.

Second, here are some pictures. [Overhead of colour pictures torn from magazines, ordered from simple to highly complex]. Please tell us what you see. [Purely descriptive response]. Good! [Any inferential quality, e.g., <u>juicy</u> tomato, are challenged gently]. Where do you see the ... (e.g., juicy)? Only what you actually see please. [Encourage increasingly refined descriptive detail]. [Quirk's Perceptual Discrimination training]. Strange to say, starting with general observations or comments, the more exact and refined the way you proceed to see or describe things, the better the control in what you do, and the more will be the success and accuracy of your actions.

Third, it's terribly important that you <u>notice</u> your <u>successes</u> and reward yourself for them. It's amazing how little of this most of us do. Partly, that's because we aren't trained in how to observe our successes, or even to know what a success is. [Hand out sample cumulative frequency charts]. Of course, we all rely on our memories to recall what we've done. Then we all forget. The trick is to record your every success, and in every area in which you are trying to succeed at the time. If you were to keep a record of each kind of action, marking one more occurrence on the chart as soon as you notice it, you will be shocked and amazed at just how much success you have – every day. [Lindsley's Precision Learning]. What kinds of things you set out to record is up to you. But pick specific things you can observe yourself doing. If you want to become more sociable, on separate charts, record smiling on seeing someone you know, conversations with others, greeting people you know, each time you express an opinion, and so on.

Fourth, a simple tool for success is Relaxation [Programming]. We all use up a whole lot of unnecessary energy in tension – energy that could be devoted to a task. If you relax, you will have more available energy, and you will be able to concentrate better on the task you are doing. Relaxation is a skill that you can learn easily. [Progressive muscle relaxation tape: Jacobson's method or Lazarus' tape; or use a guided imagery method: Schutz'

Autogenic Training]. [If the former, add differential relaxation; if the latter, add some mnemonics training – e.g., from Page-a-Minute Memory Book].

Fifth, planning is essential. [Goal-Finding program]. Life is a journey, not a destination. If you are going anywhere, you had better know where you are going – or you may end up at the North Pole and freeze to death. If you know where you want to go, you had better know how to get there – or you are likely never to make it. This is true in your life just as it is true in travel. [Hand-out materials]. How always to succeed:

(1) Set achievement goals, and work out sub-goals for each, objectives for each of them, and action plans for each of them. Suddenly, the unachievable dream becomes eventually achievable reality. Make sure you keep working through the action plans, and recording completion of each. The record works as a reward to keep persistence up.

(2) Use Personal Development goals to become the person you want to be – your ideal self. If you like, you could spend years trying to figure out who you are. Or you could define the person you would like to be and the qualities you would like to have as your identity, and then, by a fairly simple (self-reward) procedure develop those qualities and become the person you would like to be. Practice exercise: suppose you wanted to become assertive. What behaviours have you seen in assertive people? [Responses might include: made a definite statement; stood erect and tall; used a brief affirmative sentence; expressed an opinion; spoke loudly, slowly and clearly; etc]. Write down the defining behaviours. Each morning read over the list of behaviours you are watching for. Reward yourself (e.g., 'Good', 'Pat self on back') every time, for every approximation to any action on the list. The behaviours will grow, and you will notice yourself becoming the kind(s) of person you want to be. Becoming your ideal self is easy, and the method involves succeeding 100% of the time. There is no failure in it.
Block 3: Therapeutics:

<u>Change history</u> [James & Woodsmall's Time-Line] procedure. If you knew, when you picture events from the past, where do you see the pictures? Point at where. [Exercise in sample past pictures, if needed, to locate direction of approach along the person's time-line]. If you knew, when you picture anticipated events of the future, where do you see the images? Point at where. [Exercise for future time-line, if needed]. It doesn't matter how your time-line lies; anything that seems right to you is perfect. Where do you see present events? Put a bright red flag there to mark the present so you can find it again. Tie a string to the flag, with the other end tied to your great toe. Drift up above your time-line, way up, until it is just a line running way below you. Now drift down again until you are floating a short distance above your time-time, but completely out of it.

Drift slowly back over your past time-line until you are over a time when, if you knew, you feel something went wrong that might have been a root cause of a problem you have had ever since. It doesn't matter for our purposes if you know what the event at the time was or not. Turn around and face the present. Take yourself by the scruff of the neck and dip yourself, just for an instant, into that event, and then pull yourself back up well over your time-line. Notice how you felt in the situation, whether or not you remember what it was. Remember how you felt. If you knew, tell yourself was this event before, during or after your birth? If after your birth, if you knew, how old might you have been at the time? Now drift back a short time, up to an hour, before the event in question. Facing the present, drift down into your time-line. Notice how you feel. Where have the negative feelings gone? Have they disappeared? Tell yourself whether you have the same feeling as before, or a different feeling or no negative feeling at all. If you have the same feeling as before, drift up again and go back until you are over another such time, and repeat the above until the feeling is different or there is no feeling. If the feeling is a different one, mark that place with a yellow flag, then drift up above your time-line and back until you are over another time that, if you knew, seems like it might be a cause of another problem. Repeat the above procedure until you find a time in which, just before the event, you have no feeling. Each of these events where you have a different feeling may be a situation that is root cause for a different problem.

When you find a time where you have no feeling when you drift down into your time-line just before the event, facing the present, walk slowly along your time-line until you are in the event. Where are the feelings now? If you find you still have some of the original feelings in the situation, drift up above your time-line and return to the present. Pick up some resources from the present. These might be your mature sense of your strength and resiliency; they might include people who feel like resources or sources of strength for you; they might include accomplishments you have made, and the like. When you have surrounded yourself with these resources, drift up again, return to just before the past event, drift down into your time-line, and walk forward into the problematic event. Where are the feelings now? If need be, back up and re-enter the situation a few times, until the feelings are gone. When that has happened, start walking slowly along your time-line toward the present, passing through all the situations that in the past aroused those feelings taking whatever time you need to re-evaluate the situations and the learnings from them, and being sure to carry along with you any positive learnings from those situations. If any feelings recur in these situations, back up again and then re-enter the situations until they too are clear. When you have reached the present, open your eyes.

The past is full of events, most of which we don't remember because they left no unpleasant feelings. It is the situations that left negative feelings that we remember and that become bothersome events in our histories. If the feelings are disengaged or removed, the memories change to neutral ones, and they can be forgotten, or remembered, without importance. If the memories change, the history changes.

Undo some <u>effects of failures</u> [NLP Phobia Treatment]. We can use a wrinkle on the last method to get rid of some of the effects of past failures. Drift up above your time-line and back until you are over a time when you came to feel you were a failure. Now, construct a theatre up over your time-line at that place. Sit down in the theatre facing the present – the direction of the screen. While you are doing that, be a video-maker, and make a film of a 'failure' event, starting well before the event, when you were still feeling OK, and ending well after the event when there was nothing happening to make you feel badly.

Leaving your body sitting in the theatre watching the screen, drift up out of your body into the projection booth or control room. Through a window in the room, look down at yourself in the theatre below. Watch yourself down in the theatre to see how the you down there reacts. Flip on the projector and run the film through, fairly quickly in black-and-white. Stop the film at the end. Then do a fast rewind in colour, so that all the action is going backwards. How did the you down in the theatre feel? If just as uncomfortable as in the original situation, leave yourself in the projection booth, drift up and out to the front of the theatre into the ticket booth. While you are selling tickets, think about the you in the projection booth, watching the you down in the theatre, and re-run the film as above. How did the you in the theatre feel? If better, repeat the same procedure from the same positions a half a dozen or more times.

If the you is improving, step back one step in the process. For example, if you are in the projection booth watching the you in the theatre, drift down into the theatre, sit beside the you in the theatre to watch that you at closer quarters. Repeat the film re-runs a few times. Then, drift back into yourself in the theatre and watch the re-runs – forward in black-and-white, then fast re-wind in colour. When that is comfortable, drift up into the film on the screen, and take your role in the movie for a few more re-runs. When you are comfortable, roll up the screen, close the theatre, and return over your time line to the present. How did that feel to you? [Obtain some experiences from participants].

Convert failure to success, disapproval to approval [Visual Squash]. Close your eyes and catch the first visual picture that flashes into your mind when you think of Failure. Open your eyes when you have that picture. Who is willing to describe the picture he/she got? [Respond to pictures given. If too concrete, ask for another picture to pop from the unconscious until the picture makes little or no sense]. That's perfect. Close your eyes and catch the first picture that pops in when you think of Success. Open your eyes when you have it. [Check a sample of these pictures too, looking for ones that make little sense]. That's perfect also. [Repeat for Disapproval then for Approval].

Do you all talk to yourselves a lot? Sure, we all do. That's what it is to think. What parts of you talk to what other parts? Oh, so you don't know. We want you to talk to a specific part of you in what follows. To talk with it, you had better be able to know what part it is and to look at it. If you knew, on which hand would you put the picture of Failure? Fine, then put the picture of Success on the other hand. Now you have two parts of you – pictures that must be parts of you since they came from within you – outside of yourself so that you can see them and interact with those two specific parts of you.

First, have a conversation with the picture of Failure. Ask it to tell you what is its highest intention for you. When you get an answer ask it to tell you why it wants that for you. Take the answer and ask the question why it wants that for you. Repeat this until no other answer is possible. Repeat the same process for the picture of Success on your other hand. Surprise, surprise! The final answer for both pictures will be to support survival and/or happiness. That is the reason for the existence of absolutely every part of every person. That is, these two opposite parts of you have the same purpose. [Confirm at each stage].

Well, if they have the same purpose, maybe they could talk to each other to work out a way in which they could cooperate to achieve their common purpose, without hurting or upsetting you at all. And perhaps the two pictures, once they have found the way to achieve this cooperation, could find a way to show you that they will work together as one harmonious part to achieve their common purpose. [This last evidence usually results in the person's two hands coming together, in what is called the 'squash', as the sign of coming together into one part].

[When the hands come together (or the eyes are open), ask the participants to close their eyes and to look at the resulting new, single, harmonious part. Ask for a sample of descriptions of the new resulting part]. [If two parts remain, ask the person to try it again on his/her own, forcing answers from each of the parts – since they are parts of you – and forcing the two parts to talk to one another, if necessary]. [If a compromise solution is found, try again]. They both want the same thing, so how can they function as one? [If a new picture is reported:] That's perfect. [When a new picture is reported, ask the participants to:]
Now imagine an infinite source of power, love, joy and contentment flowing down through your head and out through your heart to the new part, and to all the other parts of you as the new part becomes integrated with the rest of your parts.
Block 4: <u>Consolidation</u>:

Design your Future for positive experiences. [Review the Personal Development Goals method and focus on positive attributes and how to achieve them]. The method always succeeds, and ends up with successes and the ability to recognize successes. Do it. The problem of succeeding is always a matter of recognizing and being pleased with successes. It also requires that you have achievable indicators of success that can actually be observed. Find them. It helps if you know what you want to achieve. What you want to achieve are called goals or objectives. And it also helps if you know what is important to you, or what your values are.

What have you accomplished today? [Answers are likely to include the treatment work done during the day]. That's great. But that's not all you accomplished. You got up to face the day. You made your bed, contributing to tidiness. You contributed to your dental health by brushing your teeth, to your peers by washing yourself, to your physical health by eating your meals. You added to your happiness and that of others by talking with others. You gave yourself a chance to improve the overall quality of your life by attending this program. On and on, you accomplished many things that you didn't even notice. It's time you began to notice just how good and successful you are, all day, every day, and you have been all through your life.

But people keep pointing out your 'failures'. Heck you keep pointing out your own 'failures' to yourself. You might recall that both they and you are wrong when they or you do that. It's their values leading them to think you were trying to do what they thought you ought to be doing. Let them do what they think ought to be done. It's just your incorporation of other people's notions that leads you to find fault with yourself. Hey, you're an adult, and you can decide for yourself what you want to accomplish and how you want to accomplish it. Freedom is just a state of mind that recognizes your right to choose freely what you want to do. You have that right. Isn't it time you exercise it? You are free.

[Summary of program and cuing observations].

Treatment 2: Creating FREEDOM

The <u>main target</u> of this program is the <u>resistance</u> of addictions to modification, which is to be seen both in their apparently intractable nature and in the fixity of attitudes ordinarily encountered among addicts. This inflexibility tends to be denied, with addicts typically preferring to assign their intractability to addictive properties of their preferred chemicals. At the same time, flexibility tends to be de-valued and routines followed. In this instance, it was felt that setting flexibility or freedom as a target would not serve as an impediment to treatment for present purposes.

<u>Block 1</u>: <u>Orientation</u>:

[Describe the nature of the human learning machine]. Unlike animal life, in human life almost everything is learned. You have even learned how to breathe, how to have sex, and how to look and listen – whether or not the learning you did was ideally adaptive.   Let's take breathing as our example.   Nearly everyone has learned to breathe in unhealthy ways. What happened was that we wanted to look good – either slim or 'masculine' or 'feminine'. To do so, we sucked in our stomachs and tightened our pectorals to expand our chests. Unfortunately, in doing so, we prevented normal diaphragm breathing – into our stomachs – and we sucked air into our chests to expand them even more. Over time, we started the habit of chest breathing. Now, chest breathing is not only shallow breathing (not using all of the lungs), it also is quick breathing. This is because, although the rigid rib cage will expand a bit, it will only contract as far as it opened. That shortens the OUT-breath to be equal in duration to the in-breath. That shortens the total breath cycle, increasing the number of breaths per minute, and not giving the low-gradient parasympathetic-controlled out-breath time to neutralize the steep-gradient sympathetic-stress-anxiety-controlled in-breath. So, we get too much oxygen in our blood streams – and become 'hyper'; we get increasingly stressed out – and anxious; and our brains don't work as well as they might – due to fogginess bred of anoxia resulting from reflexive vaso-constriction of the brain's blood vessels to protect the brain cells from danger from the increased blood oxygen levels.

The experience of fogginess feels as though we are dizzy or faint or not quite clear about what's going on around us. Nobody can stand being uncertain or confused too long – ambiguity is the most common and intense source of fear. The way all of us deal with being uncertain is to use our habits of understanding and thought from the past. And the result is that we use over-learned or habituated attitudes and beliefs and, by satisfying ourselves they worked, add more habit strength to them. The result is increasing fixity or inflexibility of our ideas, attitudes, and beliefs. And that's just one part of the effects of only one of our habits – how we learned to breathe maladaptively.

How many of you believe that the cause underlying abuse of chemicals is a chemical cause? Of course you do. Heck, it's obvious that chemicals cause chemical reactions in the body to which the body becomes addicted. The trouble is that this idea is wrong. Believe it if you wish. However, if you believe that, the only way to change addiction is never again to touch an addictive substance, which doesn't change the fact that you are an addict. Also, there is a wonderful big bridge in Brooklyn I'd like to sell you. The trouble with some of our beliefs is that we hang on to them desperately in order to avoid having to feel responsible for the things we do that we don't like the idea of doing and, in believing them, we give up our control and ownership of our lives.

Today, we want to look at some of the gains and losses that we have due to ideas, attitudes and beliefs we hang onto. We hang on to ideas and beliefs not only because they have a lot of habit strength from previous learning. They also give us something that is rewarding, and this strengthens the learning of them. One of the main things they give us is a sense that we 'understand' or 'know' our worlds. Knowing or understanding feels good and is rewarding because uncertainty is for everyone the greatest source of fear. At least three great human enterprises are motivated by fear of the unknown, namely, languages, sciences and philosophy.

Languages and their words structure the uncertain and moving universe around us. Sciences set out to predict events after finding the laws that control the universe. Philosophy bridges gaps in our knowledge by careful reasoning about our universe. When we get a concept, law or prediction, or an idea that seems reasonable, we cling to it to help make sense of our world.

Another way we get a faulty sense of assurance about our ideas and beliefs is that, having found a way to understand something, any upset or stress we have been feeling tends to get less. We are inclined to attribute the reduction in stress/upset to the idea or understanding. It is more likely to be due to the fact that the arousal from stress cannot continue forever. The body adapts to the ongoing stress or stressor no matter what idea we formulate to help in living. That is, the feeling better we experience may have nothing whatever to do with the understanding or idea we achieved.

Still another way we satisfy ourselves that our ideas must be right, and thus reward our ideas, is if other people agree with us. We've all heard the slogan: 'if a million people believe something it is bound to be right'. And we act as though that statement were true. It seems to us more likely that if a million people believe anything, it is bound to be wrong. Still, consensual validation of our ideas by others is a powerfully rewarding experience. And, if we get ourselves in 'the right' groups of people, we can quite easily get their agreement with our attitudes and beliefs. First, in a group, where everyone wants to be accepted, any attitude expressed by one of the members is likely to be agreed with by the others – if only to maintain group cohesiveness. Second, other, especially new, members are just as uncertain as you are or were about the accepted mores of the group – and they will 'yea-say' anything for acceptance, perhaps starting a wave of yea-saying in the group. Third, groups exist for a purpose, sometimes for status, sometimes to gain access to something like wealth or drugs, and sometimes to dispel loneliness. The achievement by a member of the group's purpose (which is rewarding) is likely to be enhanced by getting into a leadership position – a position established by offering opinions and having the group agree. These are only some of the rewarding factors involved in a clique or group.

Block 2: Tools:

Our question now is one of finding how to allow ourselves increasing degrees of adaptability, variety, freedom and fun. One way might be to do the adult thing, or to take back from others to ourselves the power to reward our actions and ourselves. This is one of the main things that the Goal-Finding group sets out to help you do. Especially in the Personal Development goals, the focus is on taking over your life to be governed by yourself.

Throughout childhood we felt we were at the mercy of what other (adult) people wanted, and we waited for what we wanted until others gave it to us. Your parents, your brothers and sisters, your teachers, your maiden aunt and the cop on the block each wanted you to become something different – had his or her own goals for you. So, each of them meted out rewards and punishments to you for the kinds of actions he or she wanted of you. Is it any surprise that we are all pretty confused about who we are and what we want out of life. Now you are grown up some, and you can decide for yourself who you want to be and what you want to be like. But it won't happen ... unless you take on the job of rewarding yourself for being and acting the way you want to be. That's what you learn in the Personal Development part of Goal-Finding.

A second way to help achieve our present purpose is for you to learn a new skill of finding the good in yourself, in those around you and in everything. And that ain't easy. You see, we all learned to find fault, to see mistakes and to criticize much better than to do the opposite. We've learned that from our interactions with adult others. Parents and teachers are not just OUR parents and OUR teachers. They are people who have many other things to do than run around after us saying: 'Good, good, good, good, good, good ...' So, being efficient people, they wait for that second and a half out of each hour when we are being roaring hellions, and then they point at us, warn us, point out our errors and the like. Our attention is repeatedly drawn to our failures and errors, and only rarely to our successes. Is it any wonder that, as we grow up, we get to know more about our mistakes or badness than we do about our successes and goodness? If we could identify and notice our goodnesses, we might be able to reward ourselves for success and flexibility instead of looking for the 'rules' by which others seek to influence, and even to run us.

But what about the world around us? You might try, every time you are going anywhere – from here to there, when the world is moving past you – to find three new things that you like. You don't have to love the things or to find things that take your breath away. It is enough that you like them OK, and that they be different things from things you noticed before. You might find the world in which you live is really quite nice and full of really quite wonderful things.

A third method is to keep yourself in the Here and Now. If you really did that, you might just live for ever. If you really lived only NOW, time would mean very little, and you would just be alive. But that is hard. The whole lifestyle involved in Zen, for example, has to do with just being in the here and now. That is, some people make a life's work out of doing this task. You see, thinking gets in the way. Thought always has to do with unrealistic things. The past is gone and does not exist. The future hasn't come yet and doesn't exist. And the future is pouring into the past through the razor-thin present. By the time you think about the present, it is already in the past.

One way to diminish unrealistic thought is to pay strict attention to the stimulus world around you, by paying attention to focusing your eyes and ears on things going on in the world outside you. Of course, if you stop for any interval of time to stare at something, naming it with words and thinking about it will follow. So, keep the eyes and ears roving, even if only to explore the micro-structure of the things you are attending to. It's an interesting exercise in exploring our incomprehensible and fascinating world – that really doesn't need to be comprehended. It's fun, and it helps to keep you in the here and now.

A fourth thing you might do recognizes that you are bound to do some thinking. Too bad! However, if you must think, you might try thinking in the most outlandish manner possible. Of course, you are a sensible person, so you can't let yourself be too outlandish. OK, how about looking for different ways to understand anything you are thinking about. Doing that might even increase your creativity. One way to think about things differently is called Divergent Thinking. You might have a little fun looking through a Dictionary for Divergent Thinkers. [Quirk's Dictionary for Divergent Thinkers].

Block 3: Therapeutics:

Let's try an exercise. Pick a sound that means nothing at all to you. If you can't get one, use the ultimate abstraction, 'one', or the universal mantra, 'om'. Close your eyes and start listening to the sound in your mind. Don't struggle to listen to it, and don't try to push other things out of your mind. If you notice a thought or sensation, you don't have to think about it now, just let it pass on by and come back to listening to your sound. [Allow five minutes of silence for this brief exercise in Transcendental Meditation, or TM]. OK, come on back. How do you feel now? [Allow a variety of responses]. TM is something you could practice for about twenty minutes each day. It is probably the best way to reduce the pressure of thinking from introversion, and it has a number of other healthy life benefits. [T.M].

A second way to reduce the amount of thinking you do, and thus to participate more fully and adaptably in living, is to focus your attention on each task you do. Of course, we know that you do that. But you have probably learned another faulty habit. You probably start a task and work away at it for long periods of time. After all, that's how we were taught to deal with tasks in school. But that's just plain nuts. A person's normal attention span for anything is under five minutes. If you are highly motivated, you might extend it to ten minutes. You might not even notice it, but as you reach the end of your own personal attention span, your mind starts to wander. You may not even know what you were thinking about, but you may be aware that you can't remember what you were just doing. This is because the nerves involved in the task get tired, or fatigue.

If you want to be able to concentrate on anything you are doing, to do the best you can at each task, and to reduce the amount of time-wasting thinking, you might timetable your day in time blocks that are never more than five minutes per task, and preferably under three minutes. That's impossible, right? Actually, it isn't. How long does it take you to get up and make your bed – that's one task. How long to brush your teeth? How long to read one or two paragraphs? How long to drive from one landmark to another? If you set yourself to go through a day, changing the focus of what you're doing in under five-minute intervals, you will concentrate better, accomplish more, and think less. [Task Focus method].

A third way to reduce the amount of internal television-watching (i.e., thinking) you do is to include the quality of 'outgoing' among your Personal Development goals. Here's the drill. Write down the heading 'Outgoing' as though it's a goal you want to achieve in yourself. Under it, list a half dozen observable behaviours that define an 'outgoing' person for you. When you meet an 'outgoing' person, what do you see that tells you the person is outgoing? [Write responses on the board. Exclude those that cannot be observed directly]. OK, let's say the behaviours include: 'approaches others', 'smiles on approach', 'initiates conversation'. Write down the behaviours that are right for you, but let's use these ones for the present discussion.

You are walking along the corridor. People are coming your way. This also means you are approaching them, so you had better, in your mind, start whacking yourself on the back with pleasure for performing one of your outgoing behaviours. "But," you may say, "that's not being outgoing." Don't worry about it. Let's see what happens. After a while of doing this and being pleased with yourself, you may actually begin to smile. Whoops! You'd better start whacking yourself on the back with both hands. The first person you are approaching sees a crazy person approaching him or her, smiling. He or she passes as far away as possible. Perhaps the tenth person, sees a nice person approaching and smiles back.

Perhaps the twentieth smiling-back person says 'Hi'. After that happens often enough, you might even be motivated to greet a smiling-back person with a 'Hi'. Whoops! You had better grow a third arm with which to whack yourself on the back since you are now approaching others, smiling on approach and initiating a conversation. As the habit strengths to do each of these <u>actions</u> increases, you will notice yourself becoming increasingly outgoing. You will also find yourself increasingly attentive to here and now events, and a bit less prone to being turned inward in thought (introversion). You may even notice that your overall social behaviour becomes a little more flexible and adaptive. [Personal Development Goal-Finding program].

A fourth way is to find the good in yourself and in others. Of course, that flies in the face of most of our learning. How can we do that? Think of someone who seems to have only faults, who seems to get everything wrong and to do everything wrong. Hey, I think I know that person too. How long was it, after you met that person, that you discovered what he or she was like? We know you're smart. You probably figured it out almost at once. Did you like the person when you met him or her? Did you categorize the person right away? Sure you did. You labelled the person as 'parent' or as 'black' or 'whitey' or as 'drunk' or 'punk' or as 'foreigner' or 'competitor' or, or, or...

The truth seems to be that we do NOT see people's faults first, and then conclude we disrespect them. It works in quite the reverse order. We decide not to respect others, and then we confirm our disrespect by finding faults in them. The decision to disrespect comes first. Now we know that it probably feels good to disrespect some people, especially those who differ from us. It helps us to feel superior, special, better than the other. But we usually fail to notice that it also increases our fear, bitterness, resentment, anger and other unpleasant emotions. Of course, when we were younger and needed to feel extra-special, we were willing (even wanted) to experience those negative feelings in exchange for feeling better than others.

Partly, it had to do with the wish to be 'different' – the primitive way we established our identities. But a funny thing happened. Check this out for yourself. You feel disrespect for the other person, and the angry or other negative feelings simply add to our disrespect – each feeds the other. But try this on for size. Now that you're grown up some, you probably have a better sense of yourself, and you may not need to feel better than other people – after all, it was just a compensatory need when you felt young and put down. Now you may be in a position to ask yourself: Who hurts when I disrespect and/or feel angry (etc.) about another? It doesn't matter all that much to him or her. We suspect that the complex involved in disrespect of others only hurts ourselves.

Strange to say, respect and disrespect are just decisions we make ourselves, and we are the only ones who feel good or hurt for making the decisions. If we simply decided to respect everybody, we would start finding the good in everybody. And respect is not a gift to others. It is a gift to ourselves. We find that we live in a world full of good people, doing good things. It is a happy world that we created for ourselves. [Respect Training].

A fifth way to increase flexibility and adaptability is by means of assertiveness. We have an Assertive Training program. But assertiveness is really quite easy. Mostly, it involves using the energies that our energy-producing bodies produce for us. Standing erect, moving instantly (i.e., decisively, without delay), talking in short affirming sentences (without explanations), using 'I' statements (in place of 'You' statements), increasing volume or clarity in speech, and the like, are all ways to be assertive. And they all interfere with and diminish thought and rationalization, and increase freedom through the variety of our responses.

Let's do an exercise. Write down on different pages three repeating situations from your life in which you feel inhibited, upset or irritated. Under each one, write down about 16 responses you might make in that situation, graded from the most aggressive ones at the top to the most under-assertive and passive ones at the bottom.

Make sure that most of the responses are somewhere in the middle, neither aggressive nor under-assertive. [Get a set of responses for one such situation on the board, making sure the responses are reasonably hierarchized].

Now here's what we want you to do. First, memorize the entire list of responses for each common or repeating life situation. Second, each time the situation occurs, STOP, run through the memorized list of responses quickly in your mind, pick the one that you would be comfortable using, step DOWN one step in the rank order of responses, and deliver that response.

The purposes of this procedure are to get you to increase the range of your responses in common life situations (i.e., increased freedom), to ensure that you are definitely comfortable with the level of assertiveness you actually use (by stepping DOWN one step), and to help unlearn the anxieties that keep us stuck in our attitudes and what we do (by pairing comfort with the whole list of responses you have just recited to yourself). It is a simple and useful way to make life better. [Wolpe's in vivo procedure for assertive training].

Block 4: Consolidation:

[Summarize the day's proceedings. Try to re-focus the presentation to model different approaches]. We talked about assertive training with a view to creating response alternatives in order to increase response freedom. But response freedom is also increased by allowing yourself to dream your own dreams freely, without having to have means to help or to enhance your dreams. In a few words, write down a dream. In doing so, pick the kind of language that most appeals to you. Draw a picture of it, if you like. A picture is often worth a thousand words. If you can't draw well enough, later find a picture in a magazine that fills the bill or get someone you know who can draw well to draw it for you. Make the dream as far out as you like. Make it really special. It is a goal of yours. Perhaps you can work out on paper the details of how you plan to achieve the dream.

There's another way to expand your alternatives. Think about any problem. Break it down into sub-problems that have to be solved to solve the whole problem, or into its parts or stages. If you have three sub-problems, parts or stages, there are probably four. Find the fourth. If there are four, there are likely five. Find the fifth, and so on. By doing this, you increase your understanding of the problem, you challenge your own toleration for uncertainty in looking for other options, you reduce the chance of missing something that is important so that you are more likely to succeed, and you reduce the pressure of thinking by writing things down – and thus put a full stop to the need to think. [Reynolds If 2 choices, then there are 3]. It also helps you to develop goals you want to achieve, and helps you achieve them.

Now, you and I believe that we have to exert control over ourselves or we are apt to make mistakes, or worse. The need for control is largely a fiction. You have programmed your brain beautifully across the years to respond instantly to all sorts of life situations. Isn't it about time you learned to trust your brain to do the right things? Chances are that if, in an identical situation, you were to act without thought, or to think carefully through how to react, you would end up reacting in exactly the same way. Letting go control is one big part of achieving Freedom.

Did you ever try this: Laugh, and then find a reason for doing so. Try it now. Have a good belly laugh for no good reason at all. Then find a reason for laughing – if you must. Did you know that it's a crime for a man to laugh? The crime is called Manslaughter. Speaking of crime, you may wonder why some of us are so fond of crooks. One reason is that if it weren't for pickpockets some of us would have no sex life at all. Laughter relieves tension and leaves a good feeling about life. Enjoy it.

[The summary should remind participants of all the methods suggested and used, and should include cuing observations].

<u>Treatment 3</u>: <u>Creating EXCITEMENT</u>

124

The <u>main target</u> of this program is on compensating for the <u>reinforcing effects</u> of chemicals in perpetuating addictive behaviour. Excitement is rewarding. It may sometimes be a need to be pursued, and many addicts consider it to be achievable only through the use of excitant chemicals. There seems to be little point trying to reduce the need or pleasure in excitement. There is some point in reducing the joylessness of depression and/or introversion in order to make excitement seeking less necessary (see Treatment 8). However, it at least seems appropriate to provide means by which other kinds of excitement and reinforcement can be experienced to replace excitant chemicals.

<u>Block 1</u>: <u>Orientation</u>:

The role of buzz or rush in addictions doesn't need to be explained to addicts. The Problem of Immediate Gratification (PIG) coupled with long-term harm, pain and discomfort does need to be explained, less with the focus on the long-term harm, and more with the focus on the optimal time delays (1/2 to 2 seconds) for reinforcement of habit strength. This fact of life, about the effects on habit strength of differing intervals between action and reward, is less a caveat, and more a reminder that the reinforcing effects of chemicals depend upon the pre-existing state of the individual. The reminder is that, for a rush or buzz to be rewarding, the person's pre-existing state has to involve learned characteristics such as sensation-seeking need, joylessness, boredom or depression. The caveat is that, if the effect of the excitant properties of some drugs is to be counter-acted, it requires that these characteristics have to be alleviated, <u>or</u> that alternative means for excitation be learned, <u>or</u> that the meaning of time has to be expanded to allow the negative consequences to counteract the excitant ones. These reminders and caveats define the task of the day. Some of the other treatment programs in the series address depression and variables such as sensation-seeking and torpor (e.g., the values treatment). This program is concerned with others of the above issues.

125

It offers one approach to joylessness by examining one major source of inhibition of the main source of joy – emotions or feelings. [Draw a large test-tube on the board]. This is not a penis; it is a test-tube. Let's pour into it all of your love feelings, in order to measure the amount of them up the side. By love feelings is meant all the needs, caring, love for others, and even your attachment to things such as a car or silver-ware. These bubbly feelings have been with you and developing since birth, and your basic amount of these differs little from anyone else's.

A funny thing happens as you grow up. You are lying in your crib helplessly, and you are hungry. You cry. Your parent is outside and doesn't hear you. You cry louder and get all tensed-up – indicating your ANS-anxiety response has been activated. Repetition of this scene conditions your anxiety arousal to the feelings (of need) you have. Let's show that by adding some anxiety feeling on top of your love feelings in the test-tube. You grow older. You feel lovingly toward a parent and you go running to him or her. He or she is too busy to take the time with you. You feel rejected, and some more anxiety feeling gets learned to be associated with your loving feelings. You tell a friend a secret, and the friend blabs it around to others. And more anxiety feeling gets attached to the loving feelings. You are attracted to another child, but he or she runs off and plays with someone else. And more mistrusting anxiety feeling gets connected to your love feelings. ['Love Test-Tube'].

For those who develop enough anxiety accumulated with their love feelings (which is almost everybody), a strange kind of reverse alchemy happens as the years roll by. When your love feelings are stimulated (i.e., you meet someone you like), so are all the learned anxiety feelings. Now you feel increased feelings of love and anxiety. If you experience this amount of feeling as the loving part, the feeling no longer is one of 'I love', but is one of possessiveness – the OTHER must love me more than I love, or it is not safe to love. If that increased amount of feeling is experienced as the fear part, the feeling is one of jealousy – the OTHER probably loves someone else. If it is experienced as the avoidant or inhibitive 'cork' over the love feelings, which is the function of anxiety, the effect is one of blocking or inhibiting feelings expressed to the OTHER, who has to 'prove he/she is trustworthy before I will trust'. The focus on how the OTHER feels adds to the inhibitive effect of the anxiety 'cork', distracting attention from our own feelings. We may feel strong feelings within, but they may not be expressed because we are by focusing on the OTHER'S feelings and the pain of rejection we feel.

We can see the problem another way. Instead of looking at the side of the test-tube to measure the amounts of feelings up its sides, we could look down the throat of the test-tube. At the greatest distance is a small circle of love feelings. Around that are radiating spines of anxiety. Around them is a bigger circle representing the top of the anxiety 'cork'. If the centre core is love feeling, then the surrounding inhibitive defences involve 'psychological distancing'. That is, we find ways to keep others away, for fear that closeness evokes the anxiety feelings. The ways by which we can keep people away, usually without noticing it, include being very clever and intellectual (who can relate to that), or being tough or gruff or aggressive, or being suspicious (paranoid), or just being cold and mistrusting. From others' perspective, all these actions seem hostile, distancing and aloof. From our perspective, they are merely reactions to how we think OTHERS are behaving or feeling. From an outside perspective, the result is an inhibition of our feelings. But feelings are the way in which we achieve liveliness and joy. So we make ourselves more or less joyless by means of the distancing defences evoked by the 'love test-tube'.

Perhaps it is time to take back control over the contingencies by which we run our lives and, in doing so, take back regulation of our own lives. We can, you know.

But how can we take control over the consequences and the contingencies that govern our lives? Consequences are future events that happen to us because of their causes. That sort of thinking is due to our presumption that causes always pre-date their effects or consequences. If we plan our lives, the effects or consequences we achieve could be the ones we want, by design. If we were to select first the outcomes we want (i.e., future purposes), and then select those actions that would be followed by the outcomes we wanted, we could control our own destinies. If we were to expand our notion of time forward into the exciting realm of 'the possible', instead of expanding our (memory) lives into the sad and bemoaned past, the consequences of the future can become events of our present lives, ensured by what we do now.

Block 2: Tools:

Strange to say, one of the things that makes our lives more joyless than they might be is the kind of words we use. The problem is that we tend to refer to events and things with nouns. What difference could that possibly make? Nouns are categorizing words. Their effect is to stop action, to make the world around us seem more static, to make the relationships among the world's parts seem easier to see, and to make the world around us appear more predictable. But action and unpredictability, while often stimulating anxiety, are also a major source of excitement, and increase the options or possibilities of response to the world. To explain how this works would take too long and would bore you to tears. Still, this strange set of facts offers a way to reduce the boredom, joylessness and lack of emotion we often feel. The trick is merely one of trying, as much as possible, to use verbs in place of nouns. This task is not as easy as it may sound. It may even take using a dictionary a lot to find the verb forms of words. An easier way is to keep a dictionary of Synonyms and Antonyms, a Thesaurus, handy and find, when possible, the most action-focused words for ideas you want to express. For example, Abaft draws synonyms like Aft, Sternwards and Behind – of which Sternwards is the most action-oriented as direction rather than place. Abaft draws antonyms like Forward, Ahead, Afore, Before – of which Forward is direction rather than place – although Advance, if it fits, might be even better. The more you manage to use verbs in place of nouns, the more you are likely to feel excitement, energy and fun in your life. Nuts, eh?

An even better, but related, way to increase excitement, fun and energy in your life would be to find yourself 'at cause' in everything in your life. We tend to attribute the causes in our lives to past events over which we had little control, and over which we no longer have any control. Indeed, we have a lot of words to convince us that we have no way of avoiding the pains we find in our lives. Words like 'victim' and 'abuse', 'rejection' and 'abandonment', and a host of related concepts paint us as helpless effects of others' actions. You may say that these kinds of events did (or do) happen. What we all tend to remember are the notably unpleasant events in our lives; we tend to forget, and often simply to overlook, the many, many pleasant and good things that also happened in our lives. By focusing on the unpleasant events, we provide ourselves with explanations for why we feel angry, unhappy, or troubled now. That's fine, but then we become the victims of our own logic. We then think of ourselves and present unhappiness as immutable effects, and we then become the effects, of former events. One nice thing about being human is that we control our own destinies by pursuing our own goals and purposes in the future. In pursuing our own goals and purposes, we become the causes of our futures, in place of others and past events. What difference does that make? Well, quite apart from giving us back control over our lives, and quite apart from the fact that purposive thinking increases the range of possibilities and excitement that our futures might hold, it tends to reduce the passivity and inertia that comes from waiting for others to have effects on us, and to increase the vitality and hope that come from pursuit of the possibility of whatever futures we might wish or design for ourselves. You are the cause of your life and what happens to you, and I am the cause of what happens to me. That is scary, in a way, since it puts the whole responsibility for your life squarely on your own shoulders; it is also exciting, since it makes possible the futures that you may design and pursue. And it does suggest that we all ought to be actively planning our futures.

Another tool we might use to increase the excitement and fun in our lives is to discover all the ways available to get a 'high', 'rush' or 'buzz'. Oh dear, I guess that means we have to list for you all the substances that can be used to get a 'high'. Sadly, we are living in an age when many people seem to think that the way to fix feeling awful is by taking a drug. Surely, any thinking person would conclude that to take an artificial toxin is the second last thing to do – the last thing to do is to cut into the body to change it.

Why not get a bigger, better, easier, cheaper, less harmful and more exciting 'high'? The only reason that some chemicals can produce an artificial 'high' is that the body comes equipped in such a way that 'highs' are possible. How about using the way the body has been created to produce whatever kinds of 'highs' you want. Of course, the best way to get a 'high' is to experience emotions fully. We'll get back to that later when we expand on what to do about the 'love test tube'. But if you don't want to have to wait until you feel free enough to experience your emotions fully, you might want to consult the small sample of 'highs' (and add your own thoughts) from this hand-out. [Book of Natural Highs].
Block 3: Therapeutics:

Values, or the things that are important to us, decide what we will do at any moment, how we will judge what we have done afterwards, and who we think of ourselves as being (our personal 'identities'). Here is a simple test to help you to find out what your values are like. [Hand-out: Values Questionnaire. Allow time to complete it]. Now, for each page, count and record the number of times you checked a value with a dot (.) beside it. Then, for each page, count and record the number of values you checked with no dot ( ) beside it. Then, count and record the number of values you checked separately for the right- and left-hand columns. In a general way, the four counts for each page give information about characteristics of your values that may have important consequences for your life, for your happiness and for the fun you could have in life.

Let's just play, for now, with the first page – concerned with work. Read through the no-dot values you checked. Close your eyes and imagine yourself having a job that involved only those values. How do you feel? [Get some responses]. Read over the dot items you checked. Close your eyes and imagine yourself having a job that involved only those values. How do you feel? [Get some responses]. Read over the items you checked from the right-hand column. Close your eyes and imagine yourself having a job that involved only those values. How do you feel? [Get responses]. How many of you noticed quite a difference between the three groups of items? Of those who did, how many felt best with the right-hand column values job? Of those who did, how many felt best with the no-dot values job? And how many with the dot values job? Of those who did not notice much difference, how many had nearly all dot values? How many had no-dot values? And how many of you could not imagine a job with no-dot values? How many could not imagine one with right-hand column values?

What does all this mean? Let's take the time to explain just one part of this material. For many (not all) people, most of the no-dot values are a real source of joy and excitement. That should mean that lots of no-dot values should result in enjoyment and fun in a job (or a relationship, or feelings). That's because, for the most part, the no-dot values are positively pursued values that give mainly pleasure and fulfilment. They are mostly free from conflict, and they are usually based mainly on positive experiences from the past. They tend to give nice 'highs'.

Next, let's go back to the 'Love Test-Tube'. The picture of the test-tube suggests three kinds of things that might be done to get rid of some of the inhibiting anxiety 'corking up' our yummy love feelings. First, we might just get rid of the 'cork'. The anxiety was learned; perhaps it could be un-learned. The main method for doing that is called behaviour therapy or systematic desensitization [Wolpe]. Second, we might consciously and intentionally 'pull the cork' for short periods of time – under our own control. That is, we might simply decide to trust that person there, to let go feelings, and to take whatever consequences follow from letting go. The psychotherapy method used for that is generally classed under cognitive therapy, using methods such as rational-emotive therapy [Ellis]. Third, we might 'drill little holes' in the bottom of the test-tube to release tiny quantities of love feeling, not sufficient to arouse the anxiety. This method is generally classed as assertive training; in this instance it is called Affective Responses training. How might we do that?   Well, the first thing to understand is that feelings are expressed to and about things that differ in the strength of your feeling of caring, and of anxiety. Look around you and find a stranger. A stranger is less likely to stimulate fear about caring than a friend. Look around you to notice <u>things</u> that you might like. Saying liking things about them is less likely to arouse fears of closeness than saying caring things about a <u>person</u>; and that is less likely to arouse fear of rejection than saying caring things <u>to</u> the person with whom you're talking. So, to make sure you don't arouse 'love test-tube' anxiety, (1) grade the strength of the emotion you are expressing (from 'it's OK', 'I like', 'It's wonderful', to 'I love...'); (2) grade what/who you're talking about (from 'objects', 'scenes', '3rd party people', to 'the person you're talking to'); (3) grade the people you talk to ('strangers', 'acquaintances', 'friends' to 'intimates'). Start off expressing to strangers, mild feelings ('it's OK') about things (cars, houses, trees), and move very slowly (over many months) through to strong feelings expressed to an intimate with whom you are talking.

But why go through all that elaborate nonsense? You are perfectly able to talk comfortably about feelings even to friends. That may be true, or it may be that the amount of anxiety involved is too slight for you to notice. It's better not to take chances, and to over-do each step along the way. But it would be plain silly to go around telling every stranger that you like cars of certain types or colours. Maybe, but remember that the purpose is not to do that so much as to practice the habit of feeling good and comfortable with your caring or closeness feelings. But people will laugh at you if you go around expressing love for cars or houses, let alone for other (3rd party) people. If you worry about that, you probably need to do the method. That is just your fear talking. Think of it this way. If someone laughs at you for expressing an emotion, what does it mean? Think about it. All it could ever mean is that the person laughing is afraid of his or her own caring emotions. The laughter hides his/her own fear, and it is not directed at you – even if it seems clearly to be aimed at you. OK, you say, so I'll do it occasionally. Remember, every time you do it is a practice trial in learning comfort – or unlearning anxiety. Why not do it all day long – often? There are lots of steps to go through in the levels of 'expression', 'objects' and 'people' just described. The more practice you get, the sooner the new habit is developed, and the sooner your feelings can be freed to allow you joy and 'highs' in life.

Take a few risks of this relatively safe kind to enhance your life. Like most people, risk-taking is a little exciting for you. This minor kind of risk is pretty safe and can add its own bit of excitement in your life – eventually. It might give you a 'rush'.

Now, if you knew, where are your images of your future stored? If you were to look at the pictures you have stored in your mind about possible or expected future events, where would those pictures be? Point in the direction of the pictures of the future you see. Any direction is fine, as long as it seems right to you. Then, close your eyes and drift way up above your future time-line. Drift down again until you are just above it, but not involved in it. Drift along the line of your future events. As you look down, there will be lots of times where you don't know what will happen. They may be represented as blank areas (let your pupils dilate to let in more light in case you can discern any events there), or as clouds behind which events may be hiding (enjoy the soft white fluffy ones, and notice the silver lining of the darker ones); or as bushes behind which events are obscured (have fun spreading the branches to peer through, or peeking around the bushes to catch glimpses of possible future events). When you have had a little trip over your future time-line, drift back and return to the present. Then open your eyes. What kind of kid's game is that?   One nice thing about being a child is that we can, free of responsibilities, enjoy daydreams and fantasies. Now, you have had a peek at your future time-line, letting things happen as they will, but being a bit curious about what's there. Let's see if that experience can be enhanced.

In your present, make a plan to achieve a dream of yours. Figure out several steps through which you would have to proceed to realize your dream. Second, think of a series of things you might anticipate in the future – you know, birthdays, trips and vacations, seeing friends or loved ones, buying things you want, and the like. Right now, paint each of these things with bright colours, put motion into each one, and listen for some of the sounds that might go along with each.

Is that done? Now, close your eyes and drift up above your time-line, way up, and then drift down until you're just over it but not in it. Drift forward over the future. Look down to see what you can see. Notice the orderly progression of events leading up to your dream. Notice the anticipated events, with their colours, sounds and actions. Enjoy your future. When you are ready, drift back and down into the present, and then open your eyes. That's perfect. How was that? Did you notice that it felt less like a kid's game? Did you notice that it felt a whole lot better than the first time? All that happened between the first and second trips over your future time-line was that you made some plans, and you enlivened the future with colours, sounds and motion – which are sensory qualities found in reality. Good for you! [James & Woodsmall's Future Pacing].

Block 4: Consolidation:

There are some quite simple methods by which to achieve excitement and joy. For example, you could write down Personal Development goals of 'excitement' or 'joy' or 'emotionality' or 'spontaneity' or 'happiness'. [Goal-Finding program]. If you wanted to achieve some of these characteristics, under each quality write down a half dozen observable behaviours that you might see in the actions of those people who you think have the quality. If you like, check the Behavioural Dictionary [hand-out] to find actions/ behaviours. Then, every morning read over the list of behaviours to remind yourself what you are looking for. Don't try to perform the actions. Just notice and reward yourself immediately whenever you notice any approximation to any behaviour on your list. The rewards can just be noticing your success, being pleased with yourself, imagining whacking yourself heartily on the back, and the like. You'll be surprised how quickly you'll learn to increase the behaviours. And increasing the behaviours increases the associated experiences. It may surprise you, but it isn't the experiences that instigate the behaviours. It works the other way around. You can increase your fun in life and your liking for yourself as well, all in the easiest kind of learning you ever tried.

But there is another way to increase your joy in life. In fact, joy is really achieved by a simple, but somewhat slow, process. It is a three-step process, and you need to have lots of practice at each step to succeed fully. Here it is.

Step 1: <u>Respect</u> everything and everybody. That does NOT mean 'looking up to' everything and everybody. It DOES mean seeing everything and everybody as equal to you, important, valuable and good. 'God don't make no junk.' And it DOES mean repeatedly simply <u>deciding</u> to do this in your mind. You may ask why you would give the gift of respect to others, especially to worthless and horrid others. The answer is that the gift of respect is NOT given to others. It is given to us – we give it to ourselves. The more we respect others, the easier it is to 'find the good' in them, and the happier we become with the world around us – so full of good things and people. Most people will say, let others respect me, if I'm to respect them. That's a mistake. That's not how we come to respect others. And others likely respect you more than you think. It's partly that we expect too much from others, and partly that we put ourselves down by expecting them to see our faults. Besides, the gift of respect is given by you to yourself in the happiness you can feel in a good world of your making. Strangely, happiness is far less a result of being respected than of respecting others.

Step 2: <u>Trust</u> everything and everybody. That does NOT mean that others will not let us down from time to time. However, if they do, it is only because we expected them to act wholly out of consideration for us – we all act out of consideration for ourselves and what we want first. We do that, and so do others. It DOES mean that we need simply to <u>decide</u> to trust everything and everyone – at this moment and every other. But why would we give the gift of trusting to others, and especially to the sleazy, treacherous and untrustworthy? The answer is that the gift of trust is NOT given to others. It is given by us to ourselves. When we trust others with our feelings, whether or not they deserve it, we feel safer – it doesn't work the other way around, as we might think. When we see good in others, it's easy to trust. When we feel safe, it's easy to go to the next step of joy.

Step 3: <u>Love</u> everything and everybody. This does NOT refer to sexual love, in case that has to be said. It does refer to the kind of emotion that draws people toward things or people. The weakest form of love is liking and enjoying things (cars, homes, trinkets, clothing). The strongest form of love is the feeling we can have for relatives and the dearest of friends. Love feelings arouse all the yummy juices and emotions of the body. They are only possible if we feel safe with others – hence the need to practice trust first. And trust is really only possible if we see the good in others – hence the need to practice respect first. When love is comfortable and easy, the experience of life is joy.

[Summary of program and cuing observations].

Treatment 4: Creating SATISFACTION

The <u>main target</u> of this program is the achievement of full <u>satisfaction</u> of needs to replace immediate gratification needs that reinforce addictive conduct. Seeking absent feelings in bodily experiences leads to enhanced physiological discomfort. Immediate reinforcements do drive habit development. There is no point denying it. Delayed reinforcements do not influence habits very strongly. It seems necessary to alter perception and concepts of time as well as the degree of fulfilment and self-regulation of reinforcers. This program is the last aimed at reinforcers. This means that the program ought to help summarize the last three, ought to be more general and inclusive, and ought to begin to move toward abstract concepts to bridge over to the next ones.

<u>Block 1</u>: <u>Orientation</u>:

What is satisfaction or being satisfied and how is it achieved? We talk about social satisfaction as when we have the satisfaction of competing successfully with another. Let's ignore that childish kind of satisfaction. We talk about satisfaction of an appetite, as when sex, hunger or thirst have been satisfied. That's closer to what we want to deal with today. We speak of the kind of satisfaction that follows when we have accomplished something we set out to do. That's closest to the kind of satisfaction we'd like to focus on now. That kind of satisfaction works like a reward to add habit strength to whatever we were doing that led to the accomplishment – whether it's eating, drinking, making love, or taking an addictive substance. That's right, whenever we take an addictive substance, we are trying to accomplish some state of mind that is comforting or enjoyable. The important things to notice in this are that WE are the active agents who are TRYING to ACCOMPLISH something – it's not the addictive substance that is doing it to you – and that if we accomplish what we set out to accomplish we feel satisfied, at least temporarily.

You may have noticed that, as you used a particular substance, over time, it took more and more of it to 'satisfy' you. How come? I know, most of us accept the idea that we 'habituate' to the substance. Of course we do, but that hardly explains how it happens or what to do about it. The term habituation refers to the addictive process, and it has little or nothing to do with need for increasing doses. Certainly, the body gets to tolerate ever increasing doses of anything. That is because the person becomes desensitized to the substance. The body starts off by reacting to the intake of the chemical as a foreign body, and the stress-immune system reacts to it. With repeated exposure, the body gets used to the substance so that the intensity of the ANS-mediated immune response diminishes. But that's just how 'tolerance' increases.

The need for an increase in dosage to achieve satisfaction is based on the person's expectations. Did you ever notice that if you repeatedly are treated a certain way by another person, you start to expect that treatment and you stop noticing it after a while. And that, in order to notice it again, the treatment has to involve more of the same? We tend NOT to notice as much events that occur as we expect them to.

But how are expectations formed? To some extent they come from experience that allows us to predict what is likely to happen. But we often form expectations from other sources. One such other source is attitudes. If I have a pre-existing attitude toward a class of events (e.g., people's race, red noses, red lights), even if I never encountered a particular event before that is an example of a class, my stereotypes are apt to come into play and create my expectations about this event. I may conclude that this red-nosed person is an alcoholic, instead of being subject today to the condition called erysipelas; or I might think the red light over a doorway means 'stop' or 'do not enter', instead of 'exit'.

Another source of expectations is beliefs. As a silly example, if I believed the world to be flat, I probably would not venture out on a sea voyage far beyond the horizon. Many of us think that our beliefs are formed from real experiences. Most often, they aren't. For the most part, they are formed as statements made by us or by others in groups that we valued. If group members do not challenge our statements, or seem to accept them, our belief in those statements is validated. Beliefs are largely results of the consensual validation of statements. Once formed, beliefs establish stereotypes, from which we derive expectations. So what? So we have expectations. What do they do? They do at least two things. First, they provide contents for thought or for 'self-talk' ('Tools'). Second, they CREATE expected outcomes. Have you ever noticed how often your beliefs proved to be true? The observation about their correctness adds more validation of the beliefs. What we rarely notice is that we tend to act in ways consistent with our expectations. If I believe or expect that members of the opposite gender aren't going to find me attractive or interesting, I will tend not to look after myself, my appearance or my presentation, or I will tend to present myself, dress or say things such that there is some minor element that turns others off – as I expected them to turn off (as though it was their action).

A psychologist tested the intelligence of kids in a class. Then, without referring to the results, identified for the teacher those kids, chosen at random, who were bright and those who were not. The reading scores of the 'bright' and 'not bright' kids were not different at the time of testing. However, a year later, the 'bright' kids' reading scores had improved by two grade levels, and the 'not bright' kids' reading scores had improved by only one-half of a grade level. How come? Could it have been that the teacher's expectations led the 'bright' kids to do better than the others?

A psychologist had students grow some grain. The students were assigned without their knowledge to two groups. The members of the two groups were assigned plots of ground at random. A bag of grain seed was divided into two separate bags. A sign reading 'fast-growing grain' was put on one bag, and another reading 'slow-growing grain' was put on the other bag. The students came to get their seed, and they were given seed from one bag or the other, depending on the group to which they had been assigned. The 'fast-growing grain' grew faster and produced more grain than the 'slow-growing grain'. How come? Could it have been that the students' expectations, based on seeing the signs, caused them to tend their plots differently in some ways?

The main point of this discourse is that expectations, formed as stated, not only create much of the world in which we live (an angry person lives in an angry world; a happy person lives in a happy world – the world we see is a reflection of ourselves), they also decide what we will notice and thus the amount of satisfaction we have in our lives. If we expect rejection, that is what we will notice. If we live in a world in which what we think we want (expecting the opposite) rarely happens, we are not likely to be satisfied with much of that world. And the sad thing is that we do it to ourselves.

Block 2: <u>Tools</u>:

Our expectations and the beliefs that underlie some of them are maintained by thinking about them. Let's speak of thinking as 'self-talk'. We talk ourselves into the beliefs and expectations we have. Sometimes we don't know what the thoughts are by which we do that – they pass through our heads too quickly to be noticed. However, if we pay enough attention to our thinking, we might be able to guess what some of our beliefs are. When we find them, they seem self-evident and true. But that's an illusion. Make a true statement, if you can. [Responses; demonstrate limitations of each as an absolute truth]. It's not even true that our beliefs aren't true. We just don't know. But surely we can find out something about truth. How about science as a way to find truth? Science tests only one kind of truth, called 'pragmatic truth', or whether something works (most of the time). If you do this, does that follow? That is the kind of question asked by science. If you were willing, you could use that kind of truth in your life.

Do you like being up-tight, scared, depressed or dissatisfied? No? Perhaps you would like to decide how you would like to feel. If you did, you could easily try out all sorts of expectations and beliefs to see what sorts of self-talk results in the kinds of feelings you want. The self-talk that works to create the feelings you want, feelings that satisfy you, refers to pragmatically true beliefs and expectations. They are true!

So, here's a tool for today. First, write down some of the outcomes in feelings and satisfactions you want. Second, try out all sorts of beliefs and expectations (whether you believe them or not, or even if you don't believe them) to find out which ones, if believed in, make you feel the way you want to feel (your feelings come from self-talk), and record them. Third adopt those beliefs and expectations as (pragmatically) true, and practice believing in them. You can decide your own thoughts, and thus your own feelings. Enjoy the true thoughts and good feelings.

But expectations come from another source too. And this source exerts a truly malignant influence on all of us. Most of us expose ourselves to large amounts of media contents, in watching television, listening to radio, reading newspapers and other print. Now, you and I know that we expose ourselves to the media for entertainment. Of course, we pay attention to the news and some articles and documentaries in order to find out the facts about what is going on in the world. And you and I know that the exposure we have to the media has no important effects on our lives. Well, regardless of the reasons why we expose ourselves to the media, those sorts of things that we all know, are just plain false. The scientific evidence about exposure to media contents clearly indicates that (i) the media almost never present any facts, (ii) the news is almost as fictional as everything else in the media, (iii) most of us are misled into a kind of belief that even the entertainment media represent facts in some way, and (iv) exposure to media contents affects the personalities of everybody exposed to it in many damaging ways. And the effect on us from media contents is not insignificant or relatively slight. It is measurable, major and affects many parts of our daily human lives. So, what can we do about the effects on us of the media? We could adopt the approach one of us takes and never turn on a radio, buy a newspaper or connect the T.V. to an antenna. That may seem extreme to you. You could censor for yourself every media exposure you allow yourself. But that's not too reliable a method – you would likely soon forget what you were doing and why.

The best method is to add some enjoyment to the media to which you expose yourself by discussing with friends every media thing to which you expose yourself. That gives you something to talk about, thus easing any discomfort you may have with others. And it gives you the chance to think objectively about what you have seen, heard or read. You might even develop a discussion group, as a social support group, in which media contents are critically evaluated – not for their aesthetic or entertainment values, but for their limitations of fact. [Media proofing]

For example, the media presents the world as a dangerous place, where three-quarters of human inter-actions involve violence and murder – if true, none of us has experienced our fair share of murder and mayhem. According to the media, murder is most commonly performed between strangers and most commonly for financial gain or sexual or other kinds of excitement. It almost never occurs in those contexts. The media suggest that there are more men in the world than women. The reverse is true. According to the media, most people in the world are rich and famous, use other people for their own purposes, and have piles of money and lots of members of the opposite sex pursuing them. You and I represent the real expectations of the real world much better than those shown in the media. One of the commonest events in life is two people sharing tea or coffee, or having a chat, called small talk. How often do you hear about that in the media? You can quite easily become adept at finding the misleading and untrue contents in the media, if you look for them.

We talked earlier about beliefs and their effects in filtering out some of the nice and normal events in life. You might want to examine some of your beliefs, and to challenge a few of them – just for the fun of it. Here are some materials that may help you do that. There is little point in talking at length about these materials here since you will either be interested or not in examining your beliefs. If, on your own, you want to examine some of your beliefs critically, you might work your way through these pages. [Beliefs Inventory and interpretation materials].

We mentioned attitudes we adopt as part of the means by which we filter out some items of information and experience, and become fixated on others. The Beliefs materials contain more pages at the end to help you work through some attitudes as well, if you wish. [Attitudes Training materials]. We won't spend time going over these materials either just now.

Another tool that can help us to get satisfactions out of life involves finding and using positive feelings, attitudes and experiences. You know how it goes. For many of us, most of our time is spent noticing and commenting on the horrors, miseries and despondencies of life. We may think that we need to notice the awful in order to be vigilant for it and to help us prevent it. That's one approach taken in A.A. and N.A. But those of us who use A.A. and N.A. know that the most valuable parts of those programs are the positive 'steps' we can take to work our way through pain to a happy and constructive lifestyle. So, how can we adopt a positive approach to all living? Here are some ways.

The easy way is, every time you are going anywhere (while the world passing you is changing), find three new things that you like. You don't have to love them – things you think are nice or you like will do. But each time, find things that are different from those you noticed in going anywhere in the past. The exercise is pleasant and fun, and it makes the time of going anywhere more pleasant than otherwise it would be.

It's a bit harder to focus your attention and thought all the time on the pleasant, good and worthwhile. Still, if you can, it also helps the quality of life and the amount of satisfaction you experience. For example, look out and see a day that is bleak, wet and miserable. You might feel good about the day if you remember that you will enjoy the next bright day more by contrast, that the rain provides us and the birds and animals with fresh drinking water and helps the plants and trees to grow, that the humidity is good for your skin, or that the cloud cover provides shade from the blistering sun. Or someone makes a nasty crack. You might realize that the reason for it is the way the other feels and not what you did (so you might feel compassion instead of being offended), that the person has suggested a brand new quality you might want to try out to increase the freedom and variety of your behaviour, or that viewing the world that way might be fun or even funny (in response to 'You rat!', you might picture a great white rat nibbling on a tiny bit of cheese). [Dictionary for Divergent Thinkers].

There are still other ways to enhance the satisfactions you get from your life. One way is to delay gratification in all sorts of things you do. Setting out consciously to postpone or delay reaching satisfaction, seems to increase the amount of satisfaction we experience in most things. This can apply to things all the way from sexual satisfaction, through eating snacks to winning a game or solving a problem. The more we put into something in time and effort, the greater the amount of satisfaction at completion. There is a useful spin-off from delaying satisfaction. It teaches us that it is NOT impossible to tolerate unpleasant feelings. In fact, if we wait out unpleasant feelings such as anxiety, which often underlie addictive behaviour for example, the feelings are likely to pass off and go away. Anxiety about a particular thing cannot be maintained even for a couple of hours. To maintain it, we have to re-prime ourselves with thoughts or more exposure to the upsetting event.

Another way is just to enhance the quality of the experience from which we seek satisfaction. This can be done by learning self-hypnosis, or just imagery creation [e.g., <u>Page-A-Minute-Memory Book</u>] and increasing the experience with hypnotic or other imagery enhancement. Or you could do it without going to all that trouble by making up your own exciting fantasies or images to call up in any experience. For example, if you want to enjoy a conversation with someone, you might imagine you are in a conversation with a person to whom you particularly like to talk. Or, while dining on food you don't really like, you might imagine yourself eating some of your favourite foods. The purpose of such images, of course, would be to increase the amount of satisfaction you are having.

<u>Block 3</u>: <u>Therapeutics</u>:

Let's play for a while. Let's do the Beliefs Inventory now. [When it is completed, ask participants to score it themselves. Then refer to the interpretations appended for the ten common thinking errors]. Now, let's suppose that one of the styles of thought you use is to expect things to be fair, and to get yourself angry when things are not. First question: Who ever said that things are supposed to be fair? Where is that rule carved in stone? Second question: Please ask yourself how you would feel if things were always absolutely fair. In such a world you and I would receive precisely and only what we deserved. Of course, you wouldn't be alive today. You did nothing as an infant to deserve the care, feeding and shelter your parenting ones gave you. Like most workers, you probably did the least you could get away with at work to 'earn' your pay – would you pay your employees well for that? You probably did the minimum amount of homework at school that you could get away with. Wasn't it lucky that the teachers took the time to teach much of the material in class? You probably wanted more back than you gave in most of your relationships. I know I did, when I'm being honest with myself. What did you do to deserve the company of some of the wonderful people you have known? Hey, maybe we should be grateful and happy that the world is NOT fair. Each of us gets from life far more than any of us gives. Thank goodness, the world isn't fair. Let's be happy for that.

Let's suppose that one of your styles of thought involves getting yourself upset when things in the world around you don't go exactly as you want them to. First, where is it carved in stone that the world is supposed to be controlled by you? Second, isn't it wonderful that the world is NOT controlled completely by you? Think of it. Suppose the world was completely controlled by you and what you want. Great, eh? Like hell it would be! You would have to devote your whole life, all day every day (at night too), to ensure that the zillions of horrors possible didn't happen to others and to yourself. If you controlled the world, everything that happened in it would be your fault. You beast you!

A large part of the satisfaction in life comes from social and intimate relationships with others. That's because we're social animals. When we do not have close relationships with others, or when we are unable to feel satisfied in our social relationships, we feel lonely. Loneliness is a motive that a thoughtful nature implanted in us to drive us to interact with others. Some of us feel that our loneliness from weak interactions with others or our lack of friends is due to what other people do – perhaps they are rejecting or don't like us. So, how might we set it up so others like us or are less rejecting, or so that we can reach out to others and gain more satisfaction in our social relationships? The answer is quite simple really. Social interactions depend on communications, and communications are not hard to improve. Communications involve two things, receiving and sending messages.

Receiving messages is quite easy. It involves hearing and seeing what the other person is saying, pacing the other, and checking to see whether you understood what the other person intended. There's no better way to be thought of by the other as brilliant, competent, friendly and nice than to be able to listen and show you understand.

The hardest part is hearing and understanding what the other person is saying. The trouble is that we become preoccupied with our own thoughts and interpretations due to introversion, emotions that interfere or just not having learned how to listen. If we want to hear what the other says, we need to do some things.

(1) We need to focus our eyes and ears on the other person. You know how to focus your eyes. You find a spot and make it look sharp and clear. But if you keep looking at the same spot, your eyes will quickly go out of focus. So you need to keep changing the spot you're looking at. Look at one eye, the other, the mouth, the creases in the forehead, the creases beneath the eyes, and so on. Let your eyes be drawn from one spot to another by the movements and changes occurring in the speaker's face. Looking in this way gives clues to the non-verbal and emotional communications from the other. But how do you focus your ears? You can you know. Partly it's done by cocking your head slightly to one side or the other. The slight turn that feels most attentive is the correct one, as it will turn your dominant ear toward the speaker. Partly it's done by an automatic slight opening of the ear's passages, which happens when you accept and want to hear a particular sound
– the other's voice. It helps if you allow yourself to like the other person. Partly it's done by wanting to pay attention. Some of us habitually 'tune out' those around us. Partly it's done by pacing. We hope you are all practising these skills right now while we are talking to you. It's a chance to learn how to listen.

(2) We need to 'pace' the other person. Pacing involves the skill of assuming attitudes and gestures like the ones used by the other. This sounds like we're saying to mimic the other person. That's not quite it. What the other person is doing and the attitudes he/she adopts are communicated partly in the assumptions made, and in the non-verbal communications and the gestures. Don't interpret the non-verbal language and gestures in your head. In fact, if you do, you are apt to get it wrong. It's better to try to live inside the other person's body – as the old saying goes: Walk a mile in

another's shoes. If the speaker turns the hand up, your head might tell you he/she is asking for something. But turning your own hand up let's your body feel what it is like to express what is being said with that gesture. It might involve weighing or judging something, or accepting something, or begging a question, or any number of other things. Pacing is not obvious mimicking, but it ought to involve some, at least slight, movement in your body as if to find out what doing that in that context feels like. Pacing ensures that you are 'staying with' the other.

(3) We need to check our understandings of what the other is trying to communicate. All too often we think we know, when, in fact, we don't. As far as we are aware, nobody has ever read anybody else's mind <u>correctly</u>. We all try; and we all fail. The only person who really knows the other's meaning is the other. To ask the other person to repeat doesn't really help. We will hear the same mistakes again, and the other is apt to think we're not paying attention. The best way is to say briefly in your own words what you think the other person is saying, and especially to say what you feel is the feeling underlying the other's communication. Start or end your brief summary by indicating that you are stating your understanding of the other's opinion, and by asking for confirmation. "If I get it, you're saying that ... Is that right?" To 'get it right' is the best-known way to reveal to the other how bright, empathic, and wonderful a person you truly are. And getting it wrong is much better for human relationships than not confirming or not 'getting it'.

The other part of communication is sending messages. If we send messages in certain ways, we will almost certainly create conflict with others and fail to get our needs met. If we send messages in other ways, we have the chance to get some of our needs met, to make and keep friends and to reduce the conflict in our lives greatly. Let's recognize and use some of the main features of sending messages.

(1) The body is an energy-producing machine. We need to use the energy produced or it creates problems in our lives. Some of

us want to be nice people who are liked. So, to keep from seeming pushy or obnoxious, we may try to hold back the energy we use in communications. Holding back our energy and being under-assertive tends to have several consequences. We may feel chronically dissatisfied because our needs aren't being met by others; we may become depressed or bitter and angry. That's one of many ways we set ourselves up to have negative feelings. To increase the use of energy in communicating, we can do some quite simple things. Try them out. Talk slightly louder until you can feel an echo from the walls; enunciate clearly and crisply; speak slowly to take more time; talk in brief, affirmative sentences, without explanations (explanations may convince you, not anyone else); make your gestures expansive with extensor movements; stand or sit in an erect posture. All these kinds of things will use bodily energy and increase your own sense of empowerment. They may also help to lift your mood. Sending communications provides an opportunity to use your body's energies.

(2) Some of us are over-assertive or aggressive. This creates conflicts with others and may prevent satisfaction of needs with others. Aggressiveness is often carried in the way we send our messages. Speaking about the other person, or using "You" statements, tends to get the other person on guard to be ready to defend him/herself. It is a 'flag' to arouse the other's defenses. Even being complimentary in the form of a "You" statement is apt to create uncomfortable defensiveness in the other. A much more effective way to send messages is with "I" statements. 'I think ...', 'I feel ...' expresses yourself, affirms a state or opinion of yours, and tends not to get anybody else's hackles up. It helps the other to listen to you rather than listening to his/her own head or getting him/her ready to be defensive. It is most likely to result in getting your own needs met, and thus in getting satisfaction for you in social relationships. Even saying, 'I think of you as an angry person' may be better than saying: 'You are angry.'

Some people would suggest that effective communication can be summarized in the 'three-part statement'. The 'three-part statement' starts with an "I" statement expressing how you understood what the other just said (e.g., 'I gather you think the world is flat'), and giving him/her a chance to correct any misunderstanding. It continues with an "I" statement about your own feelings on the subject (e.g., 'I feel annoyed that some people still have that opinion'). And it ends with an "I" statement about your response or intended action (e.g., 'I guess we ought to take a trip around the world some time').

(3) Some of us are afraid or anxious in social situations. We may fear how others will react to us or how we will judge our own actions. It's not a bad idea to get rid of that interfering fear. There are several ways to do this.

On separate sheets, write a one sentence description of a couple or three repeating situations in your life where you feel scared, uptight, frustrated or angry. For this exercise, let's take the situation (page) where you feel most upset. Under the descriptive sentence for that situation, write down about 16 responses you might use to that situation. Take some time with this task, and make sure your responses are graded from the most aggressive ones at the top to the most under-assertive (doormat-like) ones at the bottom. Make sure that most of your responses are in the middle, neither aggressive nor under-assertive. [Make an illustrative hierarchy on the board from responses offered by participants].

Now, here's the drill: (a) To prepare yourself for future occurrences of this situation, memorize all the items on your list, in their right order. (b) When the recurring situation occurs in the future, each time, (i) STOP and (ii) quickly in your mind run through the whole memorized list of responses, (iii) pick the level of response that you would be comfortable giving, (iv) step <u>down</u> one step and (v) deliver that response. OK, what's all that about? The main thing that goes wrong to create our psychological problems is that we become fixated on responses many of which are apt to be maladaptive. Treatment involves increasing the range of available responses, and thus freedom. Forcing a list of many (16 is ideal) different responses, increases the range of possible responses greatly. But, you say, I couldn't use most of the responses. It doesn't matter. You choose your own response level each time. Following the steps ensures that you'll be comfortable with not only the response you give, but also with the whole list that you have just run over in your mind. That is, each time you go through this exercise, you give yourself another practice trial in reducing your anxiety in that situation, about the whole list of responses (thus increasing the available response range) and about assertiveness in general. This does not mean that you will ever use extreme responses at either end of the list. It is most likely to mean that you will increasingly use mid-range reactions (that is, assertive reactions), that you will likely be less prone to anger and depressions, and that you should become less socially anxious over time. [Wolpe's in vivo Assertive training].

Let's try another exercise. Picture (one of) the other situation(s) you have written down. Picture yourself in it. Notice where the picture seems to be seen in relation to where you are now. Move the picture until you seem to see it squarely in front of you, anywhere from 1 to 4 feet away. Now start pushing it away from you. As it moves away, it gets smaller ... and smaller. Let it drift farther and farther away until finally it is just a little dot on the horizon. Now bring it slowly back again, getting bigger and bigger, until it is just in front of you again. Now push it back again, way back until it is just a dot on the horizon. Notice how you feel when it is close to you and when it is far away. Move it back and forth a few times from up close to way off on the horizon. Finally, just leave it out there at the horizon.

Let's try that a different way. Put the picture on a T.V. screen in full colour. Down in one corner of the screen put a tiny black-and-white picture of yourself looking and feeling comfortable and satisfied. When I say 'go', zoom up the little black-and-white picture of yourself until it fills the whole screen, and is in bright colour. Go! Clear the T.V. screen. Return to the screen the coloured picture of the uncomfortable repeating situation and the tiny black-and-white picture of the comfortable and satisfied you. Repeat the zoom of the little picture until it fills the whole screen in colour. Do that sequence again, say, a dozen times. Tell us what happened. [In the usual case, the person has difficulty getting the uncomfortable situation's pictures back again]. That's perfect. [James & Woodsmall: The Swish].

Block 4: <u>Consolidation</u>:

Would it be nice to have lots of joyful, happy and positive feelings? We know. How would you ever feel important and special if you didn't feel awful and suffer the whole time? Of course, if you were to have lots of positive feelings, and expressed them, other people would probably want to be with you more, like you better and notice you more. That too might help you feel important and special. If you noticed, you could be creating positive feelings for yourself just by finding the self-talk that makes you feel positive, recognizing the honesty of those self-statements as pragmatically true. If you could find such self-talk, you could create positive feelings almost instantly whenever you wanted to. If you could let yourself do that, you could then create positive feelings at will with which to reward yourself for any desired behaviour or characteristic you noticed in yourself or your daily life. Think of it. You could pile satisfying rewards on top of satisfaction for your satisfying actions and characteristics. Goodness, you wouldn't want to do that, would you?

Try this. Close your eyes and drift up and out of your body. Drift yourself away until you find yourself over a hill with a gentle slope, on a bright, warm day with a cool breeze. Drift down onto the top of the hill. Start to run slowly down the hill, leaping up and forward from time to time. Notice that you seem to float through the air with each jump. You leap and you find that, if you tilt your head back a bit, you keep floating up and up. Float away until you are over a place from your childhood where you felt safe and cared for. Tilt your head forward and drift down at that place. Visit the place and recover the good feelings of that time and place. When you're ready, leap up again and drift off to any place on or off the earth you would like to visit. Float over it, looking down at the passing scenes that your mind knows you will find there. If you want to, tilt your head down and land lightly to look more closely at people, places or things. Be part of that place and its people for a while. Enjoy it completely. When you are ready, leap up again and glide to another place or time. And when you are ready, leap up again and drift back and down into yourself. How did that feel. It was a trip, wasn't it? You can have that fun, at no cost, any time you like. See how easy life and its dreams are. [Autogenic Training].

But how do you get real satisfactions, right? That's easy too. All you need to do is to discover what you really need. It is always within your power to acquire. You see, what we do all day every day is pursue the things that are important to us – our values. And our satisfactions come from whatever it is that makes us feel fulfilled or 'actualized'. Those needs that actualize us, our self-actualizing needs, have been listed by various people. One list of self-actualizing needs might help us to find some of the means by which we can gain increased satisfaction in our lives. [Hand-out: List of Maslow's self-actualizing needs].

[Summary with cuing observations].

Treatment 5: Creating VALUES

The <u>main target</u> of this program is adaptive and mature <u>values</u> development. Years of investment in values of childhood and then in those of the addictive sub-culture need to be countered. Some of the common attitudes and values of the sub-culture need to be challenged, and any void created thereby filled with other values. James and Woodsmall's (1987) work in this area is drawn on heavily in designing this program.

<u>Block 1</u>: <u>Orientation</u>:

Values, or the things we consider to be most important to us, are (1) the most general and abstract feature of ourselves that affect everything about us, (2) the best means by which to define or identify ourselves (who we are), (3) in advance, the means by which we motivate what we do and thus determine what we do, and (4) after the fact, the means by which we evaluate what we have done, or how we judge ourselves and our actions. Thus, they are perhaps the most important quality we possess.

And most of what we prize most in ourselves and our lives, including our beliefs and our attitudes, depend upon our values. One of the most worthwhile and useful things we can do is to examine our values, find out in detail what they are, and find out if any of them need to be changed or assigned a different importance to us. This may be <u>the</u> most crucial thing we can do to ensure our future joy, happiness, effectiveness and adjustment. But then, you wouldn't want to go to all that trouble, right?

But perhaps your values are already ideally suited to your optimum future adjustment and well-being. Permit us to question some of the values you may have. There are several ways to do this. First, let's consider some of the attitudes and beliefs which tend to be common among people who exhibit various kinds of addictions. While attitudes and beliefs are not values, they depend upon and are derived largely from our values. Since it's sometimes easier to recognize attitudes and beliefs than to recognize values, it may be best to start with attitudes and beliefs, to see if any problems exist.

Many addicted people believe themselves to be mainly physical entities comprised of anatomy and chemistry. They often act as though they believe that they are controlled by their own chemistry and/or the physical events of the past. Commonly, they act as though they had little or no control over their behaviour, and they seem to have an attitude that immediate relief is needed to correct unpleasant feelings. These are a few of their beliefs and attitudes that are maladaptive and false, and they are based on values

154

by which they deny their ability or right to control their own lives or which involve conflict and avoidances. Would anybody share things he/she KNOWS to be true about him/herself (beliefs) with us? [Discuss offerings]. We will identify some of the values that create such beliefs and attitudes later. For now, if you recognize any such beliefs or attitudes to be part of your personal make up, you might want to consider them to be useful indicators of your need to examine your personal values. That is today's task.

Let's play a game. Obviously, we have no basis for knowing what your personal values are. But let's try to read your mind. Please score us on a piece of paper to see how good we are as mind-readers. Put a check mark beside the number of each of the values that apply to you out of the ones we are about to suggest, by mind-reading, are important values for you and your life. Here we go. Hocus Pokus. You highly value (#1) Precision, (#2) Power, (#3) Strength, (#4) Intelligence/Cleverness, (#5) Efficiency, (#6) Dependability or Reliability, (#7) Size (e.g., tallness) or Amount (e.g., of money), (#8) Effectiveness or Success, (#9) Acceptance by Others, (#10) Recognition/Importance.

OK, out of 10, how did we do? [Obtain scores]. So, we did pretty well, huh? Well, here's the kick in the head. None of these are, strictly speaking, values. They are all really 'evaluators' by which we measure how well we are doing in achieving other things, including values. Really, they are the kinds of evaluators used by parents and teachers – by adults dealing with children – as markers of growth and development of children. Precision in performance, power in influencing other children, physical strength (as in sports), successful use of intelligence, speed in completing or accomplishing tasks, dependability in doing anything, success in anything, being accepted by peers, achieving recognition among peers, and growth in size and amount of earnings, are all used by parents as bench-marks to celebrate growth in children toward maturity and independence. These evaluators are left-overs from having been a child. They may make one appear <u>useful to others</u> and may help us to feel important or useful in work settings. But they do not work too usefully as personal values. If you believe those to by your main values, you really need to join us in sorting out just what your <u>real</u> values are.

Once a value has been developed, it tends to persist. This is partly because it becomes an important part of our attitude-thought (cognitive) system, partly because we commit ourselves to anything we do or think for a while, partly because it is self-reinforcing, and partly because we are usually not all that aware or conscious of our basic values. Besides, values are not easily changed just because we think we ought to, or might like to, change them. We need an effective strategy to change or adjust our values.

We would like to offer a brief warning before we get on with this day's tasks. There is one pervasive and insidious source of values from which we all need to protect ourselves. And part of the problem is that we are mostly unaware of the values the media teach us. Every day, we are all subject to learning media values. The media are commercial enterprises whose primary task is to make money for media people and to inflict their beliefs and attitudes on others. Any business tries to maximize income and minimize costs. Consequently, media contents are characterized by (a) glitz, glamour and sensationalism (to acquire audiences) and (b) minimized expense in production, especially at the point of writing scripts. Consequently, quick-write scripts are adopted that are weak in characterization and plot (and especially in values), and that are carried in large part by flashy, rich and colourful action (which best controls attention). Watch out for the effects the media are having every day on your values, and thus on your life.

<u>Block 2</u>: <u>Tools</u>:

[Hand out Values program package and ask participants to get to work on the materials and exercises]. We would like to take a few standard life experiences (work, relationships, feelings, etc.) and identify your important values in each one. First, put a check mark in front of each of your important values in each area, adding those we have missed at the bottom. Second, rank the order of the importance of the checked off values in each area. Third, do the exercises to find missing important values. Fourth, make a final rank ordering of your important values in each area. Fifth, check to discover how your values make you feel. Sixth, let pictures pop into your mind of the top 6 to 10 values in each area. In all of this, please do NOT try to think reasonably, to choose values you think we or others are looking for, or to select what you think 'ought' to be your values. For present purposes, you need to know what your real values actually are. To find out, go deeply inside yourself and let yourself be guided by whatever 'pops' into your mind, or that 'seems right to you.' Trust your unconscious to tell you what you need to know. We trust your unconscious to tell you the right things. This is a voyage of discovery, and probably the most useful and worthwhile task you have ever done.

[When that is done, finally, ask participants to list their values in each area as they think they 'ought' to be by whatever rules they want to use for themselves].

<u>Block 3</u>: <u>Therapeutics</u>:

You have developed a notion about what your main values are, and pictured images to represent each of your main values. Let's use that information. First, there is some understanding about your values that you need. What do your values do for you? Why is it important to you to hold each value? [Ask these questions about a sample of the values participants offer for discussion. Work through enough offered examples to get one or two in each of the following:]

(i) Some values are <u>reflexive</u> values. To obtain their benefit we depend on others to give something to us. We may be able to work to achieve the valued feedback from others, but we only gain from these values if others do what we want of them. Recognition, appreciation, respect, and the like, if it is important to us to receive them, depend on others to give them to us. Reflexive values are nice to have, but they put us at the mercy of others, subject to the whims of others, and therefore potentially feeling disappointed and victimized. Also, they make us feel dependent on others. Please identify each one of your reflexive values with an "R". [Give participants the opportunity to discuss their values to identify the reflexive ones correctly].

(ii) Some values are <u>conflicted</u>. This means that we are most aware of failures to achieve the values. And pursuit of these values involves avoidance of their opposites or getting away from their opposites. For most people (not for all; check each for yourself), values such as trust, respect (R), safety, recognition (R), and the like, if we want them for ourselves, involve <u>avoiding</u> mistrust, disrespect, danger, being ignored, or imprecision, powerlessness, and the like. All the values you selected where you have expressed the value as a 'Not ...' are conflicted values. 'Not ...' values are things it is important to you to <u>avoid</u>.

Some people believe that <u>avoidance</u> values are formed from many earlier experiences with the value's opposite pole – that is, with not being trusted or able to trust, not feeling respected, not feeling safe, not receiving recognition, or making mistakes. Each of these unpleasant or uncomfortable <u>experiences</u> is stored in memory with a negative or upsetting 'charge' or feeling. Each of these feelings cumulates with the earlier experiences' feelings to increase the amount of negative feeling attached to the value's negative (opposite) pole. But the personality is always in a state of balance. So, as the amount of the negative feeling attached to the opposite pole (mistrust, disrespect, etc.) increases, so does the need pressure or the importance of the positive pole (trust, respect, etc.). The two poles are conceptual parts of ourselves (mistrust–trust, disrespect–respect) that pull farther apart with each new negative experience, creating an approach-avoidance conflict and increasing the value or importance of the ideas or ways of seeing things that are involved.

If you have many conflicted values, several things will follow. You will NOT enjoy your values, or the area of life in which they are important to you (e.g., work, relationships, feelings).

158

You will be fairly constantly 'on edge', vigilantly watching out for evidence of the negative poles (mistrust, disrespect) and finding them fairly often – while failing to notice evidence of the positive pole (trust, respect). You will spend a lot of time putting yourself and the world down (i.e., feeling guilty or being depreciating or critical). You won't have much joy in life. You will worry a good deal. And you may fail to achieve much of what you might have expected yourself to achieve. Mark these values with a "C". If you're not sure whether a value of yours is conflicted, ask yourself 'why' it's important to you (many times if need be), or why you want that. If any answer you give yourself involves 'avoiding' anything, or a 'not ...', the value is a conflicted one. Mark it with a "C".

(iii) Some values are wonderful, <u>approach</u> values. When you value opportunities, joy, love and the like, you will likely tend to notice instances of these values, to enjoy the experiences associated with them, and to enhance the quality of your life with them. It is worthwhile to ensure that you maximize the number of positive or approach values you pursue in your life. Mark these values with a "P", or just write JOY beside them.

[Spend some time with individual's values, helping them to check on the 'type' of each of their values. For example., 'You say Trust is important to you. When you think of Trust, what does it do for you; what do you get from Trust? ... Why is that important to you? ... And why is that important to you? ... What evidence would you accept that Trust and its associated things are present or absent? – List on the board the responses given. Then examine each to find out what the person notices (approach-positive pole or avoid-negative pole) and how it makes the person feel (happy-positive pole or scared/unhappy/angry-negative pole). If on negative pole, the value is a 'C' or avoidance value – important to addictions].

Survey your values. Are they as you would want them to be, or would you like to change them? There is no point just deciding to change them and expecting them thereafter to be changed. They won't be. But there are ways to change them. Let's play.

Find a value in your lists that you would like to keep, but which ought to be lower or higher in the rank order of your values. Let's take a couple of examples. If 'money' is at the top of any area's rank order, you are probably a pretty boring and bored person. You might want to shift it down to second or third place in your rank order. If you have too many reflexive values among the first 6 to 10 top values for any area, you likely feel a bit anxious, helpless or at the mercy of others. You might want to pick one or more of these reflexive values to move much farther down in your ranking. If you have too many conflicted values toward the top of your list, but you are hesitant to get rid of the cautiousness they maintain, you might wish to move some of them a bit farther down in your ranking to get some other, more enjoyment giving, values to higher rank order places. How is this done?

First, pick a value you want to move, select the level of importance to which you want to move it, and note the value above and below the position into which it will be inserted. Remember that, by shifting its position downwards, you automatically increase by one the position of all the values above its new position. Close your eyes and let a picture pop into your mind when you think of the value you're going to move. If the picture you get makes obvious sense, or represents a given example or concrete instance of that value, try again to see what picture pops into your mind when you think of that value. Let's have a few examples of your pictures. [Get a few of the participants' images and ask them to try again if the pictures are too concrete. If they are satisfactory: That's perfect]. Now close your eyes again, and let pictures pop into your mind for the other two values – those above and below the new location. [Get some examples of these pictures, reacting as above]. [When it appears that all participants have three different pictures to represent the three values, proceed].

Bring up the picture representing the value you want to move. Notice whether it is in colour or black-and-white. Notice its colours or shades. Notice whether it has bright or dark spots. Notice whether it is clear and sharp or cloudy, vague or in pastels. Notice if it's framed or has a background. Notice where it is located – its direction and distance from you. Notice any background, any movement or any sound. When you have identified its sensory qualities, start moving it around, noticing how you feel as it takes different positions – in front of you, higher, lower, to the side, closer, farther away. What you need to discover is how it's different positions affect you and how they make you <u>feel</u>. You're trying to find out where you can locate it to increase, and also to reduce, its impact on your <u>feelings</u>. Once you have found that out, change its other sensory qualities to see how they affect how you feel. Add, remove and change colours, increase and decrease its clarity and sharpness, add and take away movement, add and reduce its background or surroundings, and add, reduce and change sounds and movement associated with it. As you do each of these things, note how it makes you feel when the changes are there. Once you know what you can do with the picture to increase <u>and</u> reduce the strength of your feelings about the picture, put it back up on a shelf.

Then, in turn, bring down the other pictures and do the same with them until you know how to increase and decrease your feelings about those pictures. If your feelings don't change as you change the location and sensory qualities of any of the three pictures, put that picture away and let another picture pop into your mind when you think about that value. Keep on finding pictures and testing them, by changing location and sensory qualities, until you have a picture for which you can notice changes in your feelings about it as you change its location and sensory qualities. When you know how to increase or decrease your feelings about the three pictures by moving and changing them, you are ready for the next step. [Allow time].

Compare the locations and sensory qualities of the three pictures, one for each of the three values. For the picture of the value whose rank order you want to change, move to different locations, and change the sensory qualities of the picture, while noticing how you feel with each change you make to the picture. Compared to the feelings aroused by the picture of the value <u>below</u> where you want to locate the to-be-moved value, try to find the location and sensory qualities of the to-be-moved picture that create in you a bit <u>more</u> intense a feeling; <u>and</u>, compared to the feelings aroused by the picture for the value <u>above</u> where you want to locate the to-be-moved value, try to find the location and sensory qualities of the to-be-moved picture that create in you a bit <u>less</u> intense a feeling. What you're trying to do is to find, for the to-be-moved value, the <u>feelings</u> the picture arouses that are sandwiched <u>between</u> the <u>feelings</u> aroused by the pictures for the other two values. Don't try to be reasonable or sensible about how you judge the strengths of your feelings. Go inside yourself, and let your unconscious tell you how you <u>feel</u>. When you've found the location and sensory qualities of the to-be-moved value's picture so that it conforms to those feeling intensities, anchor the picture for that value in that location and with those sensory qualities. You can do that by any method that works for you. One way is to put the picture on the screen of a very heavy television set, and then nail the television set in just that location with huge spikes, or anchor it with a big, heavy anchor. When you have done that, open your eyes and look around you. Then close your eyes again and check to make sure that the to-be-moved value's picture is where and how you wanted it in relation to the other values and their pictures. If things have changed, go back and re-anchor any picture that has moved or that has changed appreciably.

With that done, go back inside yourself and relist your values from that area in the right order as they feel to you now. If the to-be-moved value is not in the place you wanted it, close your eyes and go back to check out whether the pictures are as and where you left them. If not, review them and re-anchor them as before.

What's all this about? Our values have been formed, and are carried to us, through images we carry in our minds. The images mostly don't make much sense because they combine all sorts of features from many memories from the past involving those values. If we want to change the locations of our values in their rank ordering of importance, we need to make the images associated with the values such that they evoke the right quality and amount of feeling in us – the amount of the associated feeling deciding how strong or important the value is to us. And, if we want the value to stay where we put it, its image or picture has to stay as and where we put it – hence the need to anchor it.

Let's play another game. Look down your list of values in the various areas of living and find an avoidance value that you would like to heal, so that it no longer drives you to avoid things in your life. Trust or respect or others' acceptance would be good ones, but you choose your own. Whichever conflicted or avoidance value you choose, it will have a positive and a negative pole. For example, the two poles of trust might be trust and mistrust, of respect might be respect and disrespect, and of acceptance might be acceptance and rejection. Find the two poles <u>for you</u> of the conflicted value you chose.

Close your eyes and let a picture pop into your mind for the <u>negative</u> pole of your value. For example, what picture pops into your mind when you think of mistrust, or of disrespect, or of rejection? Keep letting pictures pop into your mind until the picture makes little sense or seems a bit far out. When you have the picture of the negative pole of your value, put it up on the shelf. Now, let a picture pop into your mind for the positive pole of the value. For example, what picture pops into your mind when you think of trust, or of respect, or of acceptance. Check the picture for your value's positive pole to make sure it doesn't make too much sense to you.

When you have that picture, put it up on the shelf too, and open your eyes. [Check a few examples].

Great! Now, you all talk to yourselves, right? We know you do. It's called thinking. The trouble with thinking, or with talking to ourselves, is that we don't know which part of ourselves we are talking with. That's no good. We want to talk to some particular parts of ourselves right now – the parts that we have created across the years involving the two poles of this one of our values. One way to talk to those parts of ourselves specifically and separately would be to place those parts outside of ourselves and to talk to the externalized parts. We could put those two pictures of the two poles of our value outside ourselves and talk to them as parts of ourselves. Close your eyes and hold out your two hands, palms up. If you were going to put the negative pole picture (e.g., that for mistrust, disrespect or rejection) on one of your hands, if you knew, which hand would you put it on? Trust your unconscious to tell you. That's perfect. Put it there. Then put the picture of the positive pole (e.g., that for trust, respect or acceptance) on the other hand. Now you have a part of yourself resting on each of your hands. Ask those parts some questions and listen carefully for the answers you get.

First, ask the <u>negative</u> pole (e.g., the mistrust, disrespect, rejection) picture to tell you what its highest intention for you is. Get the answer. If necessary, demand that it gives you the answer – after all it is part of you and subject to your will. When you get the answer, ask it <u>why it</u> wants <u>that</u> (new purpose) for you. When you get the answer to that, ask it <u>why it</u> wants <u>that</u> (next purpose) for you. Keep asking the 'why' question until the answer is always the same. Then open your eyes. What was the final answer? [If a person is stuck, either push for the answer, or get him/her to try again with another popped picture].

Now close your eyes and ask the picture of the positive pole (e.g., trust, respect, acceptance) what its highest intention for you is. When you get the answer, ask it as often as needed <u>why it</u> wants <u>that</u>

(next purpose) for you. When you get the final answer, open your eyes.

Strange, isn't it, but the final answer is always the same. It is for your survival and/or happiness. You see, every part of each of us exists always and only to support our survival and happiness. [Most people are surprised to find that even the negative side of any value or feeling or part exists for that purpose, regardless of its apparent negativity].

Surprising isn't it that such different pictures of such different poles have the same purpose for you? Since they have the same purpose for you, perhaps they could talk to each other to reach some agreement about how they can each help to achieve their common purpose for you while contributing to your joy. And perhaps they could find a way to express their coming together in agreement so that you and they will know that they will work together as one part of you in the future. So, close your eyes, and ask them to talk this over with each other, and to find a way to show to you that they will cooperate together as one part of you to achieve their common purpose. [The two hands tend to move together as the sign. When that happens, proceed. If some hands do not come together, ask those people if they have experienced a problem in this. The answer may be that the two pictures changed to the same one on both hands, or that the pictures no longer contradict each other. If not, the person should be encouraged to demand the two parts reach an agreement and show that they intend to cooperate].

Now, close your eyes again and look at the picture you now have of that new part. Who is willing to describe the new part? [Get a few examples]. That's perfect. Now, imagine an infinite source of power, love, happiness and contentment shining and coming down through your head and out through your heart to that new part of yourself, and also to all the rest of the parts of yourself as the new part integrates itself with the rest of the parts of you. When you are done, open your eyes. [James and Woodsmall: Visual Squash].

<u>Block 4</u>: <u>Consolidation</u>:

Did you feel better after the earlier exercises? [Allow brief discussion and comments]. Do you feel there remains some pain or distress associated with your early experiences related to the conflicted value you changed? Close your eyes and scan back over all your memories of the past. Get an idea of where they lie in relation to where you are now. Whatever direction they approach you from is perfect, but do get a direction. Drift up, way up, over your time-line and then drift down a bit but staying well out of and above your time-line. Drift back over your past memories until you find a place that you think might have been the root cause of your pain or distress about this value. Drift about twenty minutes back before that time, and drift down into your time-line facing the present. Where are those feelings now? If they are still there, drift up and back to find an earlier time that might have been the root cause. Drift back twenty minutes before that time and drift down into your time-line facing the present. Repeat this until you do not have that feeling of pain or distress. When you have found the time, walk slowly forward into the root cause situation. If the feelings are still there, drift up and back again to about twenty minutes before, and walk into it again. If the feelings are just as strong in the situation, drift up and back to the present. In the present collect some resources around you, such as your more mature understandings, your relative invulnerability, loved ones with whom you feel safe, some of your accomplishments, and the like. And then return to try again. If that doesn't reduce the feelings in that earlier situation, please drift up and back to the present, and raise your hand. When you're done, come back to the present and open your eyes. [If any participants raise their hands, get the group to go back above their line-lines and construct a theatre over the critical place. Perform the trauma procedure as described in treatment #1: Creating Success, Therapeutics]. [Alternatively, try the Swish procedure used in treatment #4, Creating Satisfaction]. [If need be, the second presenter can take the individual aside and ask about the problem. Some familiarity with other NLP and behavioural methods may be needed in order to find solutions to the problems identified].

Remember that reflexive values place you at the mercy of others. Let's think of an example. In prison, it is common practice to look up to the 'solids' and down on the 'rats' or 'pigeons'. We all know that the 'solids' are the tough and courageous inmates who 'do their own time' and don't bother with other people's time. We all also know that the 'rats' and 'pigeons' are the weak, timid and cowardly inmates who 'do everybody else's time'. That's true, right? Actually, the reverse is more true. The 'solids' are those who are so fearful of others that they have to pump iron to feel strong and safe, who are afraid of being caught and unwilling to live with the consequences of their own behaviour, and who insist that others 'dummy up' – thus trying to 'do other people's time'. The 'rats' and 'pigeons' are those who don't worry about the consequences of their behaviour, and who are not afraid to come forward when someone breaks a rule. Maybe we have some of our ideas all scrambled up. Of course, the conventional views of 'solids' and 'rats' are based on <u>beliefs</u> that are adopted in order to feel accepted or part of the inmate culture. They are not values. But beliefs are developed from values. The values involved in these example beliefs are the values of the inmate or counter-culture that involve rebellion against rules and authorities. Commitment to values such as these ensures that we perpetuate our participation in whatever is involved in crime and its associated sub-cultures. If we want to change our lifestyle, say, of crime or addiction, it is probably necessary first to change our commitment to their values. That's what we have been trying to do today.

But what's the point of changing our commitment to particular values? Partly the point has to do with acquiring new lifestyles for ourselves that are continually rewarding and enjoyable and thus getting to like and respect ourselves a whole lot more than we do; partly the point is to become useful and contributing members of the community of people that has bred us, kept us alive and that offers us much more than any of us gives. If that seems like a worthwhile goal, one of the better ways to achieve that goal is to know our values, to adjust our values to suit the lifestyle we want, and to get rid of the conflicts within some of our values – conflicts within us that are reflected in the conflict with others in our lives and in the pain and distress that drives us to seek 'feeling better' with the help of our addictive substances.

[Summary and cuing observations].

Treatment 6: Creating INNOCENCE

The <u>main target</u> of this program is <u>guilt feelings</u> and the complications that can develop surrounding them, including those of criminality and addictions. The paradoxical manner in which the treatment of conflict must be approached is nowhere clearer than in the treatment of guilt intolerance. Increasing guilt feelings tends to increase defensive denial (intolerance) of guilt, and thus to increase the risk of crime (Reynolds & Quirk, 1996) and the felt need for an addictive. Decreasing guilt feelings directly is almost impossible since they tend to be denied or unacknowledged. Decreasing innocent feelings is tantamount to increasing guilt with its consequences (above).   And increasing innocent feelings, if incautiously done, feeds directly into the strategy offenders and addicts already tend to adopt, namely the defensive denial or the suppression of guilt. Paradoxical means need to be adopted to 'get around' this paradoxical state of affairs.

<u>Block 1</u>: <u>Orientation</u>:

Who never feels guilty?   Who enjoys feeling guilty? Whether or not we deny feeling guilty now, everybody has felt guilty in the past. And we all hated feeling guilty. Guilt feelings imply a sense that we have done wrong or have been bad. At least, we all know what being bad or doing wrong is by other people's standards. What percentage of your life have you been bad or done wrong? [Get estimates of percentages. They tend to vary from 5%

to 99%]. OK, let's decide who is the worst person who ever lived. My nominee would be Adolf Hitler. Let's use him as our example. What percentage of his life was he bad or did he do wrong? [Estimates tend to vary from 50% to 100%]. Now here's a kick in the head. It seems likely that Adolf Hitler was a bad person for under 2% of his life. And, though we hate to insult you in this way, your badness probably doesn't get anywhere near even 1% of your life. Think of it this way. You and Adolf slept away about one-third of your lives. Were you bad then? For the first nine or ten years of your life you were being a kid, just learning how to be good. Were you bad when you didn't know any better? Let's see, that brings your possible bad time down to, let's say, 50%. Of course, you spent a couple of hours each day eating and another hour travelling to and from school and work. Were you bad then? That brings us down to a maximum of 40%. You probably spent four hours a day watching television and talking to friends. Was that bad? Now we're down to a maximum of about 20%. How about the time at school and work? Were you bad then? Whoops, we're now down to under 1%.

Let's do it differently. Add together all the seconds and minutes in your life that you have been bad. Include only the time of doing your bad actions. Does it amount to 24 hours' worth? Was it more? How about two weeks' worth, twenty-four hours a day, seven days per week? Let's even give you that excessive an amount. How old are you? Multiply your age by 52 weeks. Say you're 18. That's 936 weeks of being alive. Your two measly weeks of being bad amounts to a little over 2/1000ths of your life, or one-fifth of one percent. What a bad person you are! Sorry, but you just don't hack it as a bad person. You're going to have to try harder if you want to shape up as the bad person you apparently think you are. In fact, poor you, you're really an enormously good person!

But where do we get the idea that we might be bad people? There is a very good reason for it. You see, whether or not you know it, you were raised by parenting adults and teachers. Of course, they were YOUR parents and YOUR teachers. So, they should have spent all their time looking after and teaching you, since that was all they did in their lives. At least, that's what we thought as children. They related to us in those roles, so that's most of what we knew about them. Now, of course, we know they were also workers, cookers, spouses, travellers, entertainees, cleaners, pet owners, gardeners, and had a host of other roles. Strange to say, few of us modify our childhood understandings of these people according to our grown-up understandings. We forget that they were people who happened to be doing an extra task in raising us. They were busy, and they just didn't have all day long to follow around after us saying, 'good,' 'good,' 'good,' 'good,' etc. So they adopted the more efficient procedure of waiting for that ten seconds to half a minute out of each good hour in which we were roaring hellions, and then they warned us, controlled us, pointed out our mistakes and took us to task. This drew our attention most strongly, clearly, and poignantly to our errors, misdeeds and (presumed) 'badness' – and we mostly ignored or failed to notice our wonderfulnesses.

The notion that we are bad or guilty comes from errors of several different kinds. First, we fail to notice that we are good by failing to notice our goodnesses and by watching out for our badnesses. Second, we fail to understand that the purpose others have for drawing our attention to our mistakes is the loving hope that we will grow into happy people – the purpose is to help us achieve happiness. Third, we fail to notice that adults have other things to do than just to be parents or teachers, so we take their negative input as applying to all of our actions and/or ourselves. Fourth, we fail to notice that, like we ourselves, everybody else, including parents and teachers, are always doing the very best we can, at every moment, given the circumstances in which we find ourselves. We or they can be wrong, but all of us does the very best he or she can at every moment. Fifth, we take into ourselves the judgements made by others around us, especially adult others. This last error needs more comment.

We-as-children love those great big adults who look after us. And they always seem to be right – heck, what do we know? Oh, of course, we-as-children probably think we know everything. However, if they judge us, their judgements must be right. If they, who love us and care for us, seem angry with us, it must be because we are unworthy of their love. So we must be bad. The child mind works in a simpler way than the adult mind. The child mind, however, is a learning mind. It learns very efficiently how to AVOID the dangers of being judged as bad. It learns to pay attention to, or to notice, those acts that will be judged as wicked or lead to loss of love (in child-eyes). It remembers the error or bad act, and hooks to it an emotional response as a way to mark or keep it active in memory. The way this is done is to 'incorporate' it as part of the self. That is, the act is taken to be part of the self – but a part TO BE AVOIDED. Then when we do the act again, we find that we are judging ourselves, and with the negative emotional charge that we have attached to the memory. We feel bad again, but this time by our own incorporated judgement. This experience is called guilt. And the part of us that does the judging is often called 'conscience'.

Now, some of us get to hate our consciences. They keep saying we are bad, making us feel like small vulnerable children once more, and making us afraid we are or will be unloved. Quite early in life we can start to hate this feeling – for which, of course, we blame those we think 'did it to us' for it. If the feeling feels bad enough, or we decide that those we think 'did it to us' were themselves the bad and wrong people, then we may come to decide that the bad feeling is the thing that is bad, and not we ourselves. There are several ways that we can then deal with the bad feeling about the bad feeling. We can set out to AVOID the bad feeling (1) by trying not to provoke it by being 'good', or (2) by means of experiencing the feeling we get from the bad actions as excitement (rather than distress or discomfort), or (3) by finding a way to stop the bad feeling as quickly as possible whenever it happens. The second of these ways to handle the bad feelings tends to result in delinquency and, later, in crime, and the third tends to result in addiction to any substance or action that helps make the bad feelings feel better (however temporarily).

Now we are grown up enough to examine our actions, and the bad feelings from our incorporated judgements of ourselves, in the light of reason and mature judgement. How much of the time are you, or have you been, a bad person? Under 1 percent? Just how bad does that make you? OK, then, how good are you? We know what part of your answer will be. How about all that use of addictive substances, and the number of times you have tried and failed to quit? And how about all the times you have hurt yourself and others with your addictive behaviour? Just for a moment, forget about the number of times you have failed to quit. Have you tried to quit? Please don't lie to yourself by saying that you <u>must</u> have wanted not to quit since you kept failing. Even thinking about quitting means you wanted to quit. Failing comes from the fact that it is hard to give up feeling better quickly, and from having to live with feeling bad. Every time, and all the time, that you thought about quitting, no matter what you did about it, was time during which you were being, or trying to be, good! You good person you! Please add that to the 'good' part of you. All we need to do to help that 'good' part of you along is to learn ways to succeed – strategies for success.

One way to do that is to notice the huge number of times when you were not doing addictive acts – when you were not smoking or drinking or doing drugs. We tend to ignore those times. But you already know how not to do addictive behaviour, since you have done non-addiction lots of times – including now. You're already good at that. Perhaps you might want to figure out HOW you did that!

Even if that doesn't work completely, all that you would need to do would be to get rid of the bad feelings, or to enjoy the bad feelings or have fun with them, so you don't need to find relief from them anymore. We know, you think that would be a hard thing to do. But that's the main part of today's task.

But before we can get rid of the bad feelings, we need to ask ourselves what purpose they serve in our lives. They do have a purpose, or else they wouldn't be there. What useful thing could such bad feelings ever have in our lives. To figure this out we have to return to the past to see the world through child's eyes again. As children, we get upset or angry when something hurts us – hurts us physically or hurts our feelings. So, when we-as-children, see adults upset or angry we can only assume that their feelings have been hurt. We love those who love and look after us. We certainly don't want to hurt their feelings. That's why we incorporate into ourselves their judgements of us, along with the associated bad feelings. So the purpose or function of guilt feelings or conscience is mainly to help us keep from hurting the feelings of those we love.

As we grow older, we tend to think of behaviours that hurt other people as angry or aggressive actions. So the purpose or function of conscience or guilt feelings tends to be to help us AVOID anger or aggressiveness, or the hurt it is supposed to cause in others. Now that we are grown up, perhaps we ought to review <u>what</u> happens when we try to AVOID aggression or anger, and how hurt is actually caused. That's part of today's task too.

But let's suppose that guilt feelings are necessary, at least some of the time. How will we be able to tolerate them, when they occur, without having to resort to the use of addictive substances? Of course, in the long run, we may have to learn to accept them and to discover that they are not all that awful. That is, expecting the bad feelings and letting then last for a while without having to relieve them can become perfectly possible. But you'd expect people who don't have an addiction to cope with to say that kind of thing. However, there is another thing we could do about guilt feelings. We might even be able to learn to enjoy them. We might even learn to enjoy other people's attempts to lay guilt-trips on us. That is nuts, right? Still, it might be possible.

<u>Block 2</u>: <u>Tools</u>:

The first tool for today is to find the good in ourselves. Are you predominantly a bad person or a good person? On paper, start adding up the time you have been 'good' to make a realistic estimate of how good you are. One way to do that realistically might be to add up the time you were a good person, doing good things, during the past day. You haven't done anything 'good' during the last day, have you? Oh no? When you got up this morning, did you make your bed, relieve yourself, brush your teeth, bathe, comb your hair, say good morning to somebody, have some breakfast, tidy or clean something up, do some work, smile at somebody and/or walk or travel somewhere? Did you sleep some during the night? Were these healthy, social, helpful, good things to do? Notice how much of our 'good' behaviours and time we simply don't notice? In another column, add the numbers of seconds and moments you did bad things. Remember that, even between the seconds of taking drinks or drugs, we are doing good things like talking to others, watching T.V., or just sitting being and feeling good. Let's try to be fair to ourselves as well. What percentage of the time of your life were you 'bad'? Make an estimate.

But other people have been or are being hurt by you, right? Let's take a few moments to look honestly at that idea. Actually, nobody hurts anybody else. We are the ones who hurt ourselves. Nobody has a right to expect anything from anybody else. What happens is that the person who is going to feel hurt THINKS that the hurting person SHOULD NOT act the way he/she is acting. By talking to him/herself that way, he/she makes him/herself angry. The anger he/she has thus created arouses guilt feelings fairly automatically, and the felt component of those guilt feelings is the feeling of 'being hurt' – attributed to someone else.

So, is it true that you and other people hurt one another? Of course it is, right? Let's use our favourite example of this. You are walking along a sidewalk. Suddenly, you feel a bump on your shoulder. How do you feel? Do you imagine you feel angry or hurt? You do not. All you feel is surprised by a sudden and unexplained event. The 'orienting response' has been activated. It almost demands that you turn around to see what happened. But that's all you feel ... yet. You turn around. What you see is a 12-foot-tall man, with shoulders 3 feet wide, with a knife in one hand and a club in the other. And he is menacing you. How do you feel? You probably feel scared out of your skull. But suppose you are twenty-feet-tall, with six-foot-wide shoulders and automatic guns in both your hands. How do you feel? You probably would feel scornful of the shrimp. Of course, in actuality, you're not 20 feet tall and you don't have any automatic weapons in your hands. But then, actually, I was wrong. What you see when you turn around is really a punk little kid who is trying to show off to his punk little friend. How do you feel? You probably feel angry at the punk. Hey, you could beat him/her up, if you wanted to. So it's safe to feel angry. Damn! I was wrong again. It's not a punk kid, it's your boss, and he/she is laughing to a friend about his/her right to upset you. How do you feel? You probably feel hurt by his/her callousness. Oh, I'm sorry, I was wrong again. It's not your boss, it's a little old person on crutches who stumbled on the sidewalk and bumped into you by accident. How do you feel? Probably you feel compassion and concern that he/she is OK. But suppose you are also a little elderly person on crutches too. How do you feel? You probably chide the person angrily for being so careless about injuring you. You see, in all these scenarios, it's NOT the event – the bump – that makes us angry. It's how we see the situation, or what we tell ourselves about the situation.

There are two general ways by which we upset ourselves, and it is always WE who upset OURselves – never other people. One way is: An event occurs –> we become aroused –> we talk to ourselves in a certain way –> we become upset or angry. The other way is:

An event occurs –> we talk to ourselves about it in a certain way –> what we say arouses our feelings –> we become upset or angry. An example of the first way was given in the situation we just described. An example of the second way occurs every time we feel insulted, put down or our feelings are hurt.

The important question is: <u>what</u> do we say to ourselves, or <u>how</u> do we talk to ourselves about events that results in our feeling upset or angry? It's hard to know what we say to ourselves. Many of our thoughts become so habitual that they just flip past us in the twinkling of an eye before we know we had a thought. It might be worthwhile to capture or notice some of these thoughts as they flip past. It's hard to do. So here are a couple of clues for us to use in this exercise to try on your own. Just saying 'that (an event) makes me mad', doesn't do it. Check to see if by itself it does. One way to find what we are saying to ourselves is to see whether saying any particular thing gets us upset. Generally, the kind of idea that works to get us upset is one that tells us that the other person <u>shouldn't</u> have said it or <u>shouldn't</u> be trying to upset us, that it is <u>awful</u> that such a thing occurred, or that some horrible <u>catastrophe</u> is about to happen. Nothing <u>shouldn't</u>, or should, happen. People say and do things for their own purposes and not to upset or hurt us (unless the person's purpose was to upset or hurt another for his or her own reasons, and it might have been said or done to anybody else). No event is inherently <u>awful</u>, unless we choose to make it so. And the only real <u>catastrophe</u> that we can do much about is the catastrophe of upsetting ourselves about an unknowable future possibility that hasn't happened. We could all profit by finding out what we say to ourselves to upset ourselves. [Ellis' Rational-Emotive Therapy].

But we have all suffered guilt feelings because we believed we were hurting or had hurt others. The function or purpose of those feelings, if you remember, is to keep us from doing angry or aggressive things that we believed hurt others. Quite apart from the fact that we were wrong in that belief, we have all learned to block our angry or aggressive feelings to keep from hurting others. The way we have done this is to use one of the many means people find to 'control' or stop themselves from doing certain kinds of things. The trouble is that the ways we find to control or stop all sorts of actions also inhibit the use of the body's energies. The body is an energy-producing machine. And inhibiting energy use results in depression or compulsive behaviour such as addictions. That's right. Depression is NOT due to the horrible events of the past, nor does it descend upon us without cause. We do it to ourselves. It is not to our advantage to block our energy use. Using the body's energies is one way to help stop depression and compulsive actions like addictions. Does that mean that aerobic exercises and fitness are good for us after all? Yes. But that's not the only way in which to use body energies, and it isn't even a necessary way. It's only one way out of hundreds of ways, many of which can be done without big strong movements of the body. The basic way in which we use the body's energies is by assertiveness. Hold it! Assertiveness is NOT limited to what this author or that one chooses to focus on in teaching assertive skills.

Assertive Training is a wide array of procedures to encourage the use of body energies. Most assertive trainers are social behaviourists. They teach ways to communicate or to send assertive messages to others. The most basic assertive method in social communication is the so-called 'I-statement' or, more generally, the 'Three-part statement'. Aggressive <u>and</u> under-assertive sentences tend to use the 'You-statement'. In its aggressive form, it attributes to somebody else the source of our own feelings. It takes the form: 'You make me angry.' In its under-assertive form, it attributes power or importance to someone else. It takes the form: 'You shouldn't have to do that, I'll do it.' In either case, the control over our own lives and feelings is transferred to someone else. We do not acknowledge our own rights and power in our own lives. The 'I-statement' expresses our own feelings, without attributing the cause of them to anybody or anything else. It asserts our own rights to have feelings of our own, no matter why the feelings are there. It takes the form: 'I am angry.' Notice that there is no explanation given for the feeling. Any explanation attributes the feeling to another person as its cause (an implicit 'You-statement') or to a general principle that takes over from the speaker responsibility for the feeling – thus making the principle (and not the speaker) the active (energized) agent causing the feeling. A useful motto for assertive 'I-statements' is: 'Never explain. Your friends don't need it, and your enemies won't believe it anyway.' Just taking responsibility for our own feelings is assertive and uses bodily energies.

The general form of the I-statement is the 'Three-part statement'. The three parts of this statement facilitate assertive communication. The first part expresses in our own words our understanding of what the other person just said. It takes the form: 'I understand you to have said that ...' This allows the other person to correct any misunderstanding of what was just said and provides the basis for what is to follow. The second part expresses how we feel about the matter being discussed. It takes the form: 'I feel upset [or happy, etc].'. It is the standard 'I-statement'. The third part expresses our intention or the position or action we will take. It takes the form: 'I think/believe that ...' or 'I will take the position/action that ...' It makes an assertive, personal affirmation. Assertive sentences such as the 'I-statement' or 'Three-part statement' foster good communications, do not arouse defensiveness, competition, enmity or conflict, and do not challenge other people.

But communications are not the only ways to be assertive. Each action or, if you wish, each element of body language, can use the body's energies effectively. Standing or sitting with the body erect, using large and expansive (extensor) gestures, maintaining eye-contact, speaking clearly and audibly, using short sentences (without explanatory clauses), enunciating crisply, and a host of

178

other minor aspects of body use, are assertive. They use the body's energies, and they expand one in space, if only by reaching out toward the other person (e.g., eye contact) or filling the area (e.g., clear and crisp speech). To some extent, assertive use of bodily energy is accomplished by one's own sense of personal impact on the world around. And such impact need not be destructive. It can even work better if it is constructive. There is one caution that may be needed. No criticism or judgement is ever assertive. It may have an impact on those around but, no matter how cleverly it is hidden, it is always in the form of a 'You-statement'.

We suggested above that each of us is almost entirely a 'good' person. Let's remember that the same applies to everyone else as well as to us. It would be to everyone's advantage if we were all able to see ourselves and the world around us as good. But how can that be accomplished? To figure out the answer to that question, we have to start somewhere else.

Your parents and ours were NOT OUR parents. Of course they were OUR parents, but that was not ALL they were or are. They were people, and people never have ONLY one identity. They were also spouses, workers, friends, relatives, entertainees, sleepers, lovers and a host of other things. They did not have the time to be parents ONLY. It was only through our child eyes that they were parents only – that's mainly what we saw them doing. Because they had other things to do, they could not go around all day long patting us on the head and saying 'good, good, good, good, good, good, ...' Instead, they went about their lives watching out of the corners of their eyes and, out of sheer love and the desire to ensure our greatest happiness, shouting out warnings or commands whenever what we were doing might lead to danger of injury, pain or irritation of others. These reactions occurred in response to those couple of seconds out of each hour when we were 'roaring hellions.' The rest of the time we were as 'good as gold.' That's how it comes to be that most adults know more about their errors and mistakes than they do about how truly good they all are.

The way in which our errors and badnesses are drawn to our attention is in the form of 'You-statements' or criticisms. Perhaps it's time to grow up and to give up criticisms of ourselves and of others. Perhaps we might even start looking around for the good things in ourselves, everybody else and the world. They are everywhere and can easily be found once we have adjusted our filter habits to find the good things.

Once we have started to find and comment on the good things in life, two other interesting other things tend to follow:

First, we start setting an example for others. Others too can learn to notice and find the good around them. That includes the good in you. Suddenly, other people are rewarding you for your goodness by noticing it. Our acts benefit us in the long run.

Second, we find ourselves in the position to make a useful and solid contribution to our communities. We find ourselves in a head-space where we are drawn to positive ways of viewing things. And positive things happen if we look for and see things in positive ways. Let's understand how this works through a rather basic example.

Let's suppose that you concluded that it is important to have peace in this world. We can't do it all by ourselves, and there are lots of pressures acting against it. In fact, our habitual preoccupation with criticism has been formalized in our society in most educational programs and in the practice of the Law. The Law seeks to 'keep the peace' by regulation and maintaining order. It finds instances of actions that contravene and punish the perpetrators. The Law indicates what not-to-do and demeans those who do the proscribed acts. This approach, far from fostering peace, fosters warfulness or crime. If we really wanted to create and maintain peace, we might better find principles that state ideals, and reward or congratulate those who act in ways consistent with those principles. By way of example, the following peace principles might serve us well in creating and maintaining peace:

1. The Golden Rule: in all things, act toward others as you would have them act toward you.
2. The Inclusion Principle: draw an inclusive circle around every person to include everyone in as part of your community.
3. The Consistency Principle: act in ways consistent with your beliefs and principles and how you hope others will act.
4. The Cooperation Principle: be liberal in cooperating and sharing all of your own with others.
5. The Conservation Principle: be conservative in the use of all resources and in the production of waste.
6. The Resource Exchange Principle: use your energies to serve others in communal exchange, and accept theirs in return.
7. The Consideration Principle: accommodate to the rights, joy and survival needs of others including all future generations.
8. The Political Principle: share power equally with all people keeping no extra power for yourself.
9. The Accomplishment Principle: achieve the best and most worthwhile you can, limited only by others' rights and needs.
10. The Respect Principle: give respect to each person (and yourself) to foster awareness of the good in all people.
11. The Trust Principle: trust every person (and yourself) in order to feel safe with everybody.
12. The Love Principle: exercise love and caring for all others as widely as possible to maximize your own joy.
13. The Positive Reward Principle: look for the positive in everything and acknowledge and praise it so you feel good.
14. The Agreement Principle: find common/shared elements in all viewpoints and merge them inclusively to find agreement.
15. The Common Purpose Principle: seek in all things common purpose to ensure cooperative pursuit of co-existence.
16. The General Principle: all other considerations, means and approaches are subordinated to these principles in

the active pursuit of   peace – if peace is our primary purpose in life.

To pick a purpose or two, such as peace, to find positive ways to achieve it/them, and to lead your life according to those ways, is the best way to make a solid and worthwhile contribution to the communities in which we live. To make such useful contributions is the best way to counter guilt or to make up for the many times we have all done dumb things. Strangely, as we pursue a positive
initiative such as peace, guilt feelings simply vanish.

Block 3: Therapeutics:

Change history [James and Woodsmall: Time-Line] to modify guilt experiences. [See under Creating Success: Therapeutics]. The purpose of this procedure, that we can do by ourselves any time we wish, is to rid our histories of the gnawing guilt feelings that, built up over the years, have made us angry and unwilling to acknowledge or to tolerate any guilt feelings we have.

Modify guilt versus innocence concepts [James and Woodsmall: Visual Squash. See under Creating Success: Therapeutics]. to de-fang guilt feelings. The purpose of this method, that we can use any time we wish on our own, is to undo some of the pain of feeling guilty that has increased our felt need to see ourselves as innocent and to value our innocence.

Who would like to serve as a victim to help us demonstrate another way to get over guilt feelings? [Accept a volunteer to take the 'hot seat' in the middle of the room]. Pick something you feel guilty about. If you can't think of anything other than your addictive behaviour, pick that. What was it you did that was wrong or bad? [Obtain answers] Who were your victims? Who hurt most because of that? [Query until the person identifies him/herself]. How did you hurt yourself? [Get answers]. Did you ever not-hurt yourself? In what ways and how? [Get responses] [If the person affirms that he/she continuously hurt him/herself, examine the progress of life]. When you were sleeping, while you were having meals, while you were at school or work, while watching T.V., etc.? Is it true that for most of your life you were not hurting yourself in that/those way(s)? How about those you love or care about? Did you hurt them more than you did them good? [If the person affirms more hurt than good, ask: then how come they stayed with you or kept on loving you?] You know as well as we do that most people accept much less 'abuse' than they get in good things. When they feel that 'abuse' exceeds 'goodness' or positive value to them (actually long before that), they simply forget the good and abandon the 'abuser.' Let's be real. You mean to tell us that you were more good than bad? Of course you were. In fact, as we pointed out earlier, you have always been many times more good than bad. If you're going to assign such importance to your badness that you play it up as greater than your goodness, you might at least have the good grace to enjoy and to be proud of your badness – heck, you didn't accomplish all that much of it. Of course, you really are a bit proud of it, aren't you? You have been willing to 'show off' your badness to us today. So you must be a bit proud of it. If that's true, it must be something you consider important, or something that makes you feel important. Hey, that's OK. But you at least have to be aware that you feel in some conflict about it. On the one hand, you think of it as bad. On the other hand, you're proud of it or think it's important. Conflict is a part of what goes on in all our heads. We fight with ourselves.

But the conflict is the most damaging thing of all. Maybe we could do whatever seems right to us without conflict over it. What purpose does your 'bad' act serve; what does it do for you? [Get responses]. And what does that do for you? And what does that do for you? [These questions seek the most general and the most important purposes or values the person has, or those that the 'badness' behaviour is instrumental in achieving]. In this pursuit, although survival and happiness [as in the Squash] are the most general reasons for anything's existence, self-actualizing or meta-needs may appear as the perceived bases for survival and happiness. Such meta-needs might include things such as power, importance, or even helplessness (as a means to maintain dependency on others). [Keep questioning until the bases for the instrumental conduct are clear]. OK, so you want to feel ... (happy, important, powerful, etc.). Are there ways you could achieve those feelings other than the ways you have tried? [Push for alternatives and suggest others].

It is surprising that, once people find what they are trying to achieve [final causes], it is relatively easy to find other ways to achieve their purposes or satisfy their needs. Moreover, once they know what they seek, most people enjoy pursuing their goals, purposes and needs in pro-social and positive ways. However, the solutions found need to provide real challenges and options, and not just do-gooder mouthed moralistic mumbo jumbo hogwash that sounds conventional and 'proper'.

Block 4: Consolidation:

Enjoying life is enhanced by finding the good in every situation and in trusting everyone. Remember to reset your filters that support beliefs, to enjoy receiving (practice the fun of being criticized) and avoid giving criticism, and to find principles for living that have a chance of achieving what we want to achieve – as purposes we choose for our lives and as self-actualizing needs. Remember the example of creating peace by setting that as a primary value or purpose or goal, finding the positive principles to achieve the positive state, and living those principles both to enhance your own life and to set an example for others. Remember that enjoying life is accomplished best in the here-and-now and by focusing on immediate experiences and events. [Perceptual Discrimination/Fair Witness Training]. For everyone, thinking about the past is at least mildly depressing (the unpleasant events stand out much more sharply in memory than the pleasant ones), and thinking about the future is scary (at the very least, it is unknown or uncertain). The present is fun. Remember to be rid of negative or unpleasant feelings or situations by using such methods as Time-Line trips, the Swish or the Visual Squash. But don't just think about doing the exercises. Do them. Remember to use your body's energies to improve your mood and make life feel happier. Using your energies includes active use of the body's muscles, either in exercise or just in expanding yourself in space by how you talk and how you carry yourself. It also includes communications in the form of 'I-statements' or the 'Three-part statement', minimizing the use of critical 'You-statements'. And remember to notice just how really good you really are.

[Summary and cuing observations].

Treatment 7: Creating HEALTH

The <u>main target</u> of this program is on maintaining and valuing <u>health</u>. Psychological and physical health are most commonly impaired by (1) stress and (2) expectations from personal beliefs. If chronic stress can be relieved, and personal health beliefs modified, future health can be improved radically. Since many of the discriminants controlling addictions relate to distress and to general physical malaise, improvement of health should serve to diminish addictive behaviours or 'self-medications.'

<u>Block 1</u>: <u>Orientation</u>:

As far back as the 1930s the role of the body's <u>stress</u> response in health and disease was pretty firmly established. The stress response of the body creates most of the chronic and killer diseases afflicting humankind. It is central to nearly all the so-called mental or emotional diseases. And it plays a central role in the body's capacity to recover from physical diseases. However, the body's stress response has been badly misunderstood in everyday ways of talking about it.

The body's stress response is a standard reaction of a very particular kind. There is a major part of the peripheral outflow nervous system called the <u>Autonomic Nervous System</u> or the ANS. The ANS is comprised of two major branches, the Sympathetic and the Parasympathetic branches. Both of these nerve tracts feed almost every organ and part of the body. However, as we will explain later, there is no parasympathetic feed to the adrenal glands. And the two branches compete with each other, so that when one is active, the other becomes inactive. The response of the sympathetic branch of the ANS is an immediate survival response. Consequently, it takes precedence over the parasympathetic and other response systems.

When the <u>sympathetic</u> branch is active, the heart rate is accelerated, breathing shifts from diaphragm to chest breathing, the blood vessels of the gut become narrower and those feeding the muscles become wider, the pupils of the eye dilate, and a host of other arousal responses occur. Also, the body's auto-immune system is activated, releasing fluid to target areas and increasing the white blood cell count. The body becomes prepared to deal with an emergency. And the subjective experience is one of arousal, of anxiety or fear (ready for flight) or of anger (ready to fight). This reaction of the body is called the stress response.

When the <u>parasympathetic</u> response is activated, among many other things, the heart rate slows down, breathing tends to return to diaphragm breathing, the pupils become reactive to the amount of light present, the blood vessels in the gut widen and those feeding the muscles become narrower, and the immune response rests. The body becomes calmer and 'vegges out.' And the subjective experience is one of calmness or pleasure.

We think it's important that you know at least this much about how an important part of your body works. There is a little bit more that you probably ought to know. We think some knowledge about our bodies is necessary to allow us to understand ourselves.

If the <u>sympathetic</u> response of the ANS occurred without any other thing happening, it would occur and vanish almost in the twinkling of an eye. However, the sympathetic response is aroused by emergencies where there might be danger. In a tropical jungle, the fleeting glimpse out of the corner of your eye of something yellow and black moving would arouse a sympathetic response. This is called the Orienting Reflex, since it activates a quick turn of the head to see what might be there that might be dangerous. If the eyes do not detect any danger at once, the sympathetic response subsides. But that might not be too wise from the point of view of survival. The tiger might have vanished behind rocks or bushes.

So the body is constructed to <u>extend</u> the sympathetic arousal for a short period of time after it is activated. This is done by stimulating the adrenal glands to pump out <u>adrenaline</u>. Adrenaline circulates through the body and keeps the arousal going, mimicking the sympathetic response. The absence of parasympathetic feed to the adrenal glands, which we mentioned earlier, means that the maintained arousal cannot be damped down too quickly. This keeps the body vigilant and ready to respond in case the emergency is a real one requiring actions of flight or fight, for which the body has been prepared by the sympathetic-stress response.

There are three more things we need to talk about before we have finished with this lecture on how the body works. Stay with us because this information is important to your life.

The first thing has to do with health. The <u>auto-immune</u> system, by which the body fights off infection and disease, is stimulated and orchestrated by the sympathetic ANS response. It involves release of a wide range of hormones that activate fluid retention and distribution, white blood cell production and cell growth to repair damage to the body. If the sympathetic-stress-anxiety-immune response is activated too often, and the adrenergic extension of it makes arousal more or less continuous, the use of the stress hormones may exceed the rate of their production. This can result in either or both of two consequences. The stress hormones can become depleted so that the body can no longer fight off disease or deal with errors in body maintenance. And the continuous activation of the immune response can create immune diseases such as arthritis and cancer. It is not to anyone's advantage to have too continuous or repeated sympathetic activation going on in the body.

The second thing has to do with personal <u>experience</u>. The activation of the sympathetic response is experienced as arousal.

The experience felt by the person depends on the person and how he or she habitually understands life circumstances. The experiences provoked can be felt as unpleasant sensations such as anxiety or anger; or they can be felt as pleasant sensations like excitement or sexual arousal. The physiological response underlying all of these experiences is more or less the same. It involves activation of the sympathetic branch of the ANS. That is, a 'high', whether it is due to activating drugs, sexual arousal, fear, anger or just plain happy excitement, involves the same basic physiological activation of the ANS. And the 'high' can be produced in all sorts of ways, either voluntarily or involuntarily, intentionally or unintentionally.

The third thing has to do with <u>how</u> the stress response is <u>activated</u>. How does it get going? [Obtain some answers]. There are three kinds of basic experiences that automatically arouse the sympathetic response. These are loss of support, as in falling, sudden and loud noise, and intense local sensory experience usually called pain. That's why you get aroused and excited by loud music. There are three sensory experiences that tend to focus attention and thus support the Orienting Reflex. They are colour, motion and sound. That's why explosions and riots get people excited. And there is one basic class of events that activates sympathetic arousal. It is change of any kind. Change of any kind in the world around us requires changes in what we do, or adaptation. That's why Selye called the stress response the General Adaptation Syndrome. All any of us needs to do to become aroused is to expose him or herself to falling, loud noise, pain, colour, motion, sound, or change. We don't have to go to the expense and loss of freedom of doing drugs to achieve a high.

But while it is easy, even commonplace, to achieve a high or to become aroused, for the sake of health, comfort, and peace in life we also need to be able to achieve calmness, rest and a strong parasympathetic response. In fact, if we don't also master the art of achieving a parasympathetic response, we will not feel or enjoy fully the sympathetic arousal. So, how can we learn to manage our sympathetic-stress-anxiety reactions? Few of us know how to do this partly because we have never learned how, and partly because we have learned erroneous ways to use our body's functions.

The first and easiest way to manage our stress responses is through re-learning how to breathe. Breathing patterns are not automatic. We have learned how to breathe, and most of us have learned how to breathe wrongly. In the attempt to look beautiful while we were young, we all, males and females, have tried sucking in our stomachs to expand the apparent size of our chests. That has made it difficult for us to 'breathe into our stomachs', to do healthy diaphragm breathing. Instead, we have tended to practice the art of breathing into our chests, or chest breathing. This, in turn, has increased the ease and speed with which we become aroused – anxious, angry or excitable. We ought to explain how breathing works before talking about how to manage breathing better.

Normal diaphragm breathing pulls the air in from the diaphragm muscle at the bottom of the lungs. It involves long, slow breaths. They are slow because the OUT-breath is about two or three times longer than the in-breath. When chest breathing begins, either by the habit of sucking the stomach in or under stress conditions, the expansion of the lung cavity is accomplished by expanding the chest. The rib cage is a rigid structure that will expand to a certain extent. But it will only contract the same amount as it has expanded. The result is that the OUT-breath is shortened to the same duration as the shallow in-breath. That means there are more breath cycles per minute. This, in turn, results in more oxygen getting into the system. In an emergency, the increased oxygen level getting into the blood stream from the lungs is desirable. It increases the amount of oxygen to be metabolized with nutrients by the muscles to permit the muscles an extra level of energy with which to deal with the emergency – from the point of view of survival, that is helpful in case in case we need to fight or run away.

But we are seldom in real <u>emergency situations</u> calling for excess supplies of energy to deal with dangers. We now live in an engineered safe society with stout tiger-proof doors, railings to prevent falling from high places and traffic lights to give all a fair chance at safe travel. There are no dangers other than those we manufacture for ourselves or for others. So, if we practice chest breathing, for reasons of aesthetics or imagined danger, we increase the body's available energy without having anything to do with the energy except to 'stew in our own juices'. The results are characteristic, commonplace and uncomfortable.

There are several effects. (1) The increased oxygen available to the muscles lowers their metabolic threshold, increasing muscle tension and the subjective sense of being 'up-tight'. (2) The increased blood oxygen poses a threat to the survival of brain cells. To protect them, a reflex constriction of the blood vessels in the brain is triggered by an oxygen receptor in the blood vessels. This reflex response results in a lessened volume of the highly oxygenated blood supply to the brain. That actually reduces the brain's oxygen supply. The resulting anoxia is experienced as dizziness, wooziness or reduced efficiency of brain functioning. This sensation scares some people. (3) Unlike the indefatigable smooth muscle of the diaphragm, the striate muscles of the chest wall react quickly to yank the chest open for chest breathing, but they also tire out quickly. Before long in chest breathing, the muscles fatigue and the person feels a tightness and/or pain in the chest and/or a sense that he or she cannot breathe easily. These symptoms, although non-significant, may be interpreted as heart trouble and may scare the person even more. (4) The rapid passage of air through the throat tends to add to the natural stress reaction of dry mouth, so the person may start to swallow in the effort to moisten the mouth. But he or she is only swallowing air. A saliva bubble may then grow in the stomach from the swallowed air. At some point the person may feel he or she can't swallow or breathe – due only to the balloon of air in the throat. This can scare the person even more. (5) The shortened parasympathetically-controlled OUT-breath affords less time for the steeper-gradient sympathetic response (controlling the in-breath) to be neutralized. This means that stress-anxiety grows with each breath. And each increase in anxiety increases the stress response and increases the tendency to shallow chest-breathing.

That's what we do to ourselves by doing shallow chest-breathing. Of course, if we want a high, all we need to do is some shallow chest-breathing. Why go for any more by way of expense? But if we are to enjoy that high instead of letting it pass by unnoticed, we had better learn how to have periods of calmness in between to permit a contrast experience. So how can we do that?

The simplest answer is to master the art of re-instituting diaphragm breathing from time to time by using long OUT-breaths. Now, we're sure you just heard us asking you to breathe deeply. Right? We did NOT say that. We said the absolute opposite. We have all been taught to breathe deeply. That is exactly the WRONG thing to do – just about always. Instead, for about three or four bursts of three or four breath cycles, push the air OUT of your lungs for three or four or five times as long as the preceding in-breath. Do NOT interfere with the in-breath. Let it happen as it wants to. Just time it in your mind. Then make the following OUT-breath three or four or five times longer, to exhaust your lungs completely. Repeat this for three or four breaths, followed by three or four uninfluenced breaths. And repeat that sequence about three of four times. By the end of that time, you will feel a slight but significant reduction in your stress-anxiety-anger intensity, and the symptoms of hyper-ventilation noted above should disappear.

Incidentally, there are some things you should know about this corrective procedure for hyper-ventilation   for shallow chest-breathing. The reason for not doing a dozen or more long OUT-breaths in a row is merely that the reflexive constriction of the brain's blood vessels is reversed slower than the reduction of the blood oxygen level. If you reduce the blood oxygen level quicker than the reflexive constriction response, you lower the oxygen level to the brain even further, and you may become more dizzy or faint. Next, by doing this corrective long OUT-breath procedure you reinstate normal and healthy diaphragm breathing to some extent and this is all to the good. Next, you may notice you wheeze a bit during long OUT-breaths, which may lead you to feel you shouldn't do them or that you are having more trouble breathing. If it persists, consult a health professional. Mostly, you will notice it goes away and you can actually breathe easier. The wheezing is likely only because you had some bronchial constriction due to the preceding hyper-ventilation. That constriction should let go as you persist in your long OUT-breaths.

Notice that in what we have just said we are using the opposite (parasympathetically-controlled OUT-breath) response to compete with the stress-associated (sympathetically-controlled in-breath) breathing response. To manage our stress reactions, we need to find various parasympathetic-associated responses to compete with and undo the sympathetic-associated responses involved in stress. There are quite a few of these parasympathetic-associated responses that can be used in addition to correcting the sympathetic chest-breathing response by using long OUT-breaths.

If we are prone to more than one or two bowel movements a day so that the bowel contents are fluid, we are creating stress for ourselves by requiring our rectal sphincters to be held tight closed (a sympathetically-controlled response). Reducing the frequency until the bowel contents are firm, permits the rectal sphincter to let go or relax (a parasympathetically-controlled response). Also, general muscle relaxation is a parasympathetic-associated response that can moderate the sympathetic-stress-anxiety response. Indeed, if deep relaxation is paired repeatedly with images of anxiety stimuli, the result may become habitual non-anxiousness in those situations – systematic desensitization. Assertive (NOT aggressive) behaviour activates a parasympathetic response that can be used to counter anxiety. There are many other competing responses that can be used to manage stress.

Now all this might sound as though we are pushing some kinds of treatments for you to get involved in. We are not. We have a quite specific attitude about treatment. You only fix things that are wrong; and you only seek treatment for something you can't do by yourself. We believe that the job of looking after you and your health is nobody else's business except your own. You are the only person who has to live with the illnesses you permit to affect you; and you are the only person who has any benefit from whatever you do to improve your health. To turn over the care for your health to anyone else, doctor, lawyer, medicine man or chief, is both unrealistic and asks for every illness and associated cost you get. Nobody should be allowed to tell you what you ought to do, or what ought to be done to you. Get information from experts, and get second and third opinions if you don't like the first information you get. Then go home and decide for yourself what you ought to do about your health. It is yours and only yours. You wouldn't think of letting a stove salesman decide FOR you which stove you ought to buy. Don't let us or any other health salesman, called doctor or nurse, tell you what health services you ought to buy. Make up your own mind. Practice consumerism in the health area too.

Block 2: Tools:

We know that you really don't care all that much about your health. You have other more important priorities. So perhaps you would be interested in demonstrating to yourself that you are in good health with only an average amount of stress to undermine your future health. If so, we have an idea for you.

We all feel sick at times, and we all feel a certain amount of stress. Whenever those feelings occur, one way to show yourself how basically healthy and together you are is to graph the growth of improvement in your state. To do this, all you need to do is to make a set of cumulative graphing tables and use them. A graph of this kind just involves a series of vertical lines with markings all the way up to show the number of times something happens. The hand-out contains some sample graphs. On each graph mark at the top what you are going to record on it. You could record anything on these graphs. For present purposes, what you might record are any kinds of indications that you are getting better, or any indicators of good health. Temperature coming down, pulse rate getting lower, sweat level getting drier, nausea feeling less, pain getting less, all might be good indicators of feeling better. Calm feelings in you, comfortable breathing, good energy level, good mood, laughing, telling jokes, friendly conversations, absence of pain, all might be good indicators of good health. Pick the indicators you want to use and, perhaps at hourly (or less or more) intervals, if the positive indicator was present during the last interval, put a mark at the next position on that day's vertical line, <u>beginning at the bottom of the table</u>. Each vertical line is for one day. At the end of the week, add together the number of marks for all the days and record that total number. You'll impress yourself with how well you are doing.

<u>INDICATOR</u> to be Recorded: ______________________________

<u>Numb er</u>	<u>Mon day</u>	<u>Tues day</u>	<u>Wednes day</u>	<u>Thurs day</u>	<u>Frid ay</u>	<u>Satur day</u>	<u>Sund ay</u>
<u>34</u>							
<u>33</u>							
<u>32</u>							
<u>31</u>							
<u>30</u>							
<u>29</u>							
<u>28</u>							
<u>27</u>							
<u>26</u>							
<u>25</u>							

24							
23							
22							
21							
20							
19							
18							
17							
16							
15							
14							
13							
12							
11							
10							
9							
8							
7							
6							
5							
4							
3							
2							
1							

TOTALS FOR EACH

DAY: _______ _______ _______ _______ _______ _______ _______

WEEK:

____

What is this graphing procedure all about? The purpose is to help yourself to encourage your body to improve and maintain its health. There was a physician once who made a lot of money just teaching his patients to repeat to themselves: 'Every day, in every way, I'm getting better and better.' Do it.

Make as many different graphs for as many different indicators as you like. You can use this method to improve your school or work performance, your social skills and anything else too. [Ogden Lindsley's Precision Learning method adapted].

The next tool is going to make you think you are back in grammar school. It has to do with the body's need to use the energy is produces. Don't worry, we're not about to recommend an active exercise program. At least one of us is opposed to any kind of exercise, considering it bad for one's health. However, you can still use the body's energies without actually doing anything very much. The founder of the Fitness Institutes in Toronto is reputed to have performed an experiment in physical fitness. People who wanted to take off weight and to increase their muscle development were assigned at random to two groups. One group practised an active exercise program every day. The other group stood for the same length of time as the exercise program each day, but all they did was actively to imagine themselves doing the exercises. Both groups took off weight and increased their muscle development, and both to the same degree.

This story does not mean that one can expect to get good results by sitting around day-dreaming about exercise or muscle use. The imagination needs to be an active imagination of the muscles doing the work. And the body needs to be held upright so the muscles are actually working. Now for the grammar school part. You can get some of the same benefits just from your posture – that is, how you hold yourself as you sit, stand and walk. The taller you sit, stand and walk, the more you extend your arms and legs, the more you balance your head in an upright position, the more you use your body's energies. Believe it or not, your teacher was right about your posture. Good posture is good for you. It does use the energy of the muscles, and it feels good.

But there's another side to that coin. Learning how to relax your body fully, and using relaxation for one or more periods of time each day, is also good for your body. Your ANS sympathetic nervous response is going to occur as you have to adapt to the many changes in what you are doing each day. The excess energy that is produced as a result of this fact needs to be used up, for your health. But you also need to exercise the parasympathetic nervous response to give the body and the immune system a rest. This is accomplished best by relaxation. Let's do an exercise in learning to relax.

Curl your toes up tight until you feel a sort of cramping sensation in the arches of your feet. That sensation locates from inside you the group of muscles we will refer to as the muscles of the arches of your feet. Now, ever so slowly, let your toes uncurl and feel what it feels like for those muscles to <u>be relaxing</u>. Try to remember what that sensation feels like because we are going to use that sensation. Now, raise your toes off the floor to flex your ankle. Keep it up until you can feel a tightness in the front of your shin, and a stretching sensation in the calf of your leg. That locates the muscles of the lower leg from inside. Now, ever so slowly, let your toes come back to the floor, and pay attention to the sensations in your lower legs as the muscles relax. Try to retain the memory of those sensations.

Let's try a couple more muscle groups. Raise your shoulders up against the sides of your head. Feel the tightness in the upper surface of your shoulders. When you can feel that, slowly let your shoulders droop down, and pay attention to and remember the sensations of the muscles on the top of your shoulders relaxing. Cross your arms across your chest until you feel a tightness in your pectoral muscles. Then let the arms come back down to your sides, and notice and remember the sensations from the muscles in the front of your shoulders relaxing. Gently, try to touch your elbows together behind you, and note the tightness between your shoulder blades. Then let your arms return to your sides, and notice and remember the sensations of the muscles on the back of your shoulders relaxing. Clench your teeth tight together until you can feel tightness in the muscles of your jaw. These muscles are on your cheek just below your ears. When you have the sensation, let your jaw go, and feel and remember the sensations of your jaw muscles relaxing. All the muscle groups in the body have sensations associated with their tension and their relaxation. And you have felt them all many times in your life. So we will be satisfied for the moment with these brief reminders of where the muscles are and how they feel as they are relaxing.

Lie on your back on the floor. Prop a pillow or the back of a chair under your head in order to stretch the muscles at the back of your neck slightly. Lie with your feet slightly parted and your legs slightly bent out at the knees. Lay your arms at your sides, with the elbows bent just a little, and your shoulders drooping.

Think about the muscles of the arches of your feet. Don't tighten anything now, just let the muscles relax. Imagine the sensations of muscle relaxation in the muscles of the arches of your feet occurring, and going further, and further and further. As you do, the sensations you'll have will be that your arches seem to come down until you feel sort of flat-footed. Let go the muscles of the arches of your feet loosely.

Let go the muscles of the lower part of your legs. Imagine the sensations of muscle relaxation in the lower part of your legs occurring, and going further, and further and further. As you do, the sensations you'll have will be that your ankles feel loose and floppy. Let them go loosely.

Let go the muscles of the upper surface of your upper legs. Imagine the sensations of muscle relaxation in the upper surface of your upper legs occurring, and going further, and further and further. As you do, the sensations you'll have will be that your seat seems to sink deeply into the floor. Let them go loosely.

Let go the muscles on the inner surface of your upper legs. Imagine the sensations of the muscles between your legs relaxing.

As you do, the sensation you'll have will be that your knees seem to roll apart on their sides. Let them go loosely.

Let go the muscles on the underneath surface of your upper legs. Imagine the sensations of muscle relaxation in the under surface of your upper legs occurring, and going further, and further and further. As you do, the sensations you'll have will be that your legs feel heavy all over, heavy and loose, heavy and limp. Heavy. Let go loosely.

Let go the muscles of your back. Imagine the sensations of muscle relaxation in the small of your back occurring, and going further, and further and further. As you do, the sensations you'll have will be that your back settles deeply down into the floor. Let your back muscles go loosely, sinking deeply, way down.

Give your fingers a stretch. Stretch them out a good one. Then let them go loosely.

Let go the muscles of your arms. Imagine the sensations of muscle relaxation all up and down your arms occurring, and going further and further. Don't do them now, but these include the muscles that bend your wrists in and out, and the muscles that bend and straighten your elbows. Let them go loosely. As you do, the sensations you'll have will be that your arms feel loose and limp, resting deeply and heavily into the floor. Let them go loosely, sinking deeply.

Let go the muscles of your shoulders. Imagine the sensations of muscle relaxation in the top, front and back of your shoulders occurring, and going further, and further and further. As you do, the sensations you'll have will be that your shoulders droop down loosely, and that your shoulders sink evenly and deeply into the floor. Let go loosely, drooping down loosely, resting back deeply. Let go the muscles of your forehead. Gently push all thoughts and worries out of your mind for the present. Lots of time to think later. Concentrate your attention only on the sensations of your body's muscles relaxing. Let your forehead become smooth and calm and relaxed.

Let your eyes rest lightly closed. Let your eyelids relax.

Let go the muscles of your mouth and lips. Imagine the sensations of muscle relaxation in the muscles of your jaw occurring, and going further, and further and further. As you do, the sensations you'll have will be that your jaw droops down until there's a gap between your teeth. Let your jaw droop loosely.

Let go the muscles of your lips. Let your lips become soft and puffy, and relaxed.

Let your tongue rest loosely on the floor of your mouth. Let it go loosely, relaxed.

Let your whole body go limp, loose and relaxed all over. Let yourself feel like a wet rag, limply draped on the floor. Let yourself feel like a great lead statue, resting heavily into the floor. Let yourself go.

[Allow a minute or so of silent relaxation. Then ask the participants to rouse themselves and to report how they felt. A few affirmations of calmness will do. Debrief the participants, since this method of muscle relaxation will be used later for purposes of systematic desensitization]. Notice we talk in a slow way, paced roughly at the speed of out-breathing. This is NOT hypnosis. It used voluntary relaxation instructions. As you practice this skill, you may notice that relaxation skills advance in three stages. The first level of relaxation involves feeling pretty relaxed, as most of you felt just now. The second stage involves involuntary twitches, you know, of the kind you sometimes have just as you are falling asleep. These happen because your body is used to being fairly tense. It is unused to getting deeply relaxed. So it momentarily reinstates its tense state in a twitch or spasm. It only means you have become more deeply relaxed than you are used to being. The third stage involves loss of awareness of where some of your body parts are. For all you will know, your arms are in Timbuctu and your legs are in China. We promise to go fetch them and return them if they take off on such a trip. This loss of awareness of your body parts occurs because you are so relaxed that the kinaesthetic muscle sensations, that tell you what your body parts are doing, are not occurring, since your muscles are doing nothing. They are fully relaxed. We would be pleased for you if you could reach that third level of muscle relaxation when we use this skill later today.

The last self-help tool we want to talk about today is purpose. Having noticed causality mostly in the physical world, most of us are most familiar with initial or antecedent causes that work in the physical world. Initial causes are the kinds of things we usually think of as the causes of events. They occur before their effects, or the things they cause. [Examples]. But in the world of psychology, or the behavioural universe, which is the real place we all live, initial causes have almost no importance or effect at all. Nearly all the causes that act in our daily lives are final causes, or the purposes or needs that we pursue. Final causes don't happen until after the effects they cause. [Give a few examples]. If we want good effects in our lives and in our health, all we need to do is to set out to achieve those purposes.

Purposes are decided on and designed by the person who has the purpose. Almost everything that happened to you in your life, you caused to happen. That does not mean that you set out with the conscious, or unconscious, intention to have everything happen as it did in your life. Everything we do has natural consequences. If you wanted to feel important or special, you did a number of things to achieve those final outcomes. Some of those things would have taken something from others or have made others feel less important or special. The natural consequences of that might well be that others did things to you that you didn't like. That is, we call down onto ourselves the costs involved in achieving each of our purposes. Only 'nothing' is free of costs. However, whether or not we intend to acquire the costs we have to pay, we bring them on ourselves by acquiring the benefits we seek from our purposes. We could decide on the purpose of obtaining, having and maintaining good health, if we wanted to. How could we design our future health for ourselves, without foregoing other things we might want to do? The answer can be found, the design made, and your future health reasonably assured. But you would have to take on the job of deciding on the purpose and designing your own future health. Only you can know what kinds of health you want, and what other things you also want to pursue. All we can do is help you to find how to design that purpose, if you choose it. [Sketch in an overview of James' (1992) The Secret of Creating Your Future and reference the availability of his program tapes].

Block 3: Therapeutics:

[Wolpe's systematic desensitization [RIT] is used for standard anxiety stimuli involving health and feeling good. The same relaxation method is used as that outlined above. The relaxation effect is amplified by additional use of lateral eye tracking back and forth across the picture being imagined. A sample of the stimuli employed is shown below].

Picture yourself feeling as if you had a cold or the flu coming on. Then check your body over, and notice that you feel pretty calm and well.

Picture yourself experiencing some pain in your body. Check your body over, and notice that the pain is slowly subsiding and you are feeling better.

Picture yourself being told by your doctor that you have a disease that can be cured by means of medication. Check your body and notice that it feels calm and better than it did.

Picture yourself being told by your doctor that you have a disease that cannot be cured. Check your body over, and notice that it feels calm and better than it felt before.

Picture yourself lying in a hospital bed feeling very ill. Then check your body over and notice that you feel calm, comfortable and better than you felt a few moments earlier.

Picture yourself at home on a muggy, humid day. Check yourself over and notice your body is comfortable, relaxed and at ease.

Block 4: Consolidation:

[Further exposure to James' health beliefs review from The Secret of Creating Your Future.   Beliefs concerning personal destiny, genetic inheritance, expected outcomes, longevity, and the like, are elicited from participants and subjected to scrutiny and analysis of the linguistics involved.   For a sample of beliefs, necessity is challenged.   Assumptions concerning the nature of causality adopted by participants are reviewed, and the predominant role of final cause (purpose) in human life is affirmed.   The role of the brain in regulating everything in the body (and in life) is stated, followed by instruction in the (verbal and imagery) means by which the brain's activities are regulated.   Participants are then asked to design specific health goals for themselves and to use standard planning methods to achieve those goals].

[Additional relaxation, coupled with further brief systematic desensitization for health-related images, is undertaken.   In this part of the program, the stimuli employed include pervasive environmental stimuli commonly associated with malaise (humidity, temperature, social isolation) and proprioceptive sensations (joint pain, headache) as the targets for desensitization].

[Summary and cuing observations for the day's learnings].

Treatment 8: Creating HAPPINESS

The <u>main target</u> in this program is to <u>counter</u> the various types of <u>depressions</u> that underlie much addictive behaviour. Alcoholism has long been linked to anxieties by virtue of its tranquillizing effects.   Depressions are almost more central to addictions, although in much more complicated ways.

Anhedonic depressions (Scale 13, occurring most commonly among introverts and obsessives) create a need for feelings and aliveness that can be generated artificially by the 'rush' or 'buzz' from some chemicals.   Reactive depressions (Scale 03, from energizing difficulties arising from depletion of stress resources) create a sense of pressure that can be relieved by soporific and mellowing chemicals. Somatic depressions (Scale 53, activating and reacting to dependent states, panic or immune problems such as allergies) interact with contemporary reliance on chemical 'treatments' to foster dependency on some chemicals. Temperamental depressions (depressed mood) are almost automatically viewed these days as being most appropriately treated by (self-) medication.

The felt depression provides the motivation to seek relief. And the relief achieved through the chemical functions as the reinforcement to perpetuate both the avoidance activity (seeking relief) and the depression (the response necessary to seek and obtain relief). This program assumes that if a fairly continuous happy, lively and calm state can be achieved, the felt need for relief from depressions might no longer exist.

Block 1: Orientation:

Who has never experienced a period of depression? Congratulations! So, you have all had a chance to develop some expertise in today's topic. It is: 'How to become (and stay) depressed'. How did you do it? [Allow some affirmations that it happened to them]. OK, so who feels at least moderately depressed right now – that is, other than the natural reaction to hearing us ask such a silly question as: 'How did you do it?' Is anybody willing to expose his/her depression in this group? [If not, play the game between the presenters].

Where did your depression come from? How do you experience it? It never comes from events of the past. Those events of the past that we ruminate about when we are depressed are not the causes of anything. The first thing we need to know about being depressed is that the depressed mood comes before the thoughts about the past. The thoughts about the depressing past serve three purposes. First, they make us feel better by finding what we think of as the 'causes' of our depressed mood – actually they are just excuses for it. Hold it! Are we suggesting that the unhappy events of the past didn't happen or don't justify our awful feelings? No, we are not. We'll come back to that. Second, they allow us to feel more depressed for a longer period of time – by bringing unpleasant feelings from the past to amplify and, through thought, extend the felt depression. Hold it! Are we suggesting that you want to feel depressed, and to amplify and extend the depression? Not exactly. But we'll come back to this. Third, the bitterness, even anger, we feel about those past events allows us to avoid feeling angry (and thus energized) NOW – since there is little that we can do now about those past events. Hold it! Are we saying that depression serves a useful purpose? Not entirely. But we'll come to the purposes it serves next.

Our next question is: What do you gain from being depressed?
Not a thing, right? It's an awful experience with no benefits at all to it. Did you ever notice that, while you may hate it when they do, you expect other people to notice when you're depressed? In fact, since we feel so helpless when we're depressed, we expect, or at least hope, that someone will do something to help us get un-depressed. In fact, don't you sometimes feel just a little bit important when you are depressed? After all, who else has had to put up with the unhappy events of your past and your present nasty feelings? It is interesting that the main gain we get from fear is the justification we get from it for avoiding situations; and the main gain we get from depression is the justification we have for being looked after by others, and the sense of importance we get from others' caring for us.

Now let's go back to the things we were not saying before. The thinking about unhappy events of the past is done partly to justify the expectation that others will 'make up' to us for the past. The intensification and extension of the depression that comes from thinking about the past increases the apparent depth of the depression, and that increases the demand on others to help. And the avoidance of anger in the present both prevents anger at those around on whom we depend to make us feel better, and provides a distraction from no-longer-existing (or manageable) things to carry the anger – helplessly. OK, go ahead and be angry at those awful and outrageous statements we just made. If you can, you might even find your mood lifting right now.

You see, not all, but just about every kind of depression is a result of ways we use to prevent anger from being felt. There are some noteworthy exceptions to this principle, but not many. The behavioural symptoms of depression mostly involve actions that impede the expression of anger – or of the body's energies. Let's play a game and make ourselves depressed. All you need to <u>do</u> is to stare downwards and into space (allowing thoughts to take over, and keeping you from noticing present events that might arouse feelings or actions), slump your body toward its own centre of gravity (making you feel de-energized, heavy and having to work just to stand up), wrinkle the forehead heavily (to enhance the occurrences of unhappy thoughts), turn down the corners of the mouth (to communicate sadness) and move very slowly and heavily (to prevent use of much energy). Try it. It's fun. You can probably even increase the depression by tightening the rectal sphincter as though you were trying to be constipated.

It's interesting that depression also increases people's impulsiveness. The reason seems to be that they are not as concerned with future thoughts, so that future consequences do not control behaviour as much as they ordinarily do. Also, it feels as though nothing can be worse than the feelings right now, so the future seems as though it doesn't matter all that much. The thoughts that occur in depression are mainly unhappy ones from the past. By way of contrast, anxiety focuses us on the future and anticipates the dangers it may hold. That is, in our business, the past is depressing, the future is scary, and the present is fun.

Essentially, the symptoms of depression express a need to depend on other people – a dependency need. In order not to prevent others from allowing dependency on them, the depressed person tends to hold back on anger in the present for fear it will interfere with reliance on others. So the symptoms of depression are merely the means by which we prevent energy or anger expression. Fatigue (increased by sleep disorder), lack of energy, depressed mood, increased thought pressure, a sense of helplessness (and crying for help), are all defensive means to suppress energy use.

But why are we on about depression? Surely the topic was one of creating happiness. It's not a bad idea to know and understand any enemy that stands in our way. If we are to create happiness, we first need to understand how we create unhappiness, sadness, or depression. That's right. We now need to return to our initial question: 'How do we make ourselves depressed?' or 'How do we do depression?' The answer to such a question differs from person to person. So we have to explain briefly some of the ways we do it.

Introverted people think a lot. Thinking competes or interferes with feelings and with actions. The more we think, the less we feel. The more we think, the less active we are. As a result of their thinking, introverted people experience less intense feelings than others – which is comforting in a way, but that leaves the person feeling joyless and empty. As a result of their thinking, introverted people use less of the energy their bodies produce – which may feel efficient, but it then increases depression. The introversion and depression together may impede use of the body's energies to the point that the person feels constantly frustrated or blocked, so that rage may develop as a means to try desperately to get out of the resulting self-imposed inhibitions, rules and other restraints.

Some people have learned that it's not nice to be angry. They may come to think of anger as a hurtful motivation that ought to be controlled. The controls they develop in themselves inhibit the use of energy, for fear that someone is hurt or harm is done. Such people try to be nice. The pleasant reactions of others to their controls and niceness serve as rewards to increase their reliance on others as a source of pleasure and reassurance. In turn, this enhances their dependency. They are then doubly prone to sadness and depression, as a dependency response and as a means to inhibit the expression of anger.

Some people have learned to fear emotional closeness to others – for fear they may be rejected and feel hurt. They may find ways to hold themselves aloof, at a psychological distance from others, so they don't risk emotional commitment. Most of these ways have a kind of hostile flavour to them, which does keep others at an emotional distance. To justify their hostility toward others and their sense of despair about finding friends who 'can be trusted', they often ruminate about the mistreatment they have received in the past from others. Whether imagined or real, the purpose of the ruminations seems to be to remain conscious of the imagined ill-will of others, to perpetuate aloofness. The thinking, coupled with the ruminations about past unhappiness, creates a bitter kind of depression that views the world in hopeless terms.

These are only some of the ways depressions form themselves out of the pre-existing approaches to life that people adopt. And, unfortunately, an angry person lives in an angry world; a depressed person lives in a depressing world. The world we live in is a mirror of ourselves. That is, the world we live in is one created by ourselves, and not the reverse.

Although we accept as axiomatic that we are always wrong, we have developed the crazy idea that you might prefer to be happy throughout your life, and that you might prefer not to get yourself depressed. If, by some miracle, on this occasion we happened to be right about you, it might be worthwhile for you to learn how to be happy, even joyful, and even all the time.

Block 2: <u>Tools</u>:

If you wanted to be happy, the first thing to do might be to discover just how you depress yourself. You see, we're from a temporary employment agency, and you have hired us to take on a job of work for you while you're taking a vacation. In this case, since you surely would not want your depression to go untended while you are taking a holiday from it, you are going to have to teach us how to do your depression thing. And, you should know that we are very conscientious employees. We want to be sure that we do our job right while you are on vacation. So, who would like to take on the job of teaching us how to be depressed just like you are (or have been)? [If nobody is willing to do the teaching, the presenters play the game of teaching by one of the other. Be very careful and critical of the effects on the learner of doing the various suggested ways of getting depressed. Seek self-talk, actions, images and the like that might be involved in creating the depressed mood. When techniques work, the learner acknowledges the extent to which they have the desired effects]. So, it just may be that you could discover just how you depress yourself. [NLP/James' Modelling Behaviour procedure]. We'll return to this later.

The next tool is one you might like to keep using for the rest of your life. Write down some qualities of yourself you might like to have in greater measure. Include 'Happy' and 'Outgoing' in your list. Two or three qualities will do for now. Under each of these qualities write down at least a half a dozen behaviours that you can actually observe that you might see in another person who you believe has each quality in large quantity.

You might want to notice that 'happy' people tend to smile, to move in a light and quick way, to focus their eyes on people and things around them, to comment on nice things happening or being said, to turn the inflections in their voices upwards at the end of sentences, to express positive feelings about all sorts of things, and the like. You might want to notice that 'outgoing' people tend to approach other people, to smile at others, to talk freely in groups, to start conversations, to ask others about their pleasant recent experiences, to listen attentively to what others say and to reflect the positive feelings in what they hear, and the like. If these are some of the kinds of observable things that you believe happy or outgoing people do, then include them in your list. If you disagree, list your own views of what such people habitually do that demonstrates to you that they are happy or outgoing.

Now, here's how to use your lists to become a happy person fairly continuously. Each morning, take a moment to read over the list of <u>behaviours</u> you have just made. This is to remind you what you are watching for all day. Go about your life. Don't make any effort to do any of the behaviours on your lists. Just pay attention to what you are doing to ensure that you notice each and every occurrence of any approximation to a behaviour on your lists. As soon as each occurrence happens, reward yourself with praise and a mental 'pat on the back'. [Use the example for 'Outgoing' cited under the third method of Therapeutics for Treatment 2, Creating Flexibility to explain how this might be done]. The important thing about this method is that you must be easy about accepting an action of yours as an occurrence of the behaviour from your lists. And you must notice and reward yourself for it by being pleased with yourself. [Personal Development Goals procedure].

How does this work? Surely, I'll only act one of those ways if I am either happy or outgoing. Not true. We know, it sounds right that I act in a certain way because I first feel that way. The reverse is more true. The actions occur first. The brain becomes aware of the actions on its internal proprioceptive senses. Then the brain experiences the feelings. It is more true that I am happy because I laugh than that I laugh because I'm happy. But each single bit of behaviour, by itself, does not create the feeling or experience. There are many actions involved in each feeling. That's why it was necessary to list several different behaviours for each of the qualities you want to achieve.

Because actions are relatively mutually consistent with one another, all we need to do is to increase the habit strength to do each separate action, and the whole bunch eventually come together to have the desired result. But you don't want to force the actions by acts of conscious will. If you do, you will learn how to force the states you are seeking, they will occur only in parts, and the whole experience will feel rather artificial. Instead, just wait for each separate action to occur, with your awareness primed to notice it, and then reward its automatic occurrence. Although you handle each behaviour separately, they will increasingly occur together with other related behaviours, fairly continuously and with a good sense of 'real' experiences.

The next exercise you might want to do every day involves assertiveness. Remember that depression involves inhibiting the use of the body's energics. Similarly, happiness involves the lively use of the body's energies – being perky and alive, as well as doing active things. Assertive training is concerned with using ways to employ the body's energies. There are all sorts of ways to assert yourself. Assertiveness is neither aggressiveness nor under-assertiveness. Assertiveness lies somewhere in between those two extremes. Let's think of it this way:

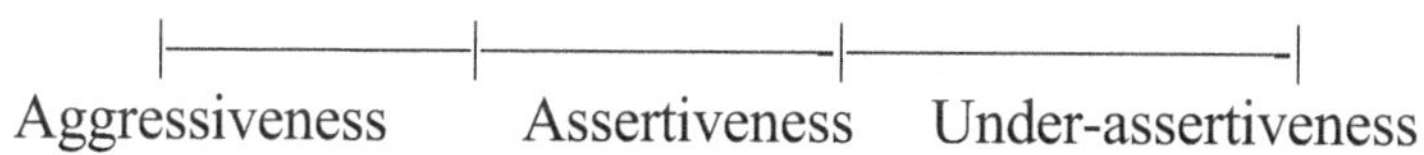

|————————|————————|————————|

Aggressiveness   Assertiveness   Under-assertiveness

Assertiveness involves the comfortable use of the body's energy. Under-assertiveness involves a fear of getting too angry or of risking hurting others. To avoid that, the person holds back from expressing feelings, especially angry ones. One of the problems with that is that the person may become depressed. Another problem is that the fear of getting angry increases the person's level of arousal, perhaps to overwhelm controls, perhaps to result in angry outbursts. That is, aggressiveness is largely a reaction to the arousal of fear of anger, such that the arousal adds to the felt anger, possibly over-riding controls. If we could get comfortable with strong feelings such as anger, we might get rid of both under-assertiveness (with its risk of depression) and aggressiveness.

But anger is surely universally accepted as a 'bad' thing. Surely it is harmful, and ought to be avoided. We would not want to contradict any beliefs you might hold in this matter. However, it may not be anger that is risky, but rather aggressiveness. We would like you to consider this idea for yourself.

Picture a test tube. Into this test tube we're going to pour all of your body's energies to measure their amount up the side of the container. The raw amount of your basic energy probably does not differ too much from that of anybody else.

But a strange thing happened across the years. You were feeling energetic, rushing about the house having fun. Your parent anxiously warned you to stop running around, to slow down a bit and to be more careful. You didn't understand that the parent was worried about knocking over precious trinkets and breaking family property. All you knew was that you were feeling energetic and having fun. Is something wrong with energy?

You were feeling energetic, so you raised your voice while talking. Your parent boomed: 'Don't you raise your voice to me!' Is something wrong with energy?

You were sitting class, feeling energetic and restless. The teacher snapped at you: 'Sit still and pay attention!' You still didn't understand that attention was important to learning. Was there something wrong with energy?

You were having fun wrestling with or swinging around one of your friends. Your parent warns you anxiously to simmer down a bit. You didn't understand that your parent was worried about how the friend's parents might react if the friend was hurt. Something must be wrong with energy?

Each of these kinds of repeating experiences aroused some anxiousness in you that, over time, was learned to be associated with the events or circumstances (in this case feeling energetic) of the time. Let's represent that learned increase in anxiety associated with energy as a kind of sticky substance poured into the test tube over the energy, increasing the amount of the experience involved. It is sticky because the fear experience is supposed to help control or inhibit over-exuberance and the use of our abundant energies.

Now, later in life, when you feel energetic, you feel the energy and all the other feelings that have habitually come to be associated with it. That increased amount of feeling, comprised of two different kinds of components, produces a new experience. If the experience of the increased feeling is that of the anxiety part, the sensation is one of being 'uptight' or tense. If the experience is that of the sticky 'corking' effect of the anxiety part, the sensation is of control or inhibition (or confinement). If the experience is that of the energy part, the sensation is one of anger – that is, energy with the bitter taste of anxiety.

If we were to view anger in this way, it may just be that we would come to some conclusions about it that are different from those we reached as children. For example, we might even conclude that anger is a 'good' thing – the feeling associated with the evocation of energy modulated by the process of socialization. It might even be worth remarking that what keeps people living together in social groups (society) is the mutual exchange with each other of energy – each doing the kind of thing he or she is best suited to or is willing to contribute to the common good.

The problem is that anger, if over-controlled, can be released periodically in aggressive behaviour. And aggressiveness may be the problem. If energy is used comfortably in assertive ways, it might serve only the common good. In case you decide to see it that way, it would be well to learn how to be assertive. [Refer to the Tools section of Treatment 6, Creating Innocence, for a method to teach Assertiveness]. [In addition, use Wolpe's method for in vivo Assertive training as appearing in the Therapeutics section of Treatment 4, Creating Satisfaction].
Block 3: Therapeutics:

[Get participants to pair off. Allow about five minutes for each member of each pair to teach the other how to be depressed. Ask for feedback about the success achieved by the teacher in showing how it is done, and by the learner in acquiring a depressed mood. Emphasize the fact that different people depress themselves in different ways, and the need for the teacher to know how he/she accomplishes depression – knowledge that needs to be expressed in words, so it can be remembered by the teacher. Get each person to make notes as a reminder about how he/she depresses him/herself].

[Administer a brief Values test for areas of living such as feelings, relationships and/or work. Our test is constructed such that 'reflexive' values tend to appear in the right-hand column of each page, and conflicted or avoidance values are marked with a dot (period). The test requests that all listed values in each area of living that are viewed as important be checked, and then the checked values ranked for their importance. Then respondents count the relative numbers of checks they have made for 'reflexive' (right column entries), 'conflicted' (dot) and non-conflicted (no-dot) items. This allows them to discover the roles of these three kinds of values in their higher priority (high ranked) values].

The purpose of the test is to discover if the values to which we subscribe contribute to depression or interfere with happiness. In general, 'reflexive' values, that depend on others for fulfilment (e.g., recognition, appreciation), foster dependency. They thus enhance the risk of depression and/or felt lack of being fulfilled in life. 'Conflicted' values, where one tends to notice, and even be vigilant for, occurrences of the negative or unpleasant pole (e.g., Not in danger, mistrust), even if stated in terms of the positive pole (e.g., security, trust), create and maintain constant stress and strain, focus the person on unpleasant or feared events, and do not contribute to happy or joyful living. In contrast, 'approach' values contribute to happy and joyful living, especially if they are active (as opposed to reflexive) values. [These distinctions are made after participants have completed the test]. [Participants are asked (with whatever help they require) to identify one of two 'conflicted' and one or two 'reflexive' values that are of paramount importance to them. Two exercises are undertaken. One seeks to change the relative position of one or two reflexive values in each person's rank order of his/her values. The attempt is made to bring their

importance down in the rank order and to elevate the rank order of one or two more active (left hand column) values. The method is described under Therapeutics in Treatment 5, Creating Values, taken from James and Woodsmall, 1987]
[The other exercise seeks to rid the person of vigilant distress associated with one or two of the 'conflicted' (dot) values, as it were to remove their negative or conflicted effects on the person. The method used is described under Therapeutics in Treatment 5, Creating Values, also from James and Woodsmall, 1987].
Block 4: Consolidation:

[Although focusing particularly on the substance of the present program's activities, and although referencing happiness as the purpose, the consolidation part of this program is equivalent to the Consolidation section in Treatment 3, Creating Excitement. The methods used are reviewed and summarized with cuing suggestions].

Treatment 9: Creating INTEGRATION

The main target of this program concerns several aspects of personal integration and consolidation. It is concerned with the consolidation of learning and integration of new habits in the person's habit-family hierarchy that might serve to counter addictions. It is concerned with the person's personal sense of integration, or of 'being together'. It is concerned with the person's integration in social groups and in society generally. It is concerned with the individual's personal contribution to him or herself and to others that, in the long run, might be expected best to consolidate any learnings achieved. It is as paradoxical in its message as any of the other treatments. It seeks to integrate and consolidate a host of factors in the person, while at the same time enhancing his/her sense of personal freedom and entrepreneurial initiative. In these ways, it is at once the most general and the most summary of the programs.
Block 1: Orientation:

Most of you know us from other types of contacts we have shared. You all know that we are crazy. However, you ain't seen nothing yet. If you think you are making any sense out of what we're going to do today, we suggest that you simply assume that you are 'getting it' wrong. Better still, you might explain it to us, since we haven't a clue what we're doing. In fact, today we're going to try to talk to your unconscious. While what we say may sound as though it means something to your conscious awareness, we are probably really talking at another level altogether. But bear with us if you can. We actually have quite a clear idea about what we're trying to do and how to do it. With that hopefully confusing introduction, let's proceed.

What we want to do today is to help your minds to use any kinds of learning or experience to serve you best in daily living. Strangely, this is NOT done best by means of understanding things consciously. It is done best by means of automatic responses that have been built into you over the years of growing up. In fact, conscious understanding of events may actually interfere with the general useability of information and experience. What happens is that our conscious understandings help us to orient ourselves in the particular situations to which conscious experience applies, whether or not the situations involved are specific or general. We have another level of functioning, call it unconscious, unaware or automatic, or spirit, if you like, that is concerned with our survival and happiness. That is the level at which we want to work today, if you will let us.

Unfortunately, for most of us, this other, let's call it unconscious, level has been tuned across the years to force us to AVOID fearsome, worrisome or awful events that, as children, we came to believe people the world. Actually, we live in a carefully engineered safe society, in which there is really nothing at all to fear, as long as we abide by some fairly simple and obvious means to regulate our behaviours. If this was a program concerned with criminality, we would call those means to regulate our behaviours, 'rules', just to get your backs up. In this program, we are going to call them 'guides', just to get your backs up. Actually, they are just ordinary bits of obvious common sense, like walking on sidewalks rather than on roads in front of cars, or waiting your turn at stop signs and traffic lights. We know that sort of thing is offensive to you since you are too special to have to do what everybody else has to do. But we aren't going to bother with that sort of thing today.

The other programs in this treatment series tried to get around or through some of the troubling things of our histories that made our guides feel oppressive or offensive, and that turned our unconscious minds to react to life by AVOIDING it. Today's program assumes that we have come to grips with some of that AVOIDING stuff, and that we are ready to advance to broader sunlit pastures, as Sir Winston Churchill expressed it. To do that, we need to address a whole bunch of tiny and important things.

Let's start with our insides. In a way, our brains are like computers. Actually, of course, it's computers that are in some ways like our brains. But let's talk about it the other way around. Computers enter the words and other things we put into them in a kind of temporary buffer memory, that we can see on the screen. The experience entered into this temporary buffer can be examined and even changed to suit our conscious ideas and wishes. After a while, when we have had time to examine, check and change those things on the screen, we may decide that it's OK, and we save the information. When we ask the computer to save the information on the screen, it goes into permanent memory, and it is stored in whatever places on the hard drive that the COMPUTER decides is right for IT. Our brain is constructed even better than that. It decides WHEN, WHERE and HOW the information we have in our conscious minds ought to be stored in our unconscious minds. This is important to each of you, so bear with us while we explain.

WHEN is information stored? This is the least important bit of knowledge, partly because we can't do much about it. However, it is stored in two stages. Conscious information waits in consciousness for about 48 hours, or two days. There it can be checked and reviewed. This first 48 hours is important because, if we let the information we have in recent memory 'mean' or 'signal' danger, fear, unhappiness, anger, or other kinds of negative emotions, when it goes into medium term memory storage it gets coded or entered into the unpleasant or danger-signalling parts of memory, where it will later be accessed first and assigned first priority. The trouble is that, AT THE TIME, the danger parts of anything ARE assigned special importance by us. It's lucky that the first stage of storage is delayed 48 hours, allowing us to use good sense after we are out of any given situation, while thinking about it, to look around and orient ourselves toward the positive and happy and rewarding aspects of each of life's events. Other programs in this series tried to teach how to do that. It is to our advantage to store in memory the positive and happy aspects of any event. And, in the 48-hour short-to-medium-term storage, each event will be coded and stored with other events and reactions that have a similar emotional or feeling tone. Let's set up our habits in the ways that serve our lives best. That is, rethink recent events in the most positive light you can find.

Medium-term, 48-hour, memory is stored as unintegrated, isolated events, coded mainly for their emotional tone. Such memories wait in medium-term memory, being checked against the rest of our personality and habits WITHOUT OUR BEING AWARE OF IT. About 6 weeks after the event, experience or learning, the brain automatically stores the surviving aspects of the event in long-term memory. And it stores it there in such a way as to make it most completely related to and integrated with the rest of our personality. Actually, it doesn't do that all at once. It may take several tries, each about 6 weeks apart, to re-integrate the new learning with the rest of the learnings in the personality. We may even feel a bit 'shook up' and troubled during each of these 6-week reintegration periods involving important and widespread learnings or experiences. Important ones are likely to include major therapeutic changes or the results of experienced trauma. The main thing to notice about this, since we can't do much about its unconscious operations, is to remember that quite often, when we feel shook up and troubled, even for up to a couple of weeks at a time, it may simply be because our minds are consolidating or integrating important things into our personalities. And that's a great thing to have happening! It means we are growing in important ways that will affect our futures. That is, we are forming important parts of our personalities – so our experiences were NOT unimportant or meaningless after all. In fact, if we do our jobs well today, you may feel shook up and troubled for short periods of time 6 weeks, 12 weeks, 18 weeks, and perhaps 24 weeks from today. Wouldn't that be fun!

WHERE and HOW the memories are stored has been implied in what we have already said. And they represent the important parts of what we have already said. The WHERE is given by the emotional or feeling tone we adopt during the first 48 hours after an event. If we view the event with sadness or fear or anger, it will be stored in the AVOID area. We try to direct most therapeutic stuff to that area, in order to fix that area's memories and images. It was partly for that reason that we started off as we did today. You would be well-advised to think about ALL <u>OTHER</u> kinds of experiences in a positive and happy way, at least finding the 'silver lining for each cloud', if only to ensure for yourself a large supply of positive memories and personality elements to help you have a happy and enjoyable life.

The HOW is given by how you handle each experience in life. You have time during the first 48-hours to find and focus on the positive aspects of each experience – so it is stored in the most rewarding places. You have a chance to make sure that you get perspective on each unpleasant situation to get the best out of it, during that first 48 hours. And you have a chance to re-interpret unexplained uncomfortable feelings you have, even if they last up to two weeks, as desirable and promising events involving only the healthy integration in your personality of new learnings that are challenging some of the old and painful learnings of your past. Enjoy disruption! It may be ... GOOD FOR YOU!

Block 2: <u>Tools</u>:

Now let's move outside our bodies. Look around you. We live in a social world, don't we, with all sorts of other people around us and interacting with us. When we were infants and children, those around us came to us, brought what we needed to us and looked after us. Most of us got the idea that we were pretty important with everybody we knew clucking and fawning over us. We liked that way of having things, and we'll be damned if it is going to stop happening that way. Though people have stopped acting that way toward us now that we're grown up, we keep acting as though that was the ONLY right way to have things. And, if things aren't the way they are supposed to be, we'll do our best to achieve that happy and comfortable state of helpless dependency as often as we think it ought to exist – that is, all the time. Oops! We've just described the state we all seek in addictive behaviour.

Funny, though! When we were children, we used to think how great it would be to be all grown up, free to choose what to do and how to do it, and in charge of our own lives. Now that we have reached that important and much-to-be-desired state of being, we act as though we want to be children again. Do we? Of course we do! And of course we don't! That's in the nature of conflict, to want and not to want at the same time. Actually, what we want is to have EVERYTHING! To have what we want AND what we want, even if they are totally incompatible, and even if we know it. There's a saying about this: 'I want to eat my cake and have it still too.' Too bad! As we are fully aware, it doesn't work like that. So, how can we 'eat our cake and have it too?' It ain't all that difficult to do, if we plan it right.

The trouble is that we have tended to plan things in ways that don't work. We do that, not because we're stupid, but because we set up most of our strategies for doing things when we were children. And children are NOT well-known for their experience, wisdom and understanding of life. If you'll pardon the expression, we got things ass-backwards. We decided to be children who grew up. Unfortunately, it doesn't work that way, and it keeps us forever in conflict within ourselves. What we would suggest as an alternative adult approach is to be grown-up children. Now what the hell does that mean? Who knows? We just made that up.

Let's look at someone sitting near us. Just pick anybody you want to look at, and look at him/her. It doesn't matter what part or aspect of the other you look at since you're not looking at him/her to interact with him/her, just to look at him/her. Hey, get your minds out of the gutter, and re-join us in this garbage! Think of this. The person you're looking at is IN FACT GROWN UP. He/she is NOT a child. You can see that. Somebody is probably, in turn, looking at you. He/she also sees a grown-up person. Keep looking at others around you, and let what you can see of each one impress itself on your mind, showing you definitely that each one is a grown-up person, and that each one, in looking at you, sees a grown-up person. OK, so we're all grown-ups. So what? IF that is true, then we had better, for the sake of not-particularly-unpleasant reality, think of ourselves as grown-ups. Of course, you KNOW you're grown up. Why make such a thing of it? The reason is because we all have a whole lot of re-doing of our habits to do – habits that were formed and strengthened all through our years of growing up. And we're asking you to change those well-entrenched habits in a few moments here and now. Don't worry, we won't forget about our other domain.

So, your PRIMARY IDENTITY <u>NOW</u> is as a GROWN UP, right? Hey, you've arrived where you always wanted to be – a GROWN UP. But we would all like to be children too. OK, so let's ADD that to our identities. For this purpose, close your eyes and go for a few moments into yourself. Think about it. On the outside, the body you have, is grown up, with all the advantages that come from that source. On the inside, that is your personality and the way you feel, is still that of a child. You still have the wonderment and fascination of the child; you still have the light-hearted, happy and contented feelings of a child; you still have the needs for others and for their love that you had as a child. PLEASE, try to focus on those parts or aspects of being a child.

We know, you're having a hard time getting past your unsatisfied needs for attention, importance and recognition; you're having trouble not noticing the helplessness, pain and mistreatment that you felt as a child; you just can't seem to stop paying attention to the fears and anger you felt about those big people around you, who were supposed (by you) to know better, but didn't. Don't try to stop yourself from attention to those things, if you must. We know you can't do a not do. But simply wait through those things, and gently try to come back to the other, happier, things such as the wonderment and fascination, the light-hearted, happy and content feelings, and the needs for others and for their love, that were also a part of childhood. Take your time. You need to find those parts of the child in you too.

If you can be a grown-up first, as you are, but with all those nice parts of being children inside you, you can be a grown-up child. And that was the first part of what we wanted you to experience today, so that you could practice that way of being every day, as the first of our self-help tools for a better life for today. But there are others to work on too.

You know, we DO spend a lot of time thinking and reviewing our lives every day. We've just suggested two profitable ways to approach that thinking and self-observation, namely, making sure we find and focus on the positive aspects of each experience (the silver lining to every cloud) at least during the first 48 hours after each event, and noticing our own and others' grown-up states while focusing within on the positive aspects and values of our childhood lives. The purposes of doing those things are to enhance the happiness and good feelings embedded in our personalities to serve our futures well, and to construct for ourselves happy and healthy identities, free of conflicts. But in both of these aims, our purpose is to learn for ourselves to benefit ourselves.

Learning is something else we could profitably learn to do better than we learned to do it as children. We often even got the strategies of how to learn wrong. Those who taught us didn't teach us how to learn. Most of us think that learning involves getting an idea in memory and understanding it. That's school learning. It has little to do with us or with living. That is learning of things OTHER PEOPLE want us to know. As grown-ups we ought to be able to choose for ourselves what we will learn, and benefit for ourselves from our learning. Let's do that.

If YOU want to learn anything FOR YOU, don't copy the information down for later review. That just tells you what we or someone else thinks you ought to know. Phooey! Write down either (a) the outcome you want to achieve FOR YOU, or (b) the things YOU want to DO more of FOR YOU. (a) If you write down the OUTCOME you want for you, the strategy to use to achieve that OUTCOME is a purpose-oriented or goal-oriented strategy. Our Goal-finding program will help you to make that strategy work for you so you can achieve the OUTCOMES you seek at any time in life. We will come back to one kind of outcome later. (b) If you write down what YOU want to DO more of FOR YOU, then the strategy for achieving more of that kind of DOING FOR YOU, is for YOU to take on the job of REWARDING YOURSELF for doing it. We're going to look at how to reward yourself in a moment. But first, just a comment about how this relates to the last exercise.

You're grown-up on the outside, right? Grown-ups DO things on the outside. That's part of being grown up. Every time you prepare for learning by writing down something you want to DO, you're exercising your grown-up side. But you're making it happen by rewarding yourself with the kinds of things you want – your inside child aspect. Inside we're all children, full of light-hearted happiness, wonderment and fascination, and needs for other people. Children want results or outcomes to happen, right? Every time you prepare for learning by writing down an OUTCOME or goal, you're exercising your inside child side. But you'll find that the only way to make things happen the way we want them to is to DO specifiable kinds of things to make them happen – your outside grown-up aspect. You can be both, but always starting with the realization that you are now grown up.

So, how to learn to DO something – a skill or a way of being? First, as we said, you need to write down what it is you want to do. Hey, you can do anything you want to do, right? If so, how come we are all so unsuccessful in making the friends, getting the jobs and acquiring personal property that we always wanted. Come on, let's be real with ourselves. We know, those are outcomes, and not what we DO. Oh yeh? We all know that's not right, we hope. Now, here's a funny thing about that. We actually all do know one kind of thing we have all set out to DO. We all know what we want to do, or have to do, to DO the addictive acts to get a high. The trouble is that most of us don't know what ELSE we might want to DO. How about talking to others comfortably; how about making love better – yes, even better than you do now; how about enjoying the world around you, like sunsets, trees and the like – yes, that's a doing too; how about reading about the wonders of the world around us and about different ideas – yes, two heads are better than one; how about writing about your experiences and thoughts well enough that somebody else might enjoy reading what you wrote; how about doing sports really well; how about doing and enjoying hobbies of various kinds; how about enjoying the company of other people; how about doing work tasks so well you are in high demand as a worker; how about making a useful contribution to others and the society that provides so lavishly for you; how about ...? All these things, and more, you might want to learn how to DO FOR YOU.

Second, after you have written down the things you want to DO more FOR YOU, each on a separate piece of paper, under each thing you want to DO, write down some (or all) of the indications you could observe that you are doing each action WELL. Examples might be these kinds of things. If you want to talk to people more, the indications might be the number of sentences uttered or statements made to other people, the number of sentences they made that you listened to, and/or the number of people you talked with. If you want to make useful contributions to your community, indications might be the different tasks you can do at the time or in the place where you are at the time that are useful to others, the number of times you help others with their tasks, and/or the number of tasks you can find and start doing that might contribute usefully to your community. The choices are yours about what you want to DO, <u>and</u> what indicators of them you will use.

Third, for EACH indicator, make a little table on the page. The tables should have numbers from one to any number up the side, and days of the week or month along the bottom. You ought to carry the paper(s) with you, along with a pen or pencil. The task is to make a mark beside the next number up the side of the table for that day. In this way you keep a record of the times you DO each of your indicators. Who needs to go to all that trouble, right? Hey, you can remember well enough what you did. Oh yeh? List all the things you did so far today that contributed to your present community, that involved talking to others, that improved your health, that increased the marketability of your job skills. You might get a few, but we guarantee you have only retained a very small percentage of the many things you have already done TODAY toward each one of those things. And that's the problem. We just don't use good strategies for learning just how good we are or to increase our value and worth to ourselves and others. That's what we're trying to show you how to do right now.

Fourth, each week or month, whatever interval you're using along the bottom of your tables, record the total numbers for that interval on master sheets under each indicator for each action you want to DO. Be pleased with yourself for your accomplishments. It doesn't matter precisely what actions you did, as long as they each qualify for one of the indicators. Know that each and every record of an action indicator is another assurance that you are learning the kind of skill or action you are trying to increase. You are just plain great! You'll soon find that, in spite of the pain you imagine this unnecessary and boring task will entail, you are really enjoying having a record of how well you are doing, and you will even, pretty soon, enjoy making the records and rewarding YOURSELF. Besides, you will soon discover something you suspected, but never really knew was true, namely, that you are an impressive and worthwhile person, who might even get to like him/herself.

There's another thing you might usefully and profitably do for yourself every day, as another kind of self-help. In other treatments we have asked the question, 'what is important to you?' The purpose of that question was to ask you to examine your own personal VALUES. We'll be coming back to that later. The question might be asked slightly differently as well. It might be asked, 'what needs or gains in life are important to you?' Of course, we all need to survive. For that, we need to gratify our basic survival needs, such as air to breathe, food and fluid to eat and drink, a place to eliminate body wastes, shelter and clothing to keep us warm, activity to use the body's energies, sleep to calm and rejuvenate us, a sexual life to reproduce our species, freedom from life-threatening dangers and severe pain, means by which to acquire basic survival resources (usually called work), and some changes occurring around us to prevent boredom. We all need those things. But that's NOT ALL of life! They might be all of life if we were animals and nothing more. But we are humans as well.

As humans, we are conscious or aware of our selves. We possess a self. And that self needs nourishment too. Most of us continue our old habits of childhood, imagining that what nourishes the self is what OTHERS DO to and for us. But that was the way our child selves got nurtured. Look around you again. We're all grown-ups now. Remind yourself in this way of that fact lots every day. It's easy to forget. How are grown-up selves nurtured? Some of us think we know. It's done by feeling different, important, special, better than others, in control of the world or at least of other people, excited, on-top-of-the-world, almost omnipotent and invincible, with other people doing things for us, right? WRONG! That's how children's and adolescents' selves are nurtured. Children get to feel important, special, better than others, and omnipotent because the adult world around them is looking after them, provides them with security and puts their needs first. Adolescents haven't figured out yet how to establish their own individual identities, and so they do it by the simplest and most obvious means, by seeing themselves as different, excited and on-top-of-the-world (a post-pubertal awakening that becomes ordinary eventually), and invincible (to feel safe, since they are still less powerful than the grown-ups around them). Perhaps there are other ways to nourish the grown-up self. Let's pretend there are. What might they be?

A guy named Maslow tried to figure out answers to that question, and came up with what he called self-actualizing needs. He believed that we don't pursue our self-actualizing needs until basic survival needs have been met. They have been met for all of us to a sufficient degree. So, what are the next set of needs we might usefully and profitably go after? [Hand-out] Here is a list of the kinds of self-actualizing needs Maslow suggested. As you look over this list, please remember something else. The needs from this list that you appreciate as the ones you want to pursue are likely to be those that are most consistent with your present VALUES. That is, if you have a strong value for money, you are likely to 'see' such self-actualizing needs as 'richness' as meaning 'being rich'. If you have a strong value for controlling others or for sexual gratification, you are apt to understand or 'see' self-actualizing values such as 'beauty' as referring to the 'sexual attractiveness' of others or yourself. Although those might be examples of particular applications of some self-actualizing needs, the NEEDS actually go much broader and deeper than just those limited applications of them.

You might usefully consider, re-consider and consider again and again over the next months the self-actualizing needs that you have and need, to create a reasonably fulfilling satisfaction of your basic human self. [Encourage some discussion of the needs that individuals might select, and examine the INSTRUMENTAL value of each for the self and for personality development].

Let's come outside ourselves again and realize something about the communities in which we live. What is the purpose or reason why people live together in societies? Is it for self-protection? Is it to give everyone other people to rip off, or to make money from? Is it because people want others to talk with? Is it just a dumb habit we follow because as children we were taught that was the way to live? Of course, it is none of these. Protection is easier in a small group than in a large one; money and ripping others off is a relatively recent invention; we really only need one other person, a mate, to talk with; and we were among those who most utterly resisted what we were taught as children.

The reason is that the nature of humankind is such that we have discovered that we can function, get along and accomplish best in societies. We come equipped with a motive, called loneliness, whose purpose is to drive us to be with others. We come equipped with varying kinds of skills and things that interest us, not being driven by instincts that would make us all the same. This means that we will be able to do one kind of thing better than other things, and we need other people to do the things we need to have done for us for our fulfilment. It is this fact of differences among us that makes social living the kind of lifestyle that works best for humans.

A society works ONLY if everybody in it contributes his/her energies to everybody else, to derive his/her needs also from the energies of everybody else. If you want to memorize something today, that is the most worthwhile thing to memorize. Society exists and works only if everybody contributes his/her energies and special talents to do for everybody else what he/she is good at, and reciprocally accepts the results of everybody else's energies and talents to help support his/her existence. In the type of society in which humans live, everybody does and contributes something different, and everybody's contribution is equally as good, necessary and valuable as everybody else's. That's not just political hogwash, moralistic egalitarianism, a personal belief we cherish or another fairy story or fable. It's the way it works, if it's going to work. That does NOT mean, as some opportunistic power mongers try to say, that we live in societies to <u>serve</u> other people. We live in societies to serve <u>ourselves</u> best. But there is a kind of moral injunction that goes along with best serving ourselves. It has to do with the CONTRIBUTIONS we make to others.

Look at your neighbours in this room. Try to remember anything you know about any of them. What does he/she do unusually well? What does he/she seem to enjoy doing? What does he/she do that might contribute something that you need to have done? It doesn't matter too much whether you know that he/she is good at, likes doing or might contribute to you. Think about this. Can you force or make each OTHER person do for you what you need from him/her? We might be able to kid ourselves into believing we can. But we absolutely cannot! The only person anybody has any real power over is him/herself. All the rest of the power over others that people like to think they have is an illusion. While I am standing over any one of you with a stick or any social skill in manipulation I may have, I may be able to enforce from you a grudging and half-hearted acquiescence in doing my will. But as soon as I am trying to do that with two people, doing different things at the same time, I leave each for half the time to do his/her own thing, and of course to resist me, while I am trying force the other person to work. We all have too many different kinds of needs to enforce contribution from others.

What we can do is only two things to <u>correct</u> our old childhood habits of trying to push others around and manipulate them. First, we can develop and foster our own helpful and contributing social groups. Second, we can find and do those things that we can usefully contribute to others. Let's try to do the second thing first to see how it's done.

How can we find out what we're good at that might contribute usefully to others and to the society that nurtures us? Of course, in the last analysis, if you really don't know what you're good at, you could undertake an aptitudes and interests assessment with any psychologist. Don't worry, we're not going to do that now. Anyway, you already know a great deal about what you're good at, if you just paid attention to that – instead of doing what we mostly do, namely, telling ourselves what we're no good at or the mistakes we've made, or that we're entirely GREAT. Think about that for a short time while we talk away at you about people's abilities.

During the long, boring process of growing up, we were subjected to three kinds of pressures from others that tended to shape some of the ideas we developed about ourselves. We want to remind you of these pressures briefly, so you can try, while thinking about what you're good at, to let the effects of those pressures go – to decide for yourself, free from the effects of those other distorting influences.

How many kinds of measurably different abilities do humans have? [Get a few guesses]. There are probably about 120 different abilities that everybody has in varying amounts. [List a few on the blackboard, as suggested by participants, and enriched from psychological lore]. You have some of each kind of ability, and nobody has full-credit in anything near every kind.

The first set of outside influences that acted on us as children, came from our parents. Some of you are, or have thought about being, parents. What kinds of abilities would YOU most like to see in your children? We'll tell you a few of them. You would like your children to do as they are told, to be obedient or to exercise their acquiescence ability, especially when they are acting in ways that risk danger or harm for them, or when they are being the roaring hellions kids often are. You would like your children to move around with good muscular coordination ability, so they don't harm nice furniture or the precious things you keep in the house. You would like your children to exercise the social skills and graces of getting along easily with others, so that they are pleasant to live with, and so they can get along well with their friends. And you would use everything in your power and knowledge to make sure your kids exercised these and other skills. But where do parents get their knowledge about child-rearing from? They get it from the silly books by other parents who think they have found the keys; and they get it by having been children themselves, from their parents and their parents' mistakes. You may think you know how to be a good parent, but you don't, any more than we do – and we're supposed to be experts in that field. We all learned faulty parenting skills from others who were using faulty parenting skills. So, parents shout at kids, find fault with kids, punish kids, or praise them lavishly. And these are some of the methods they have learned by which to try to influence their children to exercise the kinds of skills they want the kids to develop, learn and use.

The second set of influences was the schools we attended. Schools, no matter of what kind, mainly emphasize only two of the 120 plus abilities people have. What are those abilities they emphasize? Reading and arithmetic, right? Since their job is basically to prepare kids for constructive work, they forget about nearly all of the many skills involved in constructive work and focus on the two that are needed in nearly every kind of work, namely, reading and arithmetic. Many of us are not particularly good in those two kinds of abilities. If we are not, we will probably have done rather poorly in school, and we will have felt like failures, no good and sources of trouble and annoyance for our teachers. In fact, if we had more than just a little difficulty with these two abilities, we probably got called bad names, like Learning Disabled or Attention Deficit Disorder, by means of which teachers blame the untaught for not having learned. Who cares what skills or abilities you <u>don't</u> have? It's only the ones you <u>do</u> have that matter.

The third set of influences was your friends and peers. What do you want your friends to be good at? That ought to tell you some of the things your friends tried to get from you. You might want your friends to have such abilities as not telling your secrets, liking you, looking up to you, accepting you, agreeing with you, spending time with you, and the like. You learned the skill of being deaf and dumb in talking to others about your friends; you learned to like and respect your friends, and to agree with their ideas and beliefs; you learned to accept only your friends, and not others' friends; and, since no group of people all want to do the same kinds of things, you learned to hang around in your groups doing nothing until everybody was bored enough they had to stir up a little shit somehow, or else to get rid of the boredom by getting high. You taught them your skills pretty well, and they taught you these kinds of skills at the same time.

But, quite apart from what you found out about yourself from those influences, what are YOU GOOD AT doing? That's a really important question. But how can we answer it? Ignoring for the present what other people have congratulated you for – for their own reasons or purposes – what kinds of things have you done where YOU regularly felt satisfied, or at least pleased, with the outcomes? What things do you do that YOU think you do well or right? If the outcomes are useful and contribute to something or to someone, the skills involved in achieving them are useful. If you feel satisfied with the outcomes, or if you think you do the skills well, your own self-satisfaction will tend to reward your efforts in such actions, and you will be able to develop skill in those activities. It's really that simple.

So, don't just think about the skills you have found in this way. Don't just sit there feeling smugly superior to the rest of us. You ARE superior in those ways, but please don't just sit and think of these skills of yours. WRITE THEM DOWN! They are gold and precious gems that will sparkle and adorn the rest of your life, but ONLY IF YOU REMEMBER THEM <u>AND</u> USE THEM! And, trust us, you may be <u>absolutely</u> certain you won't forget them, but you will. You will forget them because you will fall back again into thinking and fretting about the failures you are reminded of as you think about what OTHER PEOPLE have thought of you. Quite apart from the uselessness of that kind of thinking, you must surely know you will do it in the future. You will do it, UNLESS you write down your wonderful skills on paper and carry it with you for frequent reference, along with your other identification records. PLEASE, write down every one you can think of NOW!

<u>Block 3</u>: <u>Therapeutics</u>:

The other question we left off earlier was the question of how to develop our own helpful and contributive social groups? Now we all know that it's up to the group of other individuals to decide whether they will accept or reject us. We can't break into groups, except by purchasing their substances or by having substances to sell to them. We have to have something they want, right? Wrong! We were children too long, feeling at the mercy of others. All we need to do is to learn, now we're adults, how to become part of groups to support us, help us and allow us to make contributions.

The most obvious way to become part of a group is to form our own group. That is, we can take the initiative to form groups just as well as anybody else. Somebody has to start any group. Of course, to succeed in forming our own groups probably requires the same skills needed to become part of an existing group. So, aside from the reminder that somebody has to start a group and it might as well be you, we haven't said anything useful about joining a group yet. And there are several things to learn.

The first skill for group involvement is skill in listening. Most of us listen <u>for</u> put-downs, rejections, insults and other indicators that we use to confirm for ourselves that others don't like us. You might remember that some of us only insult our friends or those we like – why bother saying anything to anybody else? But listening <u>for</u> those sorts of things is not a skill of listening, it is a skill to confirm prejudices or pre-judgements.

The main skill in listening involves listening <u>to</u> what others say. You don't have to agree or disagree, praise or criticize what another says. In fact, if you do, it may well turn him/her off. What we do need to do is to check our understanding of what the other said. This is called 'reflection' or 'pacing'. It simply involves repeating in your own words a summary of what the other said, especially the feeling part of it and asking for confirmation of your understanding. We might say: 'If I got it right, you believe that ...' A little practice makes you comfortable with reflection and, amazingly, the other person will quickly consider you highly intelligent, very understanding, terribly interesting, and one with whom he/she wants to have conversations. Heck, you're interested and understanding and preoccupied with the most important things and ideas there are – his/her interests and ideas. You are worthy of being part of a group with him/her.

The second skill for group involvement is to listen <u>for</u> the things that are important to the members of the group – that is, the groups values. What do they talk about a lot; what do they all seem to agree about; what gets them excited or emotional? You don't have to part of a group to overhear that sort of thing. Just watch what they do. When you have a pretty clear idea about some of the group's values, before you try to join the group, you ought to consider whether YOU agree with their values. If you don't, look around for another group. If you do, this might be a group to try to join. If you're not sure, either you're not too clear about your own real values, or you might take some more time listening <u>for</u> the group's values.

The third skill for group involvement is to 'pace' their actions. If they're sitting erect in serious conversation, sit erect and look serious; if they're walking or running in some direction, do so too; if they're slouching around doing nothing, that's what you might do. Contrary to all the contemporary hype about racism, what marks people as at least potentially in-group or out-group members is what they <u>do</u>, and not what they look like. If you <u>act like</u> group members, you are half-way into the group; if you don't, you're out of the group, and probably due for some disparagement, perhaps referring you to another group that acts the way you do. Being like others is mainly acting like others.

The fourth skill for group involvement is to find something you can contribute usefully to the group. This may take a little time to figure out, perhaps while you are still hanging out at the periphery of the group – not yet part of the leadership or the core. But it's not too hard a thing to do. Once you have figured out what's important to the group, or what its common values are, all you need to do is to use your perfectly fine brain to figure out <u>what</u> the group is NOT doing that it could usefully or enjoyably do <u>as an expression</u> of its values. You would have to do this also if you were forming your own group. The task is one of finding a <u>mission</u> or <u>purpose</u> or <u>outlet</u> for the group members' energies. If you have the group's values, what might you want or like to do as an expression of those values? Answer that, and without expecting immediate agreement or response from the others, express the idea, and tentatively lead off the action. Even let others say the idea as if it was their own – they may not remember you suggested it, but they will feel warmly toward you, if only for letting them seem to have originated the idea. You do this, and you're in.

Please break up into small groups of four. Don't get together with your friends. Pick others you don't know. The exercise is for each person, in turn, each for about three minutes, to serve as the outsider trying to get into a group of two others, where the fourth person takes his/her turn as observer. The two playing the group talk about anything they want; the one outsider tries to use his/her skills to 'get in with them'; and the observer makes brief notes about how the outsider is doing. Change places about every three minutes, timed by the observer, so all four have a chance to play each role.

[Allow about 15 minutes for this exercise, and walk around observing the small groups].

How did you do? [Allow brief remarks]. Who found he/she could use some of the skills of group involvement? Did they help? Did you discover that FEELING part of a group isn't all that hard if you approach it smoothly and well? Great!

But we expect that each of you felt a bit uncomfortable while playing each kind of role – talking with a stranger, trying to join, and not participating as an observer. The reason is simply that we all feel a certain amount of social anxiety that we have learned over the years. Even the few of you who have well-honed social skills, who feel good at joining others, have developed those skills BECAUSE you felt socially anxious. Whether or not you've noticed it, the body-builder who has become expert in the martial arts is usually the one who was most afraid of being attacked or hurt; the person who brags about him/herself and his/her accomplishments is usually the one who felt inadequate or inferior; and the outgoing social butterfly was usually pretty scared of other people and of rejection by them. We all feel anxious about some things. And sometimes that anxiety gets in the way of our being able to make the effort to try things, so we avoid them instead. If that's true of you, you might need some means to reduce your anxieties whenever you want to.

You have all tried some methods for relaxation, and probably some kinds of special breathing techniques. The trouble is that most of those methods need to be done when you are not in a crisis or emergency, or when you are not in need of getting settled down. There is one thing you can do right along with anything else you are doing, right in the situation, and without anybody else needing to know. We all breathe without having to think about it, right? Right! And your body needs oxygen obtained from breathing IN. So let your body breathe IN just exactly as it would without being noticed – only notice it, and time it in your mind. Then, make the OUT-breath following a half-a-dozen natural IN-breaths go on for three to five times longer than the IN-breath. We know, you all thought we just said to practice DEEP BREATHING. We did NOT! We asked you to do the opposite – to make long OUT-breaths for about 6 breath cycles. [Demonstrate while counting durations out loud]. You don't have to make it obvious as we just did to illustrate the idea. Just sit as you are now and, without making it obvious, make 6 LONG OUT-breaths. As you're doing that, please notice that you start to feel (i) a bit less anxious, (ii) a bit less breathless, (iii) a bit more relaxed, and (iv) a bit less tight in the chest. It happens automatically that it calms you down a bit. Hey, you've mastered an important bit of psychological First Aid you can use for yourself.

Here's another bit. Did you ever notice that all anxiety is anticipatory anxiety. None of us knows what the future, or even the next moment holds for us. What if the group rejects me ... or insults me? What if my spouse shacks up with somebody else? What if I make a fool of myself ... or I pass out ... or he/she hits me? The 'What ifs ...' we tell ourselves create all the fears that beset us. Every time you are afraid of something, ask yourself what it is you fear, and how you made a 'What if ...' out of it. Then, <u>say</u> the 'What if ...' statement under your breath, adding only one word to it – the word prefix 'So'. Now your statement to yourself is: 'So what if ...' If that doesn't take away enough of the anxiety, perhaps even with a chuckle, think through the 'What ifs' ALWAYS in terms of <u>pairs of possibilities</u>.

For example, 'What if I'm sick?' 'So what if I'm sick?' 'I might get worse; or I might get better, in which case there was nothing to worry about.' 'If I get worse, the doctor might not find out what's wrong; or he/she might find out what it is and cure me, in which case there was nothing to worry about.' 'If they can't find out what's wrong, I might just get better on my own, in which case there was nothing to worry about; or I might die, in which case I won't have anything to worry about anyway.' Try it out now on something you are worrying about.

Next, think about something you are or have worried about or that upset you pretty badly. Close your eyes and get a clear picture in your mind of the situation you were upset about. Shove the picture slightly to one side. Push it straight in front of you. Pull it in a bit closer, and notice that it upsets you a bit more. Push it a bit farther away from you, and notice that it seems to bother you somewhat less. Keep pushing it farther and farther away. It gets smaller and smaller as it moves farther off into the distance. Push it back until it is just a tiny dot on the horizon. Hey, it doesn't bother you much way out there. Isn't that fun. You could probably even do that with your eyes open so nobody could tell what you're up to.

There's another way to do this. Close your eyes. Get the picture of the upsetting situation back in front of you. Put it in a television set, filling the whole screen in full glorious colour. Down in one corner of the screen, put a tiny little black-and-white picture of yourself feeling just exactly the way you would like to feel. Got it? When you're ready, with a swish of action, zoom up the tiny black-and-white picture of yourself as you would like to be so it fills the whole screen in full colour. Look at the colour picture of yourself as you would like to be for a second or two. Clear the screen. Get the coloured picture of the upsetting situation back filling the screen, with the little black-and-white picture down in the corner. Then when you're ready, zoom up the picture of you as you would like to be to fill the screen in full colour again. Look at it for a couple of seconds. Repeat this a dozen or so times. It only takes a minute to do. What happened? [Get reports until someone says he/she couldn't get the upsetting picture back on the screen]. Great! That's what happens after a while with the Swish.

Hey, why not use the Swish right now to get rid of some of the qualities you see in yourself that you don't like, or that you feel others don't like. Get the picture of you <u>with</u> the quality you don't want covering the screen in full colour. Put the little black-and-white picture of yourself as you would like to be down in one corner. Zoom up the picture of the you that you want to be to cover

238

the screen in full colour. Look at it for a few moments. Clear the screen and repeat the Swish procedure over and over again.

There's another thing you might try. You want things to happen right when you want them to happen, right? Hey, we're all 500-pound parrots, and Polly wants a cracker NOW! That too is a left-over from childhood, when we had to wait until parents or teachers thought it was the right time for things to happen. We mostly have not noticed that waiting for things actually increases the joy in having them. Relaxing and holding off sexual climax not only extends the period of enjoyment, it actually increases the strength of the enjoyment, if not the excitement feeling. Waiting until you're really hungry increases the joy of eating. And not buying something you want for a while, increases the anticipation and the fun of finally getting it.

Hold it, but that doesn't work in substance abuse. Oh yes it does. The trouble is that we have given ourselves the message that we just can't tolerate not having the substance NOW. Is there a child crying in that message? Of course, we can tolerate almost anything we set our minds to do. Have you ever been straight, or off addictives without wanting them ... even for ten minutes? Of course you have. You're not using right now. <u>How</u> did you do that? Seriously, how did you do it? The first thing you did was to know perfectly well that you could do without the shit for an hour or two. <u>How</u>? Well, you could take that much time off it. Of course you could! It even makes OTHER things you do while off it more pleasant, and more fun. It really does! The second thing you did was use your 'being straight' skills. You didn't know you had any, did you? Well, you do! We spend so much attention and energy on HOW we do the addictive thing, and HOW MUCH we need it, that we don't notice that we can do the straight thing, or HOW we do it, and HOW MUCH we enjoy the rest of life while we are FREE from the addictive thing. It pays off handsomely to figure out in complete detail HOW you do the straight thing. And you can, and you DO!

But how can we possibly deal with the urge, the hunger, the need or the craving for the addictive thing? That's what gets in the way of doing the straight thing. Let's get back to that after our break.

Block 4: Consolidation:

You have already learned a wide array of things you can do to reduce the strength or pain of any craving, feeling or pain. It's not a bad thing to use any and all of them. You know LONG OUT-breaths calm you down quickly. You know it helps if you add a 'So' in front of the 'What ifs' that scare us or that we worry about. You know the Swish can cut down on any unpleasant feeling. You know that you can last for an hour or two through anything, and delaying gratification may add to the fun of the rest of life. You know that really talking to others simply takes away part of the discomforts from other things like cravings. You know at least four skills for joining groups, and that you could even form your own support groups. You know what you could do with your time to make it enjoyable for you and contributive and useful to others, because you know what some of your skills are, and that you are very successful in using the skills you have. You know why we live in societies, that you get much from others and that you feel best when you are usefully contributing your energies to others. You know what some of your own self-actualizing needs are, as well as some of the values that motivate you – and some of those that get your tail in a knot to screw up life for you. You know that there are ways to get rid of those last values that foul up your life. And you know that the only person who can or will help you improve your life for you is YOU and what YOU DO. [Extend these summary statements to offer reminiscences and reminders].

Almost most importantly, you know that your life and what you do are NOT governed by the past events of life, and that the real causes of what you do and how you feel lie in the PURPOSES and VALUES you SELECT for YOURSELF. They are easy to select to suit the lifestyle you want, and they decide how you will act and live

NOW. Your future is entirely in your own hands, and you can make it anything you might want. If you convince yourself that your future is in the hands of Fate or of others, you will be waiting, bored out of your skull for things to happen the way you think they should, and instead things will happen to you exactly as you think they should not. Your choice, and only yours! We know, we're being mean. Remember, we have formed so many of our ideas as children, and we forget they might well be badly formed or ill-taken. We can try to be children who grew up, in which case we will remain feeling like children at the mercy of others – who are no longer paying much attention to us. Or we can be what we are, grown-up former children, with the emphasis on being grown up adults. Good luck! Have fun!

APPENDIX E: DISCUSSION OF SOME OF THE TREATMENT COMPONENTS

In this appendix, we would like to tell you a bit about some of the treatment available for use in treatment, since the average clinician may not be familiar with them. These descriptions are intended to be illustrative only, and anyone who cares to duplicate these programs in other settings should refer to the original works from which these procedures were drawn.

1. <u>Cognitive Restructuring/Reframing</u>: Guilt feelings are experiences in which everybody shares. Guilt is learned early in life as a result of reproval and criticism, and it serves as a means to remind the child to inhibit some actions in order to avoid pain from the future consequences of his actions. The reproval is offered as an act of love, seeking to protect the child from injury and embarrassment, but it is commonly misunderstood as evidence of absence of love. Feelings of guilt, and the incorporation of self-depreciation and fearful avoidance of other's judgements about "mistakes," may be taken to heart. Consequently, most of us know more about our "bad" than our "good" selves. Each of us has been "bad" for much less than one percent of his or her life. Others' and our own guilt-provoking judgements are simply wrong. Feeling guilty now is the judgement now that a past event should have been done differently. But it could not have been done differently. <u>Everybody</u> always does the very best he or she can at every moment, given the circumstances and the person's condition, including both their parents and themselves. Therefore, since nothing could have been done differently, we are all perfect. Indeed, perhaps the only real sin is guilt itself. The loving intention behind a guilt-trip, and the fact that the judgement made is always wrong, suggests that guilt-trips could be enjoyed.

Similarly, everybody feels or thinks he has failed at times. Mostly, failure is a judgement made by others which we believe to the extent we value the others or their opinions. We expect to be punished or put-down by others for our failures, and we sometimes take on the role of judging ourselves either to avoid failures or to anticipate punishment (punishing ourselves). But there really is no such thing as failure, only feedback. In addition to the fact that we all always do the very best we can, we are all magnificent learning machines, and everybody is always growing and improving his skills and actions every moment of every day. The trouble has been that we have been raised in a society which over-values competition – in the family, at school, in sports, in activities, with friends, and even in court. For example, we who are in jail are all failures in competing with the prosecution, i.e., defending ourselves before the Law. But society hasn't "got it": competition is one of the main sources of war and of crime. Identify (on paper) several repeating situations in which you most either feel like a "failure" or fear failing. Take each in turn and (a) reverse your view of failure in it into success – enjoy the fun of trying to fail or make the mistake, and (b) reverse the contingencies involving failure – enjoy trying as an objective to achieve the very thing you fear may happen (Use examples such as Ellis' "objective" of being turned down as often as possible in requests for dates.) Pair off in dyads to play the game of enjoying failing.

Everybody feels a certain amount of distress every day, and a great deal of distress from time to time. Suppose you had no means at all by which you could reduce your distress. You would live with it and tolerate it, right? In fact, one of the things that sets us up to risk becoming addicts is that we think we can't stand our distresses, and that we have to get rid of them NOW. (Examples, such as being scared while driving, and the consequences of stopping and leaving the car versus keeping on driving.) We can all tolerate distress just fine and, if we do, it passes – almost never lasts longer than 90 minutes. In fact, let's have some fun enjoying distress.

Wouldn't it be nice to enjoy being free ... to be warm, friendly, concerned and close with everybody. The trouble is you can't trust any person ... to be consistently caring the whole time. (Use the logic of Pascal's Wager to demonstrate it is always a mistake of thinking not to trust other people with your feelings.) (Use "the love test tube" model (Quirk, 1991) to explain how it gets to be hard to trust, and easy to create "distance" from others emotionally.) So we all make mistakes of thinking which create havoc and trouble in our lives. It might be well to examine some of our mistakes of thinking, and even how we could find ways out of our problems.

Thought is the single main source of personal distress and thus interpersonal and other trouble. Thought is always a waste of time. In fact, when we are wasting time, the way we keep ourselves from boredom is commonly by thinking. Thought, however, never has to do with reality, if only in that by the time we think about the present, the present is already past. What happens to many of us, who have been taught that we ought to think and that our thoughts should be organized, is that we confuse ourselves trying to organize our thoughts. Another use we often make of thinking is to manufacture faults in ourselves and others, and we justify our fault-finding on the grounds that we have been trained that it is desirable to maintain a critical attitude of mind – it is not. By finding fault we manage to find ways to disrespect others, and thus to justify our cold and distant attitudes toward others by which we avoid "getting close" to others. Finally, we often use thought to find justifications, rationalizations, excuses and intellectualizations about ourselves and what we do.

Of course, since there are as many different logics as there are people, nobody except ourselves is convinced by our impeccable arguments and incisive logic. Just because thought is a waste of time, however, does not mean that cautiousness and precision should not be used in the things we say and do. We can enjoy being cautious and precise. But we don't need any "self-control," or to concern ourselves about the ways we think others want us to "conform." Our brains are already programmed beautifully, so that we will do what we are going to do whether or not we have thought it through first, and no matter how much self-control we exercise. Of course, self-control too can be fun. Use it for that purpose. Most of what we believe and say is achieved through the exercise of what we are pleased to call "common sense." All that "common sense" really tends to mean is that we jumped to a conclusion on the strength of impression, emotional attitude and imagined consensus of opinion – that is, attitudes we think are in fashion or are popular. Common sense commonly misleads us all. It is probably true that, if a million people believe something, it is bound to be wrong.

We are all in some sort of jail. This means that our freedoms and choices have been denied us, and we are restricted from doing anything interesting or useful, right? Wrong! There is just as much freedom in jail as in any other life setting. Freedom is only the freedom to choose or decide. But we can't decide freely to go home or any number of other things. Of course we can. The only thing that restricts us is our own unwillingness to accept the consequences of making certain choices. We restrict ourselves because we aren't willing to pay the costs of making certain decisions. But that's always true for everybody, at every moment of his life. Moreover, in jail we actually have MORE freedom than on the street. We are free from the requirements of supporting ourselves, those complexities which we don't handle well of deciding how to use our leisure time, the demands of life's distractions by which we prevent ourselves from pursuing our own best interests and things which might later contribute to the quality of our lives and, for some of us, from the constraints imposed by our relationships with others – that is, we are free to make new lives for ourselves with new choices about those we will relate to in various ways. So, maybe it's time, while you have the opportunity freely to feel confined, to enjoy your restraints.

Actually, all confinement and restraint comes from within ourselves. "Stone wall do not a prison make, nor iron bars a cage. Hearts innocent and quiet take that for an hermitage. If I have freedom in my love, and in my soul am free, angels alone that soar above enjoy such liberty." Even when prevented movement of our bodies, we are free to exercise our minds – where all of anybody's reality exists. Inhibition comes mainly from thought, but also from habits of self-control and of avoidance. Since action and thought compete with one another, the confinement that comes through thought impedes the use of the body's energy – the body is just an energy-producing machine. The felt restraint from this source creates an increased pressure for bodily energy to be used, which can eventually lead to a sense of rage. To combat rage, use up the body's energies in actions (restlessness, pacing, exercise or any vital activity). Self-control is necessary, right? It is not. We are well-programmed to act as we will act, and all the extra burden of self-control does is increase the ANS-stress arousal which increases anger. Trust your well-programmed brain and enjoy doing crazy things. Avoidance habits are learned to keep us from doing things we fear, but the fear and the avoidance result in situations and reactions of ours which result in robbing ourselves of joy and justifying for ourselves hostile attitudes and feelings toward others. We live in an engineered safe society. There is nothing to fear, except the effects of fear itself.

2. "Personal Development" Goals Development (Quirk, 1993): To discover your perfection, take on the job of noticing and rewarding your "goodness" so that you become your "Ideal Self." List all the qualities you would like as your ideal self. Under each quality, list a half-dozen observable behaviours which define that quality. Each morning read over the behaviours to remind yourself of them. During the day reward yourself ("pat on the back"), and even record, every time you notice yourself, even

for an instant, doing any (even) approximation to any act on your lists. You will soon discover how good you are, and become your ideal self.

3. <u>Values Development</u> (James and Woodsmall, 1987): List all your values – everybody has lots – and extend them to include as many "replicative" (positive only) values as you can. If unfamiliar with considering your values, you might consider those listed in the multiple-choice values checklist (Quirk, 1992) – made available to the participants. Values are the most general guides for living, the best means for self-definition, the motivators which determine how we use our time, the means by which we evaluate how we have done (thus, values underlie guilt feelings), and the most abstract or general issues affecting everything in our lives. It is well worthwhile discovering and developing your own values.

4. <u>The "Visual Squash</u> (James and Woodsmall, 1987): Consider "guilt" and its opposite (e.g., "innocence"). What picture pops to mind when you think of guilt? What picture pops to mind when you think of its opposite? Close your eyes and hold out your hands, palms up. Choose one hand on which to place the picture of "guilt." Place the picture of its opposite on the other hand. They are both "parts of you" (images through which you process personal experiences) and they are placed on your hands to externalize them so you can talk to parts of you and know which parts you are talking to. Ask the "guilt" part what its highest intention for you is ... and why does it want that for you? ... Ask the opposite part what its highest intention for you is ..., and why does it want that for you? ... (Proceed according to the method outlined by James).

5. <u>The "Swish</u> (Bandler, 1985; Andreas and Andreas, 1987): Picture a common situation in which someone tries to "lay a guilt-trip on you." Set that picture aside for the moment. Picture yourself feeling just the way you would want to feel – confident, relaxed, etc. Now, with the camera of your eye, zoom

the picture off into the distance, way off until it is just a dot on the horizon. Bring the "guilt-trip" picture back in front of you, then zoom it out to the horizon at the same time as you zoom the other picture (the one of yourself looking just the way you would wish to feel) back in again. Look at it closely. Let that scene fade away, and then do it all over again, but faster. Picture a common situation in which someone tries to "lay a guilt-trip on you." Set that picture aside for the moment. Picture yourself feeling just the way you would want to feel – confident, relaxed, etc. Now, with the camera of your eye, zoom the picture off into the distance, way off until it is just a dot on the horizon. Bring the "guilt-trip" picture back in front of you, then zoom it out to the horizon at the same time as you zoom the other picture (the one of yourself looking just the way you would wish to feel) back in again. Look at it closely. Let that scene fade away, and then do it all over again. Repeat this process, switching the pictures very, very quickly – swish – half a dozen times, or until even the very thought of guilt-trips makes you think of feeling confident and relaxed.

6. "Time Line (Andreas and Andreas, 1987; James and Woodsmall, 1987): Everything exists in your mind, in images of the past, present and future. Imagine your past to be a long series of pictures stored in order so you can tell which came ahead of which. Imagine your future as a series of pictures of possible future events – future memories, as it were. Imagine a line running forward through the past pictures, through the present, and on through the future pictures. Leave that line of pictures where it is, and drift up, way up, above that line. Look down and see the line below. Drift down to just above the line, and float back until you're over a time when you first felt guilty about anything (a time ...). Float farther back in time, say another fifteen or twenty minutes or so, and turn so that you are facing the present with that memory below you and in front of you. Where are those feelings of guilt now? (If you still feel guilty ...). Step

forward, with your adult understandings and resources, into that first experience, and notice how you feel. When you're ready, move on through similar events toward the present only as fast as you can experience that and each similar situation with peace and relaxation.

7. Media-Proofing: In adulthood, one of our most usual ways of comparing our lives with those of others is through the eye of the media, especially T.V. But the world as shown to us in the media is entirely make-believe. (Data on the distortions of reality found in the media, e.g., murder rates and characteristics, sex and race roles, etc., etc.) Our expectations are shaped by the lifestyles of people as they seem to be in the media. Life is just not like that. For example, each of you has heard and told stories about all the violent acts you and your fellow inmates have been involved with. For your own stories, you know they are rarely ever true; and the same is true of others' stories. We all believe there is much more violence out there than we have ever experienced. So we make up for the imagined deficiencies in our lives. (Data on the effects of exposure to the media on people's lives and behaviours.)

8. "Achievement" Goals (Quirk, 1993): The essences of a method to develop (linear) achievement goals, objectives and action plans for one's own life are shown, with special emphasis on checking off action plans as completed. Examples of today's accomplishments are given.

9. Cumulative Frequency Graphs: The use of cumulative frequencies to display all sorts of recorded actions and experiences is illustrated, and recording sheets and graphs are provided with suggestions about events to tally and how to use the tallies and the graphs.

10. Meditation: The largest source of distress for everybody is thinking – our thoughts are what upset us. But how can you stop thinking? Don't think about a purple hippopotamus. To NOT think of it, you must think of it. In fact, nobody can do a

not-do. But it is possible to reduce the pressure of thinking, and thus disturbance from thoughts, greatly. You can do it by thinking ... about something that has no meaning to you. But everything you can think of means something, right? One thing that means nothing might be a word from a language you don't know. Sanskrit in a dead language that nobody knows, so any word from it, listened to, might distract you from other thoughts. Some methods for meditation are explained and tried briefly, with a focus on Transcendental Meditation (T.M.).

11. <u>Stress Management Training</u>: Explanation of how the ANS works, with particular emphasis on breathing IN as a sympathetic response and breathing OUT as a parasympathetic response. Long out-breaths (NOT deep breaths) are explained and practised for their effects in creating calmness.

12. <u>Relaxation Training</u> (Jacobson, 1938): Specific muscle-group progressive muscle relaxation training is selected to permit controlled group relaxation, and explanation and practice in it is provided.

13. <u>Systematic Desensitization</u> (Wolpe, 1958): All participants are induced to relax, and relaxation-mediated desensitization (sometimes enhanced by eye-movement desensitization) is employed, using "standard hierarchies" of anxiety and distress stimuli common among offenders, and asking for hand-raising signals if anyone's SUD (Subjective Units of Discomfort) level exceeds 30 on a 100 point scale. Any presentation is terminated when anyone in the group either raises his hand or exhibits "voluntary" restlessness.

14. <u>"Rapid Phobia Treatment</u> (Bandler and Grinder, 1979; Bandler, 1985; Andreas and Andreas, 1989): Select a situation in which you might feel upset. Make a video movie of it, starting from when you feel safe, and ending with you in a safe place. Make a theatre, and seat yourself in it looking at the screen. Drift up and out of yourself, leaving yourself in the theatre, and drifting up into the projection booth. Look down from the projection

booth at the you in the theatre watching the screen to watch how the you in the theatre reacts. Ask the projectionist to run the film you made on the screen fairly quickly through in black-and-white. How did the you in the theatre seem to feel? (If uncomfortable, drift up and out of yourself in the projection booth and ...) Ask the projectionist to rewind the film fast, in colour so that everything happens in reverse. How did the you in the theatre seem to feel? Repeat the process several times. Drift back down to sit beside the you in the theatre and watch that you more closely. Repeat the process. Drift back into yourself in the theatre. Repeat the process. Drift up into the action on the screen, playing your role in it. Repeat the process.

15. <u>Rational-Emotive Therapy</u> (Ellis and Harper, 1961, 1975): Having handed out a Beliefs Inventory and a Resiliency Inventory to be completed (during the inter-hour break), the inventories are now self-scored, and common errors of thinking identified are examined. The suggestion is made that both inventories be repeated often, each time thoughtfully considering whether each item answered in the direction of "error" or "non-resiliency" could be thought of differently, and only changing the answer given if it is honestly believed to be in the other direction at that time. To the extent that you can "change your mind" on any item, to that extent you either reduce the extent to which you upset yourself with "error" ideas or increase the freedom and ease with which you adapt to life's changing circumstances. Either improves quality of living.

16. <u>Problem Solving</u>: How many of you are "stuck" in acting or thinking in a particular way, or cannot solve a problem in your lives? How come? The answer is simply that we keep using the same strategies in life over and over again, or that we have not yet found the right strategies to achieve what we want to do. The role of language and words in creating and perpetuating problems is outlined. The role of sentence syntax, especially negative format instructions, is outlined and solutions suggested.

The consequent reliance on avoidant strategies is outlined and alternatives discussed. The role of externalizing responsibilities and control is illustrated and reframed.

17. <u>Enhancing Functioning</u>: In that a central theme in Factor 4 has to do with concrete and simplistic thought, apparently associated with motivated insensitivity, some training is offered in intelligence functioning to foster improved success in problem-solving and human interactions. A few exercises and strategies are introduced to enhance concept-formation and thus abstract thinking, perceptual acuity and discrimination, and thus accuracy of responses, and mnemonics to aid in retention and retrieval of information.

18. <u>Assertiveness Training</u> (Lange and Jakubowski, 1976; Jakubowski and Lange, 1978): In addition to the usual elements of assertive training programs (the nature of assertiveness, "I" statements, 3-part statements, etc.), a particular emphasis is placed on (1) the use of bodily energy (in exercise, vocal impact on the environment, definiteness of statement, clarity of enunciation, etc.), and (2) the syntax of linguistics in sending communications (brevity of sentences to exclude explanatory clauses, positive and permissive statements to counter negative format statements and criticality, decisiveness in instant response to counter rumination and foster trusting of the good programming of one's brain, rapidity of repartee to enhance activity and energy use, etc.) "Mottos" are offered as aids to application, such as "Never explain. Your friends don't need it, and your enemies won't believe it anyway."

19. <u>Assertive Training II</u>: Personal rights, common to many assertive training programs, are presented and explained, along with extended focus on freedom in using the body's energies, particularly the energies of emotions and loving. Participants list recurring situations, in which discomfort, joylessness or strong negative emotions are felt. Under each, 16± alternative possible responses in the situation are listed, ordered in

a hierarchy from most aggressive to most under-assertive, with most in the middle. Each list of responses is committed to memory. When one of the situations recurs, stop, run quickly through the associated list of responses, choose the one you would be comfortable with, step one step down from it and deliver that response.

20. <u>Empathy Training</u>: Methods from Assertive Training are used to enhance "empathy" in responses (sending messages), and extended by training in effective listening and in non-verbal reception and expression. Participants try out listening dyads.

21. <u>Divergent Thinking</u>: In order to reduce the fixity of ideas commonly encountered in introversive-obsessional-conforming people (part of what Factor 5 seems to represent), encouragement is offered to employ divergent thinking actively, both to provide alternative points of view and to view events with humour and objectivity – Factor 5 people act as though they were "objective" to create "distance" from emotions and from others, but in fact view events in highly subjective ways. Various tools for divergent thinking were offered, including fragments from a Dictionary for Divergent Thinkers (Quirk, 1989).

22. <u>How to Achieve Joy</u>: (1) Respect everyone. If you choose to respect everyone, you will discover the good in them (always vastly exceeds anything else). But the gifts which flow from giving respect are NOT given to the other person, they are given to yourself by yourself – you find yourself living in a world full of goodness which, contrary to expectations, makes you feel good. (2) Trust everyone. If you choose to trust everyone, contrary to expectations, you will feel safe in life and in human relationships, and the gift of trust is NOT given to others, it is given to you by yourself in feeling safe. (3) It is then possible to love everyone. If you choose to love everyone, your body's energies become invested in everyone and everything around you. The gift of loving is NOT given to the other, it is given to you by yourself, as you find joy for yourself.

23. <u>Achieving Freedom</u>: Jump up and fly in the air around the room. Accept fair returns for what you have given others – whoops, we all get many times more than we give. Put a sign on your weekly canteen supplies: "Steal all of this." Wear a sign on your back: "Kick me." Do you think that's funny? You do? Good! You have begun to achieve freedom. Whenever you have to do something, play it as a game. Could you do that? You could? Good! You're well on your way. Do you think it's right that people should treat each other as equals? Could you be the first person to act that way? Could you keep it up? You could? Good! You're almost there. Could you start practising the three steps to joy? Could you find three different things you like every time you are moving from one place to another, as a start? You could? Good! When you've done those things for a few short weeks you will have arrived; you will know what freedom is.

REFERENCES

Andreas, C. and Andreas, S. (1989) Heart of the mind. Moab, Utah: Real People Press. Barber, J. & Adrian, C. (1982) Psychological approaches to the management of pain. New York: Brunner /Mazel.

Barber, J. & Adrian, C. (1982) Psychological approaches to the management of pain. New York: Brunner/Mazel.

Beck, AT., Rush, AJ., Shaw, B.F. and Emory G. (1979) Cognitive therapy of depression. New York: Guilford.

Brown, D.P. and Fromm, E. (1986) Hypnotherapy and hypnoanalysis. Hillsdale, N.J.: Lawrence Erlbaum Associates.

Brown, D.P. and Fromm, E. (1987) Hypnosis and behavioral medicine. Hillsdale, N.J.: Lawrence Erlbaum Associates.

Carkhuff, R.R. and Pierce, R.M. (1977) The art of helping trainer's guide. Amherst, Mass.: Human Resource Development Press.

Egan, G. (1986) The skilled helper. Pacific Grove, Cal.: Brooks/Cole.

Eysenck, H.J. (Ed.) (1960) Behavior therapy and the neuroses. New York: Macmillan. Eysenck, H.J. (Ed.) (1964) Experiments in behavior therapy. New York: Macmillan. Ellis, A and Harper, R.A (1975) A new guide to rational living. Englewood cliffs, N.J.: Prentice-Hall; and Hollywood, CA: Wilshire Books.

Figley, C.R. (1985) Trauma and its wake: The study and treatment of post-traumatic stress disorders. New York: Brunner/Mazel,

Goldstein, AP. and Glick, B. (1987) Aggression replacement training. Champaign, Illinois: Research Press.

Gordon, T. (1970) Parent effectiveness training. New York: New American Library.

Hoff, B. (1982) The Tao of Pooh. New York: Penguin Books.

Jacobowski, P. and Lange, A.J. (1978) The assertive option. Champaign, Illinois: Research Press.

Jacobson, E. (1938) Progressive relaxation. Chicago: University of Chicago Press. James, T. and Woodsmall, W. (1988) Time line therapy and the basis of personality. Cupertino, CA.: Meta Publications.

Korzybski, A. (1933) Science and sanity, 4th edition. Lakeville, Connecticut: The International Non-Aristotelian Library Publishing Company.

Kroger, W.S. and Fezler, W.D. (1976) Hypnosis and behavior modification: Imagery conditioning. Philadelphia: J.B. Lippincott.

Lange, AJ. and Jacobowski, P. (1976) Responsible assertive behavior. Champaign, Illinois: Research Press.

Lickona, T. (Ed.) (1976) Moral development and behavior. New York: Holt, Rinehart & Winston.

Maslow, A.H. (1967) Self-actualization and beyond. In James F.T. Bugental (Ed.), Challenges of humanistic psychology. New York: McGraw -Hill.

McCary, S.P. & McCary, J.L., (1984) Human sexuality, 3rd, brief ed. New York: Wadsworth.

Mitchell, J.J. (1971) Adolescence: Some critical issues. Toronto: Holt, Rinehart and Winston.

Peniston, E.G. and Kulkosky, P.J. (1990) Alcoholic personality and alpha-theta brainwave training. In C.L. Sheridan and J. Sargent (Eds.), Medical Psychotherapy Year book, Vol. 3, 1990 (pp. 37-55). Toronto: Hogrefe and Huber.

Quirk, D.A. (1985) Motor vehicle accidents and post-traumatic anxiety conditioning. The Ontario Psychologist, Vol. 17, No. 5.

Quirk, D.A. (1973) An automated desensitization. In Advances in Psychotherapy, Vol. 4 (103-115). New York: Academic Press.

Quirk, D.A. (1983) Developments in biofeedback treatment. Paper presented at the Ontario Psychological Association Annual Meeting, Toronto.

Quirk, D.A. (1991) Manual for the goal finding group. Brampton, Ontario: O.C.I. Program Reports.

Rokach, A. (1982) Anger and aggression control training: A cognitive-behavioural intervention in group psychotherapy. Paper presented at the 34th annual meeting of the American Society of Criminology, Toronto.

Selye, H. (1958) The stress of life. New York: McGraw-Hill.

Siegel, B.S. (1986) Love, medicine and miracles. New York: Harper and Row.

Skinner, B.F. (1953) Science and human behavior. New York: New York Free Press.

Snygg, D. (1941) The need for a phenomenological system in psychology. Psychological Review, 48, pp.404-424.

Sterman, M.B., MacDonald, L.R. and Stone, R.K (1973) Biofeedback training of sensorimotor cortex EEG in man and its effects on epilepsy. V.A. Hospital, Sepulveda, CA: Author.

Tansey, M.A (1990) Righting the rhythms of reason: EEG biofeedback training as a therapeutic modality in a clinical office setting. In C.L. Sheridan and J. Sargent (Eds.), Medical Psychotherapy Yearbook, Vol. 3 (pp. 57-68). Toronto: Hogrefe and Huber.

Watson, D.L. and Tharp, R.G. (1977) Self-directed behavior. Monterey, Cal.: Brooks/Cole.

Wolpe, J. (1958) Psychotherapy by reciprocal inhibition. Stanford: Stanford University Press.

Woolfolk, R.L and Lehrer, P.M. (Eds.) (1984) Principles and practice of stress management. New York: Guilford.

Yochelson, S. and Samenow, (1976,1977) S.E. The criminal personality, Volumes I and II. New York: Jason Aronson.

Reg M. Reynolds, Ph.D., C.Psych. (Retired)

Reg Reynolds was born in Grande Prairie, Alberta. He attended London Normal School (teacher training) before becoming interested in psychology and special education. He received his B.A. and M.A, from the University of Western Ontario, and his Ph.D. from the University of Waterloo.

He was a psychologist for almost sixty years. At various times during his career, he functioned as a counsellor and psychotherapist for individuals, couples, and groups; as lab technician in a reserve medical unit; as personal office in a reserve army unit; as Director of Vocational and Recreational Services at Lakeshore Psychiatric Hospital; as Chief Psychologist at the Vanier Centre for Women, the Oakville Reception and Assessment Centre (for juveniles admitted to training school), and the Ontario Correctional Institute; as Coordinating Psychologist for the Central Region of the Ontario Ministry of the Solicitor General and Correctional Services; as a consultant regarding the assessment and treatment of sex offenders; as a consultant regarding ethical issues; as a researcher; as a college lecturer; as an intern in, clinical member of, and board member of the Halton Centre for Childhood Sexual Abuse; as an intern, co-therapist and therapist in the treatment of spousal abuse; as a member of the Council of the College of Psychologists of Ontario; as a member of the Ontario Society of Clinical Hypnosis and president of its Southern region; as a developer of biofeedback equipment and as a provider of biofeedback; as a student of education and special education; as a student of Applied Behaviour Analysis (ABA) and its application in the treatment of children with autism; as psychologist and Supervising Clinician in the Ontario Government's Intensive Behavioural Intervention program for children with autism; as an educator of parents of children with autism; and, more recently, as clinical supervisor of ABA-based programs for children with autism.

He is the author of *An ABA Primer, An ABA Primer with Application to Teaching Children with Autism, A Measure of Moral Development, Miscellaneous Musings,* and *The Great Reynaldo Sees All, Blabs All*; co-author with Douglas Quirk of *A Simple and Effective Cure for Criminality, Freedom from Addictions,* Large-Group Treatment of Addictions, and *Creating Peace*; and editor of Douglas Quirk's *Adventures in Pragmatic Psychotherapy, Life Management by Objectives,* and *Large-Group Treatment of Psychological Problems.*

Douglas Arthur Quirk (1931-1997)

Douglas A. Quirk was born in India, the son of missionary parents and, if I remember correctly, spent some time in boarding schools, in England. In any event, he was educated in the classics as well as in the classical English music hall ballads.

He received his B.A. and M.A. from the University of Toronto and completed all of the requirements for his Ph.D. except for his dissertation – and he subsequently taught Psychology to Psychiatrists and Nurses in the U. of T. Department of Psychiatry for many years. He was a Clinical Fellow of the Ontario Society for Clinical Hypnosis, the Behavior Therapy and Research Society, and the American and Ontario Associations of Marriage and Family Counsellors, and he was a Fellow of the Royal Society of Health.

Doug was a prolific writer. Here is a small sample of his many publications:

(1966) The Application of Learning Theories to Psychotherapy: Component Therapies and the Psychoses. Paper read at the Canadian Psychological Association Annual Convention

(1968) Former Alcoholics and Social Drinking: An Additional Observation. The Canadian Psychologist, 9, 498-499

(1976) O.P.A.'s Brief to the Royal Commission on Violence in the Communications Industry. The Ontario Psychologist, 8, Supplement

(1980) Nutrition and Crime: a review. Prepared for The Solicitor General of Canada

(1982) Biofeedback in Dangerous Offenders: Learning Normal Functioning of the Nervous System. Poster Session Paper, Ontario Association, Annual Convention

(1986) Nutrition and Violence. Invited Address, John Howard Society of Canada Conference

(1991) A Practical Measure of Offence Seriousness: Sentence Severity. Ontario Correctional Institute Research Report (RR91-1)

(1994) The nature and modification of criminality. Paper presented (with Reg Reynolds) at the Annual Convention of the Ontario Psychological Association.

At various times during his career, he served as consultant to the World Health Organization, (S.E. Asia Region), the Scarboro Foreign Missions Society (Toronto), the Canadian Institute of Stress (Toronto), Toronto Catholic Children's Aid Society, York-Lea Mental Health Project (Toronto), the American Society for Humanistic Education, the Institute for Applied Psychology, Humanitas Systems (New York), Biomedical Engineering Associates (Toronto), North York General Hospital (Toronto), and the Green Valley School & Hospital (Florida).

From 1959 to 1967, he was Senior Psychologist at the Ontario Hospital, Toronto and, from 1961 to 1967, Director of the Behaviour Therapy Unit there. From 1967 to 1971, he was Director of Clinical and Research Labs at the Clarke Institute of Psychiatry. Briefly, he was in full-time private practice; and then from 1975 to 1995, he was Senior Psychologist at the Ontario Correctional Institute.

He is the author of *Large-Group Treatment of Psychological Problems*; and co-author with Reg Reynolds of *Freedom from Addictions, Creating Peace,* and *A Simple and Effective Cure for Criminality.* A compilation of some of his case studies, *Adventures in Pragmatic Psychotherapy,* was published by Reg Reynolds in 2019